Making Los Angeles Home

The publisher gratefully acknowledges the generous support of the Lisa See Endowment Fund in Southern California History and Culture of the University of California Press Foundation.

Making Los Angeles Home

The Integration of Mexican
Immigrants in the United States

Rafael Alarcón
Luis Escala
Olga Odgers

Translated by Dick Cluster

UNIVERSITY OF CALIFORNIA PRESS

University of California Press, one of the most
distinguished university presses in the United States,
enriches lives around the world by advancing scholarship
in the humanities, social sciences, and natural sciences. Its
activities are supported by the UC Press Foundation and
by philanthropic contributions from individuals and
institutions. For more information, visit www.ucpress.edu.

University of California Press
Oakland, California

Library of Congress Cataloging-in-Publication Data
Alarcón, Rafael, author.
  Making Los Angeles home : the integration of
Mexican immigrants in the United States/Rafael
Alarcón, Luis Escala, Olga Odgers.
    pages cm
  Includes bibliographical references and index.
ISBN 978-0-520-28485-2 (cloth : alk. paper)
ISBN 978-0-520-28486-9 (pbk. : alk. paper)
ISBN 978-0-520-96052-7 (e-edition)
    1. Mexicans—California—Los Angeles—Social
conditions.   2. Mexican Americans—California—Los
Angeles—Social conditions.   3. Immigrants—
California—Los Angeles—Social conditions.   4. Social
integration—California—Los Angeles.   5. Los Angeles
(Calif.)—Emigration and immigration—Social
aspects.   6. Mexico—Emigration and immigration—
Social aspects.   I. Escala, Luis, author.   II. Odgers,
Olga, author.   III. Title.
  F869.L89M5105 2016
  305.8968'72079494—dc23
                                    2015035772

24 23 22 21 20 19 18 17 16 15
10 9 8 7 6 5 4 3 2 1

Contents

Foreword

The last hundred years comprise the century of Mexican migration to the United States. Though ebbing and flowing and often changing in size, characteristics, organization, destination, and origin, the movement of people al Norte has been a constant, one that has transformed both the immigrants and the country on which they have converged. So large and persistent a migration is an event of unusual social significance. It is also the material for a fascinating, moving, and human story, one of interest not simply to migration scholars but to anyone concerned with the ways in which international migration is changing our world.

For all its impressive dimensions, the magnitude of Mexican migration has confronted scholars with a difficult challenge. Students of Mexican *emigration* have risen to the occasion: over the past several decades, they have produced a rich, interdisciplinary literature, using the full social science toolkit. Thanks to these efforts—of which the binational Mexican Migration Project may be the most notable accomplishment—we possess a deep understanding of the causes and mechanisms of emigration and of the consequences of both *emigration* and *immigration* for the emigrants' kin, their home communities, and indeed, for Mexico writ large.

By contrast, the students of Mexican *immigration*—that is to say, the experience within the United States—have found it more difficult to come to grips with the phenomenon and its salient characteristics. To be sure, monographs of high quality addressing a multiplicity of topics—whether having to do with transnationalism, gender, labor, sexuality, the borderlands—have proliferated. But for the most part, the big picture seems to have been neglected, suggesting that this migration is of such size and complexity that it overwhelms the scholarly capacity at understanding.

In this light, the present book represents a new, daring departure in migration scholarship, as it seeks to comprehend the totality of the experience of Mexican immigrants in the very capital of contemporary immigration to the United States: Los Angeles. Fascinating, informative, and original, this book brings a fresh and badly needed perspective to migration studies. Coauthored by three distinguished Mexican scholars of migration—Rafael Alarcón, Luis Escala, and Olga Odgers—it looks at the phenomenon in a distinctive way, asking a series of questions that their US counterparts have generally not yet posed.

Readers encountering the pages to come will have a great deal to learn. They will certainly appreciate the multimethod nature of this study, which combines quantitative and qualitative material in a unique way. Drawing on the American Community Survey, the authors paint a statistical picture of Mexican settlement and adaptation in Los Angeles, demonstrating both the progress that the immigrants have achieved and the limitations that they have encountered. The authors then delve deep into that process, drawing on a unique set of interviews with immigrants from three different Mexican states—Zacatecas, Oaxaca, and Veracruz—each representing distinct stages in the history of Mexican migration to Los Angeles, from the oldest to the most recent. The authors bring a deft touch to the analysis and presentation of the interview material. The text gives voice to the immigrants, doing so in such a way that the reader is confident that the respondents have not been guided to answers sought by the researchers—as is so often the case— but rather are telling their own stories, in the way and with the words that they have chosen. At the same time, the authors take appropriate distance, attending to the contradictions, tensions, and conflicts that appear in the respondents' narratives.

But the core contribution of this book stems from its analytical perspective, which sets it apart from so much of the literature. Though focused on a single migration converging on a single place, the book engages with a question that arises wherever mass migrations occur: how the outsiders from abroad will belong. For the most part, scholars have answered that question with their backs to the border, looking inward—a tendency especially true of US researchers. Consequently, the *international* and the inherently *political* nature of population movements across national boundaries falls out of view.

By contrast, the authors of this book work with a more encompassing framework, one that extends across borders, which in turn allows them to show the ways in which migration builds cross-border connections even as integration *into* the *national* society of destination leads to *dis*-integration from the *national* society of origin.

Thus, socially, the people opting for life in another state are not just *immigrants,* but also *emigrants,* retaining ties to people and places left behind. Though the *immigrant* search for a better life yields long-term changes likely to complicate interactions with the people left behind, the short- to medium-term effects take a different form, increasing the *emigrants'* capacity to help out their significant others still living in the home society—thereby encouraging further immigration and the ethnic densities that facilitate continued home country ties. Moreover, in moving to another country, the migrants pull one society onto the territory of another state, leading "here" and "there" to converge. As the home country society gets transplanted onto receiving states, *alien* territory becomes a *familiar* environment, yielding the infrastructure needed to keep up here-there connections and providing the means by which migrants can sustain identities as home community members while living on foreign soil. Thus, international migration both brings "them" "here" and imports aspects of "there," a phenomenon that many researchers—whether for better or worse—understand as "transnationalism."

As readers of this book will see, the cross-border dimension is a salient aspect of the experience of *mexicanos* in Los Angeles. Consequently, the relevant identities are those that spring from the place of origin, not just those that are meaningful in the place of destination. Place of origin in Mexico affects experiences in the United States, for reasons having to do with regional differences in the history and timing of emigration. Moreover, origin remains socially meaningful, even if the *gringos*—hard of perception as always—fail to notice. Spouses are more likely than not to be *paisanos;* friends, acquaintances, workmates often share a common local or regional background; indeed, the strength of those ties generates resources crucial for settling down and getting ahead. Place of origin also structures interactions of a more formal kind, whether cultural, as among the *oaxaqueños* or *veracruzanos,* or political, as among the *zacatecanos.*

But it is not simply that ties originating in Mexico influence experiences in the United States; connections *to* Mexico remain vital, indicating that migrant social relations have not yet been captured by the society where they live, but rather continue to span across borders. Thus, most of the respondents interviewed for this book reported that they sent money to relatives in Mexico and continued to travel home for a variety of reasons, whether to visit ageing or sick relatives, to relax while on vacation, or to participate in patron saint festivals. And not only did the Mexicans in Los Angeles attend to their relatives and home communities, they also continue to care about Mexico and to keep themselves informed about politics nationwide. A minority of immigrants also seek active political engagement.

Nonetheless, the importance of the cross-border dimension is steadily weakening, as the locus of social life inevitably comes to coincide with the boundaries of the territory where the immigrants actually reside. Though origin in Mexico remains a source of meaning, its importance is on the decline. Thus, while the typical couple involved spouses from the same town or state, a growing minority of couples took the form of mixed marriages involving partners from two different Mexican states. More importantly, the boundaries that may have been important in Mexico no longer seemed so important to these Mexicans living in the United States. As the authors note, none of the interviewees referred to mixed marriages "with concern or with any suggestion that they constitute a social disadvantage."

To some extent, the greater diversity represented by these mixed marriages is a natural consequence of displacement to a different interactional structure. Movement to a huge, heterogeneous, cosmopolitan area like Los Angeles creates the potential to meet a whole range of people, many of whom—Iranians, Armenians, Pakistanis, Chinese, Koreans, not to mention Mexicans from opposite corners of the country—would never have been encountered had the migrants stayed home. Under these circumstances, moreover, identities change: since the core self-identity *imported* from Mexico often fails to convey a meaningful signal in the new environment, the immigrants have no choice but to adopt other identities that are more meaningful. As explained by one of the respondents: "It depends on whom you're talking to. With people from other countries, we call ourselves Mexicans. If I'm among people from Mexico, I identify myself as Oaxacan, and if I'm among Oaxacans, then I say I'm from Macuiltianguis." For many immigrants, of course, the relevant identity expands beyond nationality, extending instead to the broader, more diverse population of Latin American origin. As the authors point out, "Mexican immigrants are not Hispanics, but they become Hispanics through integration." Though the new social context encountered in Los Angeles creates a meaningful framework for a Latino identity, the latter also results from the political environment. Classified as Latinos and organized as Latinos, the immigrants have little choice but to accept the official categories that they encounter.

Thus social integration *into* the United States yields social disintegration *from* Mexico. Moreover, despite the force of the many cross-border connections, *territorial* dis-integration from Mexico is also well advanced, as the immigrants' lives are increasingly confined to the territory where they actually live. To a large extent, the attenuation of cross-border ties reflected the overwhelming power of the tendencies toward settlement. As the authors explain, many respondents had displaced the entirety of their families to the United States. Though many retained property in Mexico, most of these properties had been inherited; by contrast, most the properties purchased by the immigrants were located in the United States. The deepening of ties to Los Angeles, as well as the immigrants' growing economic commitments in the United States, meant that fewer resources were available for spending in Mexico. As explained by one of the authors' Zacatecan respondents, "But now the bills, the debts you take on, they don't allow it, although you want to go, but you know how much you're going to owe every month, and that limits you." And of course, there are the children, who may have grown up speaking Spanish and may think of themselves as Mexican, but nonetheless have been so thoroughly Americanized that return to the home country is inconceivable. As one of the respondents recounted, an effort to return home to Jerez foundered on the resistance from his children: after a year and a half, "they really didn't want to be there because they missed *their* country, Dodgers games and things like that, or McDonalds, which they like, and all those minor things."

But the immigrants are not just emigrants; they are also *aliens*, a condition shared by every foreigner crossing national boundaries, whether as legal permanent resident, temporary worker, tourist, or undocumented immigrant. As emphasized by the American sociologists Richard Alba and Victor Nee (2005) in their classic *Remaking the American Mainstream*, the social boundaries separating immigrants and natives may be blurry, allowing for extensive interaction across ethnic lines. Indeed, that is often the experience recounted in this book, which in so many ways testifies to the permeability of the society that the immigrants encounter in the United States.

By contrast to the blurry *social* boundaries, the *legal* boundaries surrounding the myriad, formal categories of alien are bright. Worldwide, the import of alien status varies by citizenship regime, exercising least weight where citizenship is a birthright; nowhere is its significance trivial. Naturalized citizens currently comprise one-third of all foreign-born people living in the United States; another third are legal permanent residents; another third belongs to some other, more tenuous, legal status. While immigrant offspring born in the United States are citizens, many young immigrant offspring *growing up* in the United States are foreign born and no small fraction is undocumented; many more have undocumented parents or siblings.

Consequently, the brightest boundaries are not imported and have nothing to do with ethnicity; rather, they are fundamentally political, made in and by receiving states, exercising long-term consequences at the individual level and beyond. International migrants begin outside the polity, remaining there long after roots have been firmly established. In a democratic society, alien status doesn't prohibit political activity, as shown vividly by the mass demonstrations for immigrant rights in 2006 or the continuing struggle by immigrant workers for rights at the job site and union representation. Nonetheless, alien status inevitably restricts rights and entitlements. Moreover, alienage leaves noncitizen immigrants vulnerable to nationals' efforts at tightening up and increasing the gap between citizens and aliens. That politics plays so central a role in determining immigrant destinies provides further demonstration of the authors' sensitivity to the dual, bidirectional nature of immigrant integration. While immigrants may integrate *into* a society by learning its language or gaining new competencies, the societal integration *of* the immigrants—or lack thereof—involves political decisions about rights and access to citizenship, decisions largely made by the nationals and their leaders.

As demonstrated in this book, those political boundaries and the changing mechanisms whereby they can and cannot be crossed have made a world of difference. The Zacatecans mainly crossed the border as undocumented immigrants; they moved to a Los Angeles where immigrants and their advocates exercised little voice and Mexican Americans had yet to gain much political influence. On the other hand, immigration enforcement both in the exterior and in the interior was lax. Crossing the border was easily attainable, making for a constant flow of back-and-forth moves to Mexico. Although undocumented immigrants were prohibited from seeking employment, employers were permitted to hire undocumented workers—opening doors to the labor market. And gatekeepers at other crucial points of access—whether having to do with drivers' licenses or even Social Security cards—then paid little attention to applicants' legal status.

Thus, at the outset, political boundaries were of very modest salience, even though there were few opportunities for direct or indirect exercise of political influence. Moreover, timing proved crucial, as the undocumented immigrants of the 1960s, 1970s, and early 1980s enjoyed the fruits of the amnesty created by the 1986 Immigration Reform and Control Act. Legalization then led to family reunification in the United States and, for a sizable share of the newly legalized immigrants, full US citizenship. Mobility followed in other domains, with significant movement into property and business ownership, and even the professions.

The later arrivals, especially the Veracruzans, had a very different experience. Externally, the territorial border had become increasingly impenetrable, making it ever harder to enter the United States, but more importantly, making it ever more difficult to try a re-entry. Hence, the newer immigrants were deprived of the circularity enjoyed by the earlier cohort. Internally, the border between persons legally resident in the United States and undocumented immigrants became increasingly bright. Consequently, unlike the earlier arrivals, the undocumented Veracruzans found themselves confined to the same sector of highly unstable, precarious jobs that they had entered at the time of arrival in the United States. And as legal status became an increasingly important determinant of life chances, it also led to the internal stratification of the Mexican immigrant population, with lines of labor market segmentation corresponding to differences in legal status.

Of course, this brief foreword only skims the surface; there is much more that awaits the reader in this rich, thought-provoking book. By going where other scholars have feared to tread, Alarcón, Escala, and Odgers have risen to the intellectual challenge confronted by anyone seeking to understand the last century of Mexican migration to the United States. While the task is immense and much work remains to be done, this effort to illuminate the Mexican immigrant experience in the quintessential ethnic metropolis of twenty-first century America represents a scholarly landmark and one to which readers will return with profit for many years to come.

Roger Waldinger
Department of Sociology, University of California, Los Angeles

This book is dedicated to our mothers Pompeya Acosta, Alba Rabadán, and María de los Ángeles Ortiz, in loving memory.

Preface

As scholars, we are always pleased when the results of our research can find an audience. It is doubly gratifying to be able to broaden and diversify that audience through the medium of translation. In the case of research about international migration, to be able to make the findings available in the major languages of the countries of origin and destination is an extraordinary opportunity. For all these reasons, we are most happy to introduce the English translation and revised version of this book, originally published in Mexico as *Mudando el hogar al Norte: Trayectorias de integración de los inmigrantes mexicanos en Los Ángeles* (El Colegio de la Frontera Norte, 2012). We trust that this opportunity not only will lead to wider dissemination (though the original version, it should be said, sold out its first edition in less than a year) but also will expose our work to scrutiny from a greater variety of viewpoints.

We are additionally pleased to be able to contribute to the discussion taking place in many parts of the world about the processes of immigrant integration. In that discussion, ironically, the perspectives of analysts in the countries where immigrants originate tend to be underrepresented. This occurs particularly in the United States, the premier destination of international migration, where the subject of immigration from Mexico has received a great deal of attention over the past several decades, not only in academic circles but also in the mass media and, especially, in the political realm.

Scholars in the United States have, for nearly a century, focused considerable analytical effort on immigrant integration; this book is written by three Mexican researchers who work in a Mexican institution located on our country's northern border. We hope this positioning lends our book a singular perspective on the study of Mexican immigration into the United States. Mexican immigrants constitute the largest immigrant group in the United States; one out of every three immigrants comes from Mexico and slightly more than half of that population is undocumented. Additionally, we see our research design as a new contribution. While most research examines immigrant integration from a given disciplinary perspective, we have adopted a multidisciplinary, multilevel approach employing a combination of quantitative and qualitative techniques to capture the distinct components, dimensions, and levels implicit in this process.

First, making use of descriptive statistics, we have analyzed the economic and social integration of Mexican immigrants residing in metropolitan Los Angeles using data from the American Community Survey. Second, from an ethnographic perspective, we have disaggregated the integration process into four analytic components (economic, social, cultural, and political), and we have similarly disaggregated the population under analysis, which we do not regard as a homogeneous group. Our interviewees belong to three different groups of Mexican immigrants, coming as they do from three different regions of Mexico. These groups arrived in the Los Angeles area in different historical periods and thus confronted distinctly different economic, political, and cultural conditions.

This methodology has led us to the fundamental finding that there is no single path toward immigrant integration, but rather a multiplicity of strategies leading to differing results. We did not find any consensus formulation about how to define the goal of integration, but rather a diversity of individual and collective projects that occupy various points on a broad spectrum that stretches from classic assimilationism to radical multiculturalism. Thus, we cannot measure economic, social, cultural, and political integration as if we were dealing with a race being run toward a single goal along a clearly delineated track.

Another important finding of our book is that, for undocumented immigrants, in spite of their heroic exploration of a variety of strategies and pathways to achieve economic and social integration, that process always remains unfinished. Only those immigrants who become legal permanent residents or naturalized citizens can take maximum advantage of their economic and social resources so as to achieve full integration.

It is important to point out that many different processes relating to immigrant integration have unfolded in the United States and Mexico since we conducted our interviews in 2008. Our research captured only the preliminary effects of the economic recession beginning in that year, which led eventually to the voluntary return of some Mexican immigrants who were not able to cope with the crisis and the reduction of employment opportunities. This voluntary return has been accompanied by the aggressive formal deportation of many Mexican men and women, a large number of them falsely accused of being criminals. These men and women had spent many years in the United States and had become heads of households there. Department of Homeland Security data reveal that since the beginning of 2003, more than two million Mexican immigrants have been removed from the United States.

Our interviewees, especially the undocumented ones, told us in 2008 they had high hopes that if Barack Obama became president, he would push for regularization of their immigration status. However, in 2012, faced with the unlikelihood of the US Congress passing such legislation, President Obama instead issued the Deferred Action on Childhood Arrivals (DACA) executive order, offering temporary relief from deportation to undocumented individuals brought to the United States as children if they could meet a number of requirements. In November 2014, President Obama announced a similar order that would offer the same type of protection to immigrant parents of US citizens and legal permanent residents through the Deferred Action for Parents of Americans and Lawful Permanent Residents (DAPA) executive order. In February 2015, a ruling by a federal court in Texas temporarily blocked the implementation of DAPA and expansion of DACA. In the case of Mexico, the continuation of violence and lack of public safety there as a result of the so-called war on drugs, in spite of a change of Mexican national administrations in 2012, suggests that our interviewees, both documented and undocumented, will reaffirm their decision to settle in the United States. This decision not to return to Mexico, another important finding, is also buttressed by a generalized rejection of the Mexican political system.

Finally, we think that books like ours will permit the promotion of greater dialogue among the academic communities of both countries about trends in Mexican immigration, the immigrants' settlement in the United States, and their efforts to integrate into US society. Equally important, as we stress in this book, is the willingness of the societies of receiving countries to undertake efforts to include their new immigrant communities, recognizing their importance and contributions. We see this as one of the central challenges facing contemporary societies, including the United States, and we hope that our book contributes in some way to a greater understanding of such processes.

Acknowledgments

The research included in this book was made possible by the generous financial support of the Fundación Banco Bilbao Vizcaya Argentaria (BBVA Foundation) through its First Grant Competition for Research Projects on Mexico–United States Migration Processes. Without this financing, the extensive and detailed fieldwork that underlies our book could not have been carried out. The support provided by our own institution, El Colegio de la Frontera Norte, was also fundamental to our carrying out this project. Thanks to the creation of the necessary conditions for undertaking ethnographic research, we were able to count on the valuable and enthusiastic participation of a number of graduate students. We are most grateful for the support of Fabiola Galicia, Mirian Solís, and Guillermo Yrizar from El Colegio de la Frontera Norte, and América Páez from the Universidad Autónoma de Baja California. In the stage of transcription and coding we depended on the work of Noelia Lorente and Ignacio Granados of the Universidad de Valencia, as well as Manuel Tapia, Carmen Martínez, Teresa López Avedoy, Olga Olivas, Laura Jáuregui, Alejandro Bonada, and Ester Espinoza. In addition, we would like to note that within the framework of the research project presented here, Fabiola Galicia (2012) carried out the research for her doctoral dissertation, dealing specifically with the process of integration of skilled Mexican immigrants in the Los Angeles region.

We are deeply grateful to Dr. Gaspar Rivera-Salgado and Dr. Telesforo Ramírez García for their support in the research and writing of this book. But without a doubt, the most important contribution, without which the entire project would not have been possible, was the generous and enthusiastic participation of the men and women born in Zacatecas, Oaxaca, and Veracruz and now living in the Los Angeles region, who in spite of their long and fatiguing workdays agreed to share their free time to speak to us of the experience of immigration, daily life in Los Angeles, and the difficulties of inserting themselves into an increasingly degraded labor market, as well as sharing with us their dreams, their life projects, and their hopes and expectations for the future of new generations. In particular, we thank the leaders of the immigrants' associations, who put their contact networks and their good will at our disposal from the first moment so as to facilitate our access to the communities of their fellow countrymen and women who have settled in Los Angeles. The opportunity to talk with each and every one of them was a privilege that we value most highly, and we are most thankful for their generosity.

At the risk of omitting some other individuals, we must also particularly thank Adriana Avelar, Rafael Barajas, Rigoberto Castañeda, Alicia and Fernando Cervantes, Luis García, Mauro García, Martha Jiménez, Fernando López Mateos, Domingo Martínez, Rodrigo Salazar, and Socorro Torres. Likewise, we are grateful to the two anonymous reviewers who shared their very valuable ideas and suggestions, which we incorporated into the text in ways we hope have improved the quality of this book. Many thanks also to our colleagues at the University of Southern California's Center for the Study of Immigrant Integration, the University of California San Diego's Center for Comparative Immigration Studies, and the Graduate Center of the City University of New York for their critiques and observations at our presentations of our research, which allowed us to enrich this work. We are also grateful to Richard Cluster for his excellent translation from the manuscript in Spanish and to Naomi Schneider from University of California Press for their wonderful editorial support.

Finally, but of no less importance, we want to offer our profound gratitude for the generous and untiring support of our colleague and friend Roger Waldinger, of the Sociology Department at the University of California, Los Angeles. Naturally, any errors or omissions in the book are entirely our own responsibility.

Introduction

In recent decades, the inexorable advance of economic globalization has been accompanied by accelerating human mobility across international borders. While some migrants plan on temporary stays, many others arrive with the idea of making a home in a different country, whether in search of new job opportunities or as an escape from violence. Within this complex new framework, international migration is a central concern both because of its magnitude and because of the challenges of managing it. While national states try to contain such population flows through ever-more-restrictive immigration policies, they confront the simultaneous challenge of integrating the new immigrants, who may come from countries with different languages and cultures. The new relations the state establishes with those who are migrating both within and outside its territories have gradually acquired such centrality that it is impossible to understand contemporary societies without observing the specific forms in which they relate to those who move from, toward, or across their borders.

In effect, unlike the states of the modern era—which assumed an identity across state, territory, and nation—contemporary states must reinvent themselves to, in one way or another, incorporate both immigrants and their own citizens who leave the national territory to live in other countries. Thus, international migration poses new demands for research and policy: To develop a new understanding of the state, citizenship, and the sense of national belonging in contexts of intense population mobility. To redefine the relationship between identity and territory when broad sectors of the population move across borders. To define the rights to be granted to people born in another country. To think about the "national" character from the point of view of global cities that are home to ever-multiplying languages, religions, and cultural traditions. In sum, to rethink social integration in the face of intense migration.

The integration of immigrants has taken many different forms over time. Today, the nation-states that are receivers of immigrants try to achieve their integration into the destination society, which implies planning and implementing initiatives that respond to the challenge of managing growing cultural diversity. Such responses have met with various degrees of success. While countries like Canada and Australia have adopted integration policies evidently oriented toward multicultural recognition, others, such as Germany, debate whether multiculturalism still works. In the United States, the leading destination of international migration, while some measures have been adopted to make room for growing pluralism in the population, in practice the task of integration is left to the market and to immigrants themselves. In still other cases, such as France, the Netherlands, and Spain, new integration policies have involved the establishment of formal contracts for immigrants in their processes of integration.

In this sense, the "problem of integration" has always existed. We might think, for instance, of debates about the status of colonized populations or the issue of excluding indigenous populations. This topic now takes on new characteristics because beyond signifying the redefinition of the rights and obligations of immigrants, it implies the need to rethink the relationships each society must establish with itself in the contemporary manner of inhabiting space.

This is surely why debates about the place of immigrants in contemporary societies have taken off in new directions. Until the end of the twentieth century, such discussion seemed to revolve around an opposition between assimilation and multiculturalism. In this sense, in its classic formulation, the assimilation of immigrants was seen as a natural process by which people from different ethnic groups eventually became indistinguishable from the native population through the adoption of the cultural patterns and participation in the social institutions of the country of destination, especially through marriage outside the ethnic group, until they had adopted a common identity with the members of the receiving society.[1]

Later, this approach gave way to others that sought to recognize the increasing complexity of that process. Such is the case with the theory of segmented assimilation, which questions the apparent connection between assimilation and upward social mobility, emphasizing the diversity of immigrant assimilation experiences. While some members of immigrant groups remain excluded from economic mobility, others find multiple paths to assimilation depending on their national origins, immigration and socioeconomic status, context of arrival in the destination society, and family social and financial resources.[2] Thus, this revision of the assimilation paradigm holds that there is no direct relation between assimilation and upward social mobility. The children of immigrants who live in poverty do not owe their situation to a lack of assimilation, but to full assimilation into a lower—and degraded—segment of the receiving society.

On the other hand, in the multiculturalist perspective, cultural difference is recognized as a constitutive element of all societies. Therefore the goal of receiving societies should not be the pursuit of gradual dissolution of cultural divisions, but rather the harmonious management of difference. The multiculturalist perspective has been nourished by such fundamental experiences as the civil rights movements of the United States, which unlike earlier sociopolitical mobilizations, have specific features: they are linked to specific ethnic groups, denounce the discrimination of which these have been objects, and demand respect for equality of opportunity while at the same time defending cultural specificity. This represents a major shift both on the analytical level and in terms of political philosophy, because this perspective upholds the need to simultaneously guarantee the right to difference and the right to equity. Such a position implies, among other things, a transformation of the relation between the individual and the state, which becomes obligated to guarantee respect for diversity in the public realm through a policy of recognition of cultural difference.

Thus, assimilationism and multiculturalism are not merely two perspectives from which to analyze diversity and social integration, but additionally they guide the design and application of public policy in particular historical and geographic contexts. Nonetheless, as the twenty-first century dawned, two of the premises that underlie both assimilationism and multiculturalism were increasingly questioned, giving rise to new approaches to the study of the incorporation of immigrants. Those premises are that social integration in the receiving societies necessarily involves a distancing from the places of origin, and that the "problem of integration" fundamentally involves the societies receiving the immigrants, while the communities of origin are relatively unimportant, progressively letting go of their connections to the emigrants.

In opposition to these premises, transnationalism proposes that the integration of immigrants into receiving societies does not necessarily involve the rupture of ties to communities of origin. Numerous ethnographic studies have demonstrated the vitality that can be maintained through transnational migration networks, allowing immigrants to live simultaneously in their countries of origin and destination.[3]

The migration of Mexicans to the United States stands out by virtue of its volume and its historic trajectory. This experience has given rise to the research project whose results are presented in this book. Mexicans are the most numerous group of immigrants in the United States, accounting for nearly a third of the total. In 2006, there were 11.6 million Mexican immigrants residing in that country, of whom seven million (60 percent) were undocumented.[4] A variety of actors within US society and politics have stressed the positive value of the presence and integration of this vast population. However, other voices have expressed concern and skepticism, including some within the US academic sector. For example, Samuel Huntington declared that the most immediate and serious challenge to the traditional identity of the United States stemmed from Latin American immigration, especially the immigration from Mexico. For him, many Mexican immigrants and their descendants simply did not seem to identify primarily with the United States, and he warned that "the Mexicans and other Latinos have not assimilated into mainstream US culture, forming instead their own political and linguistic enclaves—from Los Angeles to Miami—and rejecting the Anglo-Protestant values that built the American dream."[5]

In contrast to Huntington's and similar perceptions, this book seeks to broaden the knowledge of the efforts, successes, and challenges involved in the integration of Mexican immigrants in the United States. The first distinguishing characteristic of this work is that it takes as a point of departure the need to analyze the process of incorporation (or non-incorporation) without underestimating the importance of immigrants' ties to their sending communities as a part of this process. The fact that our research team is located in the border region of Mexico contributes to our emphasis on this perspective, distinguishing this study from others carried out within the classic approach to integration that has occupied a central place in US social science.

This perspective has also clearly affected the selection of metropolitan Los Angeles as our research site. In spite of a recent broadening in the destinations of Mexican immigrants within the United States, the Los Angeles region, made up of five counties in Southern California, has continued to be their most important destination. In that sense, Los Angeles is paradigmatic. As the second largest metropolitan area in the United States, it is the largest destination of international immigrants after New York, and Mexicans constitute the largest group of immigrants in this California metropolis.

In 2007, the estimate for Mexican immigrants living in the Los Angeles metropolitan area stood at slightly more than 2.6 million. Thus this area constitutes the fourth most important concentration of Mexicans, after the metropolitan areas of Mexico City, Guadalajara, and Monterrey. Similarly, with the Mexican immigrant population accounting for 14 percent of the total population of metropolitan Los Angeles, it far outnumbers the other immigrant groups.[6]

This book analyzes the integration of Mexican immigrants in metropolitan Los Angeles with three principal goals: (1) To analyze these immigrants' economic and social integration from a quantitative perspective, using data from the 2007 American Community Survey. (2) To examine the immigrants' economic, social, cultural, and political integration from an ethnographic perspective. Toward this end we analyze the integration experience of three groups of immigrants—from the Mexican states of Zacatecas, Oaxaca, and Veracruz—which settled in the Los Angeles region at different times in different historical contexts. (3) To document the public policies that recent administrations of the city and county of Los Angeles have implemented to facilitate or restrict Mexican immigrants' integration.

This book presents an analysis that differs from other studies of immigrant integration in that it approaches that process from a multidisciplinary perspective, examining four distinct dimensions: economic, social, political, and cultural. In addition, by looking at the revision of public policies implemented at several levels of Los Angeles government, we seek to illustrate local governments' capacity for action within the processes of integration. Although it is true that immigration policy as such in the United States is defined by the federal government, the states, counties, and cities administer federal policies of integration through their regulation of the daily interaction of natives and immigrants at work, in school, and in public spaces in general. In this sense, the strategies of integration carried out by immigrants respond specifically to the particular contexts in which they live. The interaction between public policies and the strategies employed by the immigrants themselves is the framework within which immigrants' integration into the city takes place.

Our research employed an array of sources. On the one hand, we used a fundamental database, the American Community Survey of 2007, to analyze the social and economic integration of Mexican immigrants in the Los Angeles metropolitan area. On the other hand, assuming that the processes of integration need to be analyzed from a broad temporal perspective, we examined the experiences of immigrants from Zacatecas, Oaxaca, and Veracruz. For each of these population groups we selected three different communities of origin with significant representation in Los Angeles. That selection enabled us to carry out ninety interviews with immigrants from the nine localities, as well as dozens of further interviews with informants who, though not from the nine selected communities, also provided important elements for the analysis. The group is not a random or probability sample, but rather one constructed according to "snowball" methodology while taking care to achieve diversity in such characteristics as age, sex, marital status, occupation, and immigration status. Although at first the support of leaders of immigrants' associations was a fundamental resource for contacting our interview subjects, we also took care to include the experiences of those who were not part of any association. Finally, in terms of the average dates of our interviewees' taking up residence in Los Angeles, our sample (as will be seen in chapter 2) reflects the longevity of the Zacatecan immigrant population and the recentness of the Verucruzan one, with the Oaxacan community in between.

The interviews reflect our interviewees' experiences in relation to their economic, social, cultural, and political integration. Most were carried in the informants' homes, and others in their workplaces or in public space. The interviews were digitally recorded and lasted an average of one hour. Finally, after reviewing a wide spectrum of reports and other materials, both journalistic ones and those carried out by a variety of organizations and government bodies, we documented various aspects of legislation that directly or indirectly have impacted the processes of economic, social, cultural, and political incorporation of Mexican immigrants in Los Angeles.

The book's structure reflects the analytical strategy outlined above. In the first part, in chapter 1 we discuss the theoretical perspectives underlying our analysis of the process of immigrant integration, and in chapter 2 we present the construction of the Mexican immigrant community in Los Angeles, stressing the particularities of this process in the Zacatecan, Oaxacan, and Veracruzan communities. Chapter 3 presents the results of the descriptive statistical analysis of integration based on the American Community Survey.

The second part of the book presents an ethnographic analysis of the process of integration. In chapter 4 we describe the economic integration of Zacatecans, Oaxacans, and Veracruzans. The trajectories they followed from the first jobs obtained in Los Angeles to their employment at the time of the interviews allow us to identify sharp differences in the achievements and strategies of the immigrants from these three different Mexican states. Chapters 5 and 6, devoted respectively to social and cultural integration, consider the importance of the strategies that the immigrants themselves developed in order to incorporate into the receiving society, which include recourse to transnational ties and to intermediary bodies (such as immigrants' associations, cultural or religious groups, and school parents' associations). Finally, chapter 7, on political integration, examines the implications of immigration law in the processes of integration, as well as the perceptions and actions of the immigrants themselves in the face of this legal environment.

The third part of the book (chapter 8) centers on public policies that impact the processes of integration. In it we examine the various laws and regulations in effect in the Los Angeles region that have a direct impact on these processes. This section allows us to stress the importance of the analysis of integration at two governmental levels: the city and the county of Los Angeles.

Finally, the conclusion discusses the main contemporary characteristics of the processes of integration of Mexican immigrants in Los Angeles, which must be understood both in relation to the contexts of the immigrants' arrival and in relation to the nature and density of their ties with Mexico. Relatively recent events such as the global financial crisis unleashed in 2008 and the increase in violence and insecurity in Mexico have impacted the integration trajectories of the Zacatecans, Oaxacans, and Veracruzans we interviewed. The results of the research presented here suggest that the transformation of immigrants' integration strategies will have an important impact not only in the United States but also in Mexico.

PART ONE

Theoretical, Historical, and Statistical Aspects of Mexican Immigrant Integration in Metropolitan Los Angeles

CHAPTER I

Theoretical Perspectives on Immigrant Integration

The process through which immigrants are integrated into their destination societies falls within a larger discussion of the problem of social integration, surely one of the key elements in sociological thought since the early twentieth century. From the Durkheimian concern with the construction of the *lien social* to contemporary debates about threats posed by immigrants to the identities of their receiving or host societies,[1] modern sociological outlooks might be classified according to their treatment of the processes of social integration and differentiation.[2] Today, however, this discussion has taken on particular virulence and unexpected dimensions.

This debate has heated up because of the inevitable ties linking political philosophy, economics, and political science. That is, alongside the analysis of social integration or differentiation, any "integration project" implies a normative social vision. How much room should be afforded—or denied—to difference? What is the minimum degree of homogeneity required to guarantee social cohesion? What legitimate strategies guarantee the integration of new members into contemporary societies?

Thus, to take one example, some fundamental disagreements about the legal status of immigrant workers do not necessarily arise from different assessments of the extent or limits of these workers' integration, but rather stem from prevailing contradictions among the social ideals being pursued.

In order to contribute to this debate, we find it necessary, following Wieviorka,[3] to distinguish among three levels of analysis that, although closely linked, belong to different realms of reflection. The first (a socio-anthropological perspective) is the analysis of concrete processes of social differentiation and integration in the context of specific historic realities. The second (political philosophy) involves the construction of models or ideals of integration, which can in turn point toward a third level (public policy), which is the creation of particular political projects.

Analysis of the specific processes that produce social differentiation constitutes a fundamental input to thinking about the societal ideal being pursued—what importance should be accorded to difference and what to the principle of equity—which in turn constitutes the point of departure for crafting strategies or public policies to promote integration. These three levels of thought, although tightly intertwined, follow three different logics that must be characterized as such.

Examining processes of social integration implies discussing the relationship between the individual and society, and more specifically the relationship between social integration and the principle of individuation. The society-individual relationship is key to analysis of the incorporation of immigrants into receiving societies because it highlights the bidirectional nature of this process: the migrant simultaneously "incorporates him- or herself into" the receiving society and "is incorporated by" it.[4] Thus, consideration of this dialectic relationship can accord a central place to social subjects as actors in the processes of integration, without underestimating the force—sometimes a crushing one—that the society exercises over the individual who is seeking integration. Or, to use the formulation of Pastor and Ortiz,[5] integration of immigrants may be defined as "improved economic mobility for, enhanced civic participation by, and receiving society openness to immigrants." Therefore it is fundamental to analyze both the immigrants' own capacity for action and the concrete actions of the society that receives them. We consider it of primary importance to employ this understanding of a two-way street—integration *by* the society and integration *into* the society—in any analysis of this process.

Equally, in examining varying analytical perspectives on integration, it is necessary to differentiate what importance each one accords to social change, distinguishing those perspectives that see society as a *corps social* from those that are focused on processes of integration. To what degree is the receiving society already a given, and to what degree is it under construction? What is the relative importance of immigration in the process of social change?

Following this general outline, with the goal of clarifying the theoretical framework that orients the present study, we shall first briefly review some of the major theoretical propositions that have guided thinking and debate about immigrant integration into host societies in recent decades. To make this discussion clearer, we divide these propositions into "classic theories" and "new perspectives." After this survey we will present the theoretical perspectives for analyzing economic, social, cultural, and political integration of immigrants that we have adopted in this book. Finally, in the last section of this chapter, we will describe our specific strategy for analyzing the integration processes of Mexican immigrants in the Los Angeles Metropolitan Area.

CLASSIC THEORIES

Over the past four or five decades, a vast literature has emerged on the subject of the status and spaces accorded or denied to immigrants in so-called host societies. Although this output has included a wide range of theoretical and normative approaches, these can be classified into two broad categories: those that take social integration as the objective to be achieved, and those that, on the contrary, emphasize the pursuit of models for the management of difference, which is seen as a central component of society. The first category is commonly labeled assimilationism, while the second is associated with the multiculturalist perspective.

Historically speaking, early theoretical approaches to the analysis of immigrant incorporation in receiving societies[6] were strongly influenced by the functionalist viewpoint, which ties integration to social cohesion. Still, even at this early stage, the Durkheimian perspective of incorporation "by" the society (or the construction of social cohesion) was being replaced by the perspective of incorporation "into" the society.[7]

These perspectives have at least two important implications. One is that the linking of integration and social cohesion assumes that assimilation is a positive phenomenon. Since social cohesion is seen as an indispensable requisite for maintaining society, integration acquires a normative character. Or, expressing this assumption in its negative form, the absence of the incorporation of immigrants constitutes a threat to social cohesion. Second, when attention is centered on integration "into" the society, it is assumed it is the migrants who will have to adapt themselves to the social context into which they hope to incorporate. This does not necessarily mean that societies must guarantee social cohesion by changing in order to make room for the immigrants. The responsibility for integration thus falls primarily on the immigrants themselves.

The theoretical approaches of this "classic" period were strongly influenced by the United States historical context because of, among other things, the important production of literature on that particular subject from the turn of the twentieth century on. In this US context, the reigning vision was the assimilationist one, well represented by the "melting pot" metaphor according to which immigrants gradually give up their cultural specificity so as to fully incorporate themselves into the host society. The fundamental thrust of assimilationism—the idea of the progressive fading away of immigrants' cultural boundaries—has at least three variants. The first, classical assimilationism, holds that the dissolution of cultural differences constitutes an irreversible and inevitable process. This classic model of integration dates to the Chicago School of the 1920s, with figures such as Robert Park, for whom that process is equated with migrants' assimilation. Though Park himself did recognize the difficulties faced in that process, he also stressed its positive aspects, which for him included immigrants' breaking with tradition and the subsequent expansion of secular individualism among their population.[8] Park and Burgess posited the existence of a "cycle of race relations" in which a period of competition and conflict would be followed by a process of adaptation that would end with the eventual assimilation of the immigrants through participation in common experiences and shared traditions.

Building on this base, Milton Gordon[9] put forward a more refined version that established different stages of the process and introduced the possibility that some groups would achieve greater assimilation than others, although he did not explain these differences.[10] Gordon distinguished seven dimensions or general forms of assimilation: acculturation, structural assimilation, marital assimilation, identification, and attitude-receptional, behavior-receptional, and civic assimilation. For Gordon, each of these dimensions would take place gradually, but inevitably and irreversibly.

Classical assimilationist theory has since been revised and reformulated in many directions. One variant is the "new assimilation theory,"[11] which takes a critical stance toward the original outlook, reconsidering whether a "cycle of race relations" continues without pause and questioning whether this cycle can be completed within an immigrant's life span.

For these theorists, assimilation is a long-term process that can be observed only over several generations.[12] For example, Alba and Nee, in what they themselves call "new assimilation theory," devote greater attention not only to the migration experience but also to the dominant population's openness to change and acceptance of the immigrant groups.[13] This approach recognizes the growing heterogeneity of US society—the authors discuss assimilation not into Anglo-American culture as such but rather into mainstream culture—which makes it practically impossible to speak of any uniform process of assimilation of immigrants into this destination society. Still, this variant emphasizes the degree of transformation that takes place at the intergenerational level.

But probably the revision of the assimilationist approach that has had the greatest impact, which we will call the third main variant after the classical and new approaches, is known as the segmented assimilation approach. It holds that "the new second generation—the children of contemporary immigrants—becomes incorporated into the system of stratification in the host society."[14]

In the work of Zhou and Portes,[15] this approach stresses the importance of structural barriers that direct immigrants and their descendants toward distinct routes of assimilation within their destination societies; in the case of the United States, intergenerational assimilation leads to the children of migrants into different segments of US society. This perspective outlines three possible paths of assimilation: "One of them replicates the time-honored portrayal of growing acculturation and parallel integration into the white middle-class; a second leads straight in the opposite direction to permanent poverty and assimilation into the underclass; still a third associates rapid economic advancement with deliberate preservation of the immigrant community's values and tight solidarity."[16]

Consequently, studies adopting the segmented assimilation perspective revolve around identifying the contextual, structural, and cultural factors that explain the unequal results in migrant assimilation.[17] Among these factors, those seen as major determinants of the degree of assimilation are greater or lesser human capital, degree of cohesion in ethnic community and family structure, and the destination society's degree of disposition toward incorporation.[18]

Alongside this approach, other analysts have adopted the perspective of racial and ethnic disadvantage. This approach conceives of the various migrant groups as minorities (the central referent being the black population in the United States) who confront persistent exploitation and discrimination by the dominant white population. This constitutes an obstacle to their economic and social mobility that blocks their possibilities of assimilation into the destination society.[19] Thus, as Portes and Rumbaut[20] demonstrate, migrants' racial and ethnic identities have a decisive influence not only on their occupational mobility and social acceptance but also on the aspirations and academic performance of their sons and daughters.

This revision of the assimilationist idea has at least two important effects. First, there is no direct relationship between assimilation and social mobility: the children of immigrants who live in poverty conditions do not owe their situation to a lack of assimilation, but to full assimilation into an inferior segment of the society. Put another way, social mobility is not an indicator of assimilation, just as poverty is not necessarily explained by a lack of assimilation. Second, the segmented assimilation perspective shows the need to distinguish different dimensions within the process of assimilation: cultural assimilation may be accompanied by social or economic exclusion, while the reinforcement of ethnic boundaries—that is, limited cultural assimilation—can be accompanied by rapid economic improvement. Thus, in the specific analyses of the process of immigrant incorporation into host societies, it is fundamental to dissociate cultural integration (expressed both in the internalization of norms and values and in the construction of life projects) from economic and social integration reflected in the usual indicators of social, educational, occupational, and other forms of mobility. The tension between successful cultural integration and poor socioeconomic integration can explain some of the most visible problems faced by the children of immigrants.[21]

By positing the existence of important social differentiation that is reproduced—but not created—by the migrants, this third variant of the assimilationist approach (segmented assimilation) brings us closer to the second large group of theoretical perspectives that we mentioned at the outset of this chapter: the multiculturalist perspective on integration.

In spite of important differences among the various theoretical approaches we include in this second grouping, their common identifying characteristic is their recognition of cultural difference as a constitutive element in every society, from which it follows that the goal of the host societies is not the gradual dissolution of ethnic boundaries, but rather the management of difference. And difference, of course, precedes the arrival of each new immigrant group. The true challenge is thus not making cultural difference disappear, but on the contrary, to paraphrase Alain Touraine,[22] answering the question, "How can we live together?" while respecting the principle of equity and valuing cultural difference.

Historically, this theoretical perspective grew out of the demands of the mid-twentieth-century US civil rights movement. Denunciation of the discrimination suffered by ethnic and racial minorities allowed for the emergence of a new discourse that sought not only suppression of social inequality but also recognition of cultural diversity. These demands were put forth within the African American as well as the Chicano and Native American movements.

Unlike earlier social movements, these movements linked to specific ethnic groups challenged the discrimination to which they had been subjected and demanded both equal opportunity and respect for cultural specificity. That is, they demanded integration based on recognition of difference. In terms of both analysis and political philosophy, this represents a major shift, one that upholds the necessity of simultaneously guaranteeing the rights to difference and to equity.

This perspective implies, among other things, a transformation of the relation between the individual and the state, whose obligation becomes one of guaranteeing respect for diversity within public space through a policy of recognizing cultural difference.[23] In the case of the United States, to guarantee equity in a context of difference, the state undertook the design of public policies specifically based on the recognition of ethnic and cultural diversity, departing from the principle of equality (racial, religious, gender, ethnic, etc.) before the law, commonly known as the principle of color blindness. Examples of such public policies are those known generically as affirmative action, which sought to reverse the historic disadvantages created by discrimination that have blocked the upward mobility of some minorities. Especially, affirmative action sought to eliminate the underrepresentation of minorities who had been discriminated against in specific areas, such as public administration or higher education, through special programs or specific regulations.

Thus, in its most radical variants, the multiculturalist perspective transforms the meaning of citizenship by replacing a fundamentally individualist relationship (of the individual to the state and society) with a relationship mediated by membership in specific subgroups that are constituted as "communities" or intermediate groups between the individual and the state, or between the individual and the society.

This "community-based" vision of cultural diversity has been criticized primarily because it encloses the individual within a community of reference that "ghettoizes" the individual and because it crystalizes difference rather than recognizing its fluid character. Perhaps one of the most notable critiques of this current of multiculturalism is the one put forward by Giovanni Sartori,[24] who asserts that multiculturalism is intrinsically opposed to pluralism, especially because it imposes affiliations on the individual and because it hardens the boundaries of communities. For example, unlike political party membership, ethnic membership is not voluntary and it is practically impossible to de-affiliate from such a community. Thus from Sartori's perspective,[25] the policy of recognizing difference is incompatible with pluralism and even with the principle of integration because it fosters the construction and crystallization of ethnic and cultural boundaries.

In addition to these criticisms it is important to note that, from the perspective of immigrant integration, processes of "hyper-integration" of specific groups with rigid boundaries could constitute a greater obstacle to individual integration into the society in a broad sense.

The criticisms leveled at this particular current of radical multiculturalism do not come only from the assimilationist camp. They come also from the current of "tempered multiculturalism," defenders of cultural difference whose approach differs from the community-based one.[26] Michel Wieviorka,[27] for instance, asserts the need to consider simultaneously that cultural difference operates within societies (not only between different societies) and that those differences are not immutable but rather created, produced, and reproduced both individually and collectively, transforming their contents and demanding recognition through a variety of means and within variable spaces.

The debate between assimilationism and multiculturalism in their various strands framed most discussion of the processes of immigrant integration into destination societies until the end of the twentieth century. However, more recently, new approaches have allowed further development of that discussion.

NEW PERSPECTIVES

If, from the mid-twentieth century on, the classic theories of integration "into" society were ceding ground to analyses of the integration of minority groups within national societies, the opening of the twenty-first century marked a shift in that debate. Now attention has turned almost exclusively to the integration process of immigrants and their descendants. This shift is probably related to intensified migration and the growth of the multicultural metropolis. Yet the intensification of these flows is only part of the explanation. The other part derives from the contradictions generated specifically by the predominant means of managing mobility and cultural diversity, which in various regions of the planet have created large population groups fully integrated into the logic of transnational labor markets yet without any of the political integration that stems from access to citizenship by virtue of place of residence.

This reorientation of the debate toward those who undertake geographical movement presents both virtues and drawbacks. Emphasizing the processes of integration of immigrants "into" destination societies, in contrast to devoting attention to the processes of integration "by" the societies of origin and destination, consigns responsibility for the success of the integration process to the individual. This gives rise to a distinction between "good" and "bad" immigrants and diverts attention from analysis of the specific and differentiated obstacles faced by each immigrant. But, including the population-in-movement in the study of integration has allowed a rethinking of the migrant's relationship to space, in at least two important ways.

First, in roundly denying the existence of contradictions between maintenance of community ties in the country of origin and incorporation into destination societies,[28] the transnationalist perspective has obliged theorists of integration to open their discussion beyond the borders of national states. In fact, the transnationalist perspective not only holds that migrants' ties with their communities of origin do not necessarily weaken over time, but proposes that such ties can coexist with successful integration into receiving societies.

That analytic perspective has been quickly incorporated into many studies appearing in specialized academic publications, which is a clear sign of its relevance to the examination of concrete realities. A growing number of studies—particularly ethnographic ones—have portrayed the process of the construction of transnational ties in a variety of migratory systems with precision and clarity.

In spite of the important acceptance of this proposition, the step from concrete analysis of the formation of transnational ties to the construction of a new theoretical perspective on integration that transcends the limits of national states is not yet evident. How can the study of the problem of integration "by" societies transcend the analytic logic centered on the nation-state? How can we think about the integration processes of immigrants into their societies of origin? How can we think about integration by acknowledging the "double presence"[29] which is also a double absence?

Clearly, this is a great methodological challenge that demands a rethinking of the logic of scales of space: the migrant may be integrated into local, regional, multilocal, national, and/or transnational space. In this sense, Jiménez and Fitzgerald[30] advance an important proposition about how to reorient consideration of processes of assimilation in spatial and temporal terms. Their proposed spatial reorientation allows for a new attempt to understand the relationship between immigrants' assimilation into host societies and their "de-assimilation" or differentiation with respect to their societies of origin. The proposed temporal reorientation, for its part, allows for observation of assimilation processes across several generations (immigrant generation, second generation, etc.) without losing sight of specific cohorts tied to specific historical contexts.

Second, recent events have signified new challenges for the study of integration processes by laying bare the contradictions crystalizing particularly around the so-called "second generations" in a variety of geographical contexts. The 2005 urban riots in outlying Parisian neighborhoods clearly showed the disparity between successful cultural integration and blocked economic and social integration.[31] The disparity between these different levels of integration requires the development of methodological frameworks that allow for simultaneous observation of economic, social, cultural, and political integration, and of the tensions that derive from disparate results along these various axes.

The existence of such disparities requires rethinking the processes of social integration not as stages along a unitary path, but as possible parallel trajectories. Or, reformulating Schnapper's[32] characterization, it is not a matter of different levels or degrees of integration, but of different modalities.

This distinction is fundamental to the effort to analyze the above-mentioned bidirectionality of integration processes. If we accept that there is no single path to integration, but rather different modalities, then it is key to observe the processes through which these modalities arise and intersect.

Naturally, this theoretical perspective does not seek to underestimate the implications of social segmentation, broadly documented in the work of the segmented assimilation school. Nor does it intend to overstate the real but limited capacity for action of the immigrants by placing that capacity at the center of the analysis. Rather, it stresses the importance of analyzing the tensions where the modalities of integration overlap and observes the edges that might incubate social change.

It would be advisable, therefore, to reorient our approach so as to focus on the formation of integration strategies developed by immigrants themselves and also to those created by the state (both that of origin and that of destination), as well as on the tensions deriving from contradictions between such strategies and the reigning structural conditions in the contexts of origin and destination.

ANALYSIS OF ECONOMIC, SOCIAL, CULTURAL, AND POLITICAL INTEGRATION

While it is possible to distinguish some general lines that have marked thinking about immigrant integration, the literature produced during recent decades has presented a growing disciplinary specialization. In what follows we present some of the analytical perspectives that have characterized the study of economic, social, cultural, and political integration of immigrants, so as to later introduce the analytic strategy that has guided our analysis.

Economic Integration

Economic integration of immigrants in their destination countries is a subject that has been taken up in the main by economists, sociologists, demographers, and planners, who in general have concentrated on analyzing immigrants' patterns of upward economic mobility in comparison to those of natives.[33] The analysis of immigrants' economic integration includes their insertion in the labor market and the parity of their salaries with respect to native-born workers, but also self-employment, which sometimes accounts for the rise of ethnic economies.[34] Such analysis must also include investments in real estate, both in the country of origin and in that of destination.

In the first place, from the economic perspective, it is essential to analyze migrants' decision making around their dilemma of staying in the destination country or returning to the one of origin. According to Piore[35] in his classic work *Birds of Passage,* the settlement of immigrants in the destination country can be understood as either a success or a failure. In general, the criterion of success is that the immigrant progresses and stays. Nonetheless, immigrants may also stay in the destination country out of failure, when they can't muster enough money to carry out their original project. More recently, Vigdor[36] has used the concept of selective emigration to describe how those most likely to depart more quickly from the destination country are young people and/or those who do most poorly in the labor market.

According to Piore,[37] the migratory pattern evolves from the individual migrant acting as *homo economicus* into a situation in which there is a permanent community of immigrant families with strong labor market ties. In the first phases, the immigrants view work instrumentally, as a means to earn income that they can take to their place of origin, but later, with the passage of time, they begin to question the ascetic life they are living, and they bring their wives and children to live with them.

Valenzuela[38] identifies three theories that can explain the distinct varieties of immigrant integration into the labor market in the United States: displacement, segmentation, and job-ladder succession, or queuing theory. Neoclassical displacement theory argues that immigrants arrive in the United States in a context of falling wages, and that growing numbers of immigrant workers cause wages to fall still further, as the aggregate supply of labor power increases in spite of a static demand for workers. In this process, immigrants displace native-born workers because (it is assumed) they serve as perfect replacements, if differences in abilities are ignored.

Piore[39] suggests the existence of a segmented labor market, in which the native workers are protected from being directly displaced by immigrants to the United States. A primary sector is home to the highest-paid, most stable, and highest-status jobs, which are reserved for native workers. Immigrants are concentrated in a secondary sector, occupying jobs that are unskilled, low paid, and often involve difficult working conditions, insecure job tenure, and few opportunities to move up the job ladder. Although the segmented labor market theory has not been empirically verified and seems insufficient to explain the high volume of skilled immigrants employed in the information technology sector in the United States, it is useful for understanding the growth of labor niches.[40] Immigrants from a given country are often concentrated in a limited number of occupations or industries, forming niches that increase their ability to find jobs while reducing the costs and risks of hiring and job training. Such immigrant niches limit the ability of native-born workers or other immigrants to find jobs in the given sector.[41]

The labor succession (or queuing) theory[42] argues that immigrants take jobs that native-born workers no longer want, which then become a path for immigrants. Over time, native workers move on to better occupations, leaving vacant posts that are taken by immigrants, giving rise to labor force complementarity.

On the subject of parity of earnings between native and immigrant workers, Borjas[43] measures assimilation as the speed with which the earnings of immigrants to the United States come to match those of natives over time. Borjas asserts that the pioneer study comparing immigrant earnings with those of native-born counterparts, carried out by Chiswick,[44] erroneously concluded that legal immigrants assimilated "too well." In contrast, based on his own research carried out in the early 1990s, Borjas[45] argues that immigrants' socioeconomic abilities (their educational levels and their English proficiency) deteriorated significantly between the 1960s and 1970s and therefore their real wages would remain lower than those of natives throughout their working lives.

One key element in understanding labor force integration today is the worsening working conditions in developed countries. Although the informal economy has been seen as a remnant of relations of production from periods gone by, it has grown in institutionalized economies at the expense of formal work relations. The question posed by Sassen[46] remains an open one: is the informal economy in developed countries a consequence of advanced capitalism or the result of immigration?

While an immigrant's buying a house in the destination country suggests a commitment to remain there, the acquisition of property in the country of origin may indicate that a transnational project is under way. Myers and Woo[47] assert that for immigrants to the United States, the acquisition of a house is an important symbol of membership in the middle class and of residential assimilation. Their study of home ownership by natives and immigrants in Southern California shows that while Asian immigrants have a high rate of home ownership within a short time after arriving in the United States, Hispanic immigrants start at low levels but show a steady growth in this statistic over time.

In accord with the above propositions, in our analysis of economic integration we will use the following indicators: insertion in the labor market, self-employment business formation in the United States and Mexico, and real estate ownership in both countries.

Social Integration

Traditionally, academic and political discussion of immigrant integration tends to refer to the degree of social integration in the destination country, which may be generically defined as the degree of mobility and inclusion that immigrants attain in a variety of spaces within their new societies. However, as a number of analysts[48] have pointed out, in the United States this facet of immigrant integration is afforded only limited space in both the public and political spheres. That is to say, despite the prominence of immigration as a subject of debate in the country and in its politics, immigrants' social integration is supported by limited legislation and even more limited budgets. This is important because it indicates that this process is little valued, even though it is fundamental to facilitating immigrants' participation in the creation of stronger communities and even to strengthening the economy of the United States as a whole.

For the many and varied academic and political positions expressed with respect to immigrants' social integration in that country, the Los Angeles region stands out as a central point of reference. Los Angeles County is the largest immigrant metropolis in the United States, especially in terms of Mexican immigration, despite the recent rise of other destinations and the drop in numbers of new immigrants since the 1990s. A fundamental point on which academics, public policy specialists, and political representatives all agree is that a process of social integration, to be worthy of the name, must include two main aspects: the way immigrants change to insert themselves into their destination society, and the ways that society changes with respect to the presence of that population.[49]

This assertion is consistent with recent research centered on the process of immigrant integration in the Los Angeles region. Pastor and Ortiz,[50] basing their study on focus groups, found that activists, businesspersons, workforce developers, foundation staff, urban planners, public officials, and trade unionists all agree on the immigrant population's importance to the region, not only for economic reasons but also for sociodemographic ones. Yet the first decade of the twenty-first century in the United States has witnessed a greater tendency to view that population as a "problem" and their chances of social integration as limited, both in the public and in the political spheres, especially in the case of immigration from Mexico.

The claims about the supposed declining social integration of Mexicans, which come from the political sphere, the mass media, and even the academic sector in the United States, refer to various traditional indicators such as legal immigration status, language proficiency, presence of social networks, use of public services, and school attendance. The resulting image is one of undocumented immigrants, monolingual in Spanish with almost no interest in learning English, immersed in social networks that keep them inexorably tied to Mexico, relatively alienated from the social settings of US society, and having little motivation to deepen their education or that of their children.

However, this image has provoked a much larger discussion. One fundamental measure that can suggest the degree of social integration of an immigrant population in the United States is English proficiency. In this regard, Telles[51] holds that such proficiency among Mexican immigrants is no different from that of other groups. At the same time, on the issue of educational attainment, this author reports that, while the second generation is more successful than the first, its success does not equal that of the native-born population. However, his data also show that this difference stems from structural conditions (for instance, the racialization imposed by the society on that population) and not from the Mexican immigrants themselves.

In the same vein, Rumbaut, Massey, and Bean[52] assert that in contrast to the position that judges Mexican immigrants' social integration to be very limited based on their alleged linguistic limitations, many studies demonstrate the value such immigrants accord to English-language proficiency, which they perceive as a fundamental requisite for any sort of mobility in their destination environment. Also, these authors emphasize that while the undocumented status of the majority of Mexican immigrants is indeed an obstacle to achievement of greater social integration, it can be attributed to the erratic immigration policies of the United States.

One additional major indicator affecting perceptions of Mexican immigrants' social integration in the United States is their supposedly limited degree of intermarriage and inter-ethnic relationships more generally. Certainly, during a considerable period of the history of Mexican immigrant communities, spouses from the same town, city, or state of origin were the norm. Still, Durand and Martínez[53] have observed the growing presence of mixed marriages among Mexican immigrants, which constitutes a change in the area of social integration, and with it a clear disposition toward building lives in the United States. Similarly, Montejano[54] points out that for the third generation in the Los Angeles region, mixed marriage prevails in more than half of the Latino population (which is largely of Mexican origin).

Another variant of the image of the supposed limited social integration of Mexican immigrants derives from the persistence of their transnational ties through social networks based on family, friendships, or common place of origin. While Montejano[55] himself finds that such processes have been a constant in Mexican immigrant communities since their origins, he asserts that existing studies do not show this to have been an obstacle to their eventual integration.

Based on the above considerations, our study seeks particularly to document and examine the degree and complexity of social integration of Mexican immigrants in the Los Angeles region. The individuals interviewed in our research explain their perceptions and practices with respect to the various dimensions of the social integration process. Analysis of their testimonies highlights not only the effort expended by Mexican immigrants and their families, communities, and associations to form part of Los Angeles society, but also the limitations they have faced in terms of policies and services intended to promote more effective integration. In the chapter devoted to social integration, we first present our assessment of the social dimensions affecting the possible integration of Mexican immigrants in the region under study, including those discussed by the above-cited authors.

Cultural Integration

A subject that has unleashed the most passionate debate is that of cultural integration. Most likely this is because, beyond the social problems attributed to immigrants, a lack of cultural integration seems to put the identity and indeed the essence of host societies in jeopardy. Probably the clearest example of such alarmist rhetoric is, once again, the position taken by Huntington,[56] which illustrates a current of thinking that, in spite of its contradictions, has achieved considerable acceptance. In essence, the idea holds that immigrants are morally obligated to give up their cultural particularity so as to fuse into the society in which they have chosen to live. This notion is so old and widespread that it seems to qualify as common sense. It can be found in the classic work *The Polish Peasant*[57] and in the work of such writers as Park and Burgess[58] and Gordon,[59] already discussed above. In the study specifically of Mexican migration, a notable representative of this tradition is the pioneering work of Manuel Gamio,[60] who set out to understand the process of assimilation or "adjustment" of Mexican immigrants in the United States.

By the mid-twentieth century, this point of view was losing its prevalence due to the climate of the civil rights movement, which gave rise to voices that vehemently insisted that cultural difference could be maintained and reinforced in spite of stigma and discrimination, as in the case of the black population.[61] On the one hand, it was argued that minorities' lack of assimilation was a product of the hegemonic group's reinforcement of ethnic boundaries. On the other, there was a gradual departure from the discourse itself, from the notion of pursuit of full assimilation through dissolution of ethnic particularities. New perspectives began to emerge that sought recognition for cultural difference in the public space.[62]

At first, the critique rested on the impossibility of full incorporation—a sense of belonging and shared identity—due to social stratification, which employed stigmas and discriminatory processes (residential discrimination, segmented labor market, etc.) to create and strengthen identity boundaries.[63] Thus stratification impedes immigrants' integration, even if they are they are willing to adopt hegemonic norms and values.

In that sense, Telles and Ortiz[64] argue that both the classic assimilation theory of Alba and Nee[65] and the segmented assimilation approach of Portes and his colleagues are insufficient to examine the integration of the population of Mexican origin in the United States, because that population has been submitted to a process of racialization, which they define as the social practice of assigning to others a stigmatized "race" that defines individuals—in this case those of Mexican origin—as having an inferior culture and lack of inherent value, which also excludes them from being able to become "full Americans."

Later the critique from the multiculturalist point of view went further, holding that the myth of acculturation or cultural assimilation rests on a fallacy: it prescribes that immigrants must adapt to the culture of the receiving country, when in fact what immigrants find on arrival is an infinity of distinct cultures that meet in public space in a conflictual manner and establish a relationship of constant tension with the discourse of the hegemonic culture—which is not necessarily a majority one. In sum, the assimilationist discourse assumes that the host society is homogeneous, stable, and unconflicted, when in truth it is a space of confrontation and negotiation in which identity boundaries are constantly shifting through interactions that reproduce asymmetric relations of power. In such a situation, far from seeking the dissolution of their cultural particularities, immigrants tend to enter into the existing network of power relations, playing the cards offered by their own cultural references and senses of belonging.

Consequently, immigrants' cultural integration cannot be understood as the gradual abandonment of their particularities, but rather as the development of strategies that allow them to integrate—according to their particularities—into the network of conflictual interrelations and conflicting senses of belonging. Such strategies permit movement from an identity of origin to another that contains the imprint both of the immigrants' origins and of their interactions with the society.

In this context, the perspective of Brubaker[66] is significant; he holds that after a quarter-century of expansion, the multiculturalist wave has begun to abate, making room for a "return of assimilation." This return, however, differs in important ways from "classic" assimilationism. The new concept of assimilation emphasizes that it is a process, restores the position of subject to the immigrants who are assimilating, notes that assimilation's multigenerational dimension unfolds within a heterogeneous society where some characteristics gradually converge (and thus shifts some emphasis from the cultural to the economic), and replaces a holistic perspective with a multidimensional one.[67] This return of the perspective of assimilation, however, does not resolve the old opposition between an idea of integration (centered on the pursuit of equity by way of recognition of difference) and one of assimilation (centered on the pursuit of equity by way of dissolution of difference).

Naturally, we are not attempting here to provide a generalized answer to this question. But we do assert that careful analysis of the specific process of integration constitutes the only possible way to propose new systems of explanation and new models for managing the process of incorporation of immigrants into the receiving society. To advance in that direction, in chapter 6 of this book, which deals with cultural integration of Mexican immigrants in Los Angeles, we try on one hand to analyze the process of "cultural assimilation" understood in Brubaker's sense, and on the other hand to observe the process by which immigrants themselves construct strategies of integration. We do so to distinguish between two different underlying logics: integration that begins with the recognition of difference, and the pursuit of assimilation through the dissolution or concealment of the differences that make mobility difficult.

The indicators that we selected include some that have been widely utilized in the literature: identity and sense of belonging, religion, residential segregation, and perception of otherness. To these "classic" indicators we have added a variable called "life projects," with the goal of providing a point of entry to an analysis of how strategies of integration/assimilation are constructed.

Political Integration

Among the various facets of the immigrant integration process, the political dimension has gained considerable visibility in recent years. To a large degree, this stems from the many transformations occurring in the second half of the twentieth century, including increased population mobility on a world scale and the subsequent modifications of immigration policies intended to regulate this flow. In this context, nation-states today—both as emitters and as receivers of migrants—confront a variety of challenges subsumed under the question of the political status of this population. Also, migrants themselves play a central role in the definition of their political condition, whether in reference to their destination or their origin countries.

The starting point of this discussion is the premise that a national state exercises its sovereignty over a given population in a territory defined by specific borders. The traditional nexus of state, population, and territory was expressed in the classical notion of citizenship, a key juridical and political status evolving out of either the principle of *jus soli* or that of *jus sanguinis* and determining whether an individual belonged to a national community or not. Such membership brought recognition of a series of rights reserved for citizens of a given state.[68]

Thus, the customary treatment of the presence of immigrants within the framework of traditional states involved assimilation, and the attainment of citizenship meant the acquisition of nationality; that is, through the principle of *jus domicile,* the immigrant acquired membership and with it was able to participate in the political community. In this traditional perspective, the central premise demanded the assimilation of minorities into a single national culture, which in turn implied access to rights in the country of destination.

However, with the intensification of migration, national states have felt obliged to redesign their discourses and policies with respect to the criteria of inclusion and exclusion. In the sending countries, the transformations that emigration generates in the social fabric have given rise to initiatives and policies that seek to reaffirm the political integration of the millions of citizens who have emigrated outside the territory. This is associated with a growing recognition that, on one hand, a sizable share of that population is hoping to live permanently outside the country of origin, but, on the other hand, this population also maintains strong ties with the country and locality of origin.[69]

The response of the receiving states has been more varied and polemical. The United States and a number of European and Latin American nations have markedly restricted their immigrant integration policies, particularly in the political realm. Political integration refers in a general sense to access to spaces and processes of influence and decision making within the nation. In academic circles, restriction of political integration has found resonance among analysts who hold that recognizing immigrants as having such political rights (that is, allowing them political integration) constitutes a threat to the national community and culture and to democracy.[70] In the political sector, one indicator of this concern is the number of sustained attempts by various nation-states to eliminate or reduce the presence of undocumented immigrants, or to maintain policies of regulation and control that render immigrants' path to citizenship more difficult. Since the events of September 11, 2001, border control in many national states has tightened drastically, and with this tightening has come a marked restriction of access to traditional and new destinations for international migration. Nonetheless, alongside these positions, the past decades have also seen other, opposing perspectives that have affected immigrants' political participation. Such is the case with the concept of human rights and the rise of international norms that recognize certain rights of individuals regardless of their immigration status. This, in turn, has opened up the possibility of international accords and laws that require sending and receiving states to protect those rights.[71]

This development has offered an underpinning to approaches such as multiculturalism, which relates directly to immigrants' political integration to the extent that it emphasizes the possibility of citizenship for all residents of a nation. Adopting a sense of diversity implies the extension of rights to all residents, including immigrants.[72]

However, regardless of shifts in perspective about immigrants' status and their access to full citizenship, a central phenomenon to be discussed is the growing visibility of immigrants themselves in the political sphere. This has been part of their struggle for recognition and political incorporation in both the sending states and—especially—the receiving ones. Although discussion of political integration always includes access to citizenship and the accompanying right to vote, the fact is that immigrants have managed to achieve political participation through a variety of other institutions and activities, such as unions and associations, public demonstrations, consultation or lobbying through immigrant organizations, and both conventional and virtual media where they have been able to state opinions and participate on a local level and even in transnational spaces.[73]

In the case of Mexican immigrants in the United States, their growing participation in the public and political sphere highlights the confluence between their demands for participation and the demands of other immigrants groups in other parts of the world (for example, the struggles of the undocumented in Europe)[74] as well as a confluence with the theoretical positions that emphasize the need for national states to transform their premises of citizenship and to create policies that make room for such demands.

In general terms, one response by Mexican immigrants themselves has consisted of their pursuing naturalization, which grants access to full citizenship, allowing them to participate in the political sphere. A significant sector of US public opinion and the US political class sees the process of integration of Mexican immigrants as a limited one, yet the immigrants have increasingly followed the path of naturalization. Alongside growth in the rate of naturalization, there has also been growing political activism on the part of Mexican immigrants in the United States, whether they are citizens or not. Although such participation in key regions like the state of California and the Los Angeles Metropolitan Area had been noted and documented in previous years,[75] the high point came in the year 2006 as part of a wave of demonstrations all across the United States in favor of a comprehensive response by the US government to the immigration issue. The two demonstrations held in the Los Angeles region, in March and May of that year, attracted hundreds of thousands of participants.[76] The importance of these events lies not only in their being the largest concentrations, nation-wide, in this unprecedented wave of demonstrations, but also on the evident centrality of the Mexican immigrants, whose vast numbers included both those with documents and those without, associations of many sorts, and members of the first, second, and even third generations.[77]

The marches and demonstrations of 2006 in areas such as Los Angeles underline the need to reevaluate the importance of the political integration of Mexican immigrants in this and other regions of the United States. Several analysts[78] have emphasized the need for US federal and state governments to promote more and better policies to facilitate the integration of the migrant population in general, so as to—among other reasons—reduce their degree of vulnerability.

Likewise, some analysts have stressed the importance of recognizing the growing interest in political participation on the part of immigrants themselves—in varied spheres of their destination societies, societies of origin, or both. This perspective points to a growing interest in immigrants as dynamic actors positioning themselves within a political community (whether national or transnational) and not as "mere victims of a process that is out of their hands."[79]

If Mexican immigrants have demonstrated their desire for political participation and yet this participation is still of a very limited character, the problem likely lies in structural limitations within the destination society. As Bloemraad[80] points out, the restricted access to citizenship among immigrants in the United States today reveals the absence of institutions and policies sufficient to facilitate political integration among this population, and with it their exercise of rights. The exercise of such rights would in turn, if permitted and encouraged, help consolidate the legitimacy of a democratic government and its institutions.

In this book, the chapter on political integration of Mexican immigrants in the Los Angeles region has as its goal to show the various perceptions and practices of the interviewees with respect to Los Angeles political life. We also consider what occurs in the places of origin, so as to have a point of comparison between the immigrants' political participation in Los Angeles and that in their hometowns, as well as to see the possible influences of the Mexican government's policies toward emigrants, and thus to judge whether that factor in any way influences the processes of political integration in their destinations. Also, in presenting the perceptions and actions of Mexican immigrants, this chapter complements what will later be presented in the section on public policies in the Los Angeles region, allowing for an understanding of the importance, in the achievement of greater or lesser political integration, of both strategies put in practice by the migrants themselves and initiatives by regional political actors.

The indicators we have selected for analysis of political integration are the following: naturalization process, political perception of the United States, participation in political action in the United States, and electoral participation.

Research Project Design

In line with the above discussion, for the purpose of our research on migrants' incorporation, we have hypothesized the following:

1. The integration process is bidirectional. That is, we must examine both immigrants' incorporation into the society and the society's incorporation of immigrants (social cohesion).

2. Integration is above all a process, not a state to be achieved.

3. Dissolution of difference is not a requirement for integration.

4. It is crucial to observe the disparities and tensions across the areas of economic, social, cultural, and political integration.

5. Integration processes may be diverse. There is no single modality of integration, but rather a diversity of strategies.

Based on these assumptions, the methodological design of this investigation was developed with an eye to observing the integration strategies of Mexican immigrants in the Los Angeles region and the integration policies that have affected this process. Synthetically, we could describe our theoretical-methodological approach as a schema drawn on four axes (economic, social, cultural, and political integration) that in turn are affected by three factors (transnationalism, participation in intermediary groups, and public policies). Although we employ this schema differently in each of the empirical chapters, our intent is to observe which factors are susceptible to aiding or restraining integration along each of the four axes.

Also, toward the goal of including a double-faceted temporal dimension (that is, the time transpired since the immigrant's arrival as well as the historical context of his or her integration), we selected three groups each from the three Mexican states of Zacatecas, Oaxaca, and Veracruz. The states of origin represent waves of immigrants who settled in the Los Angeles region in different historical contexts.

We should point out that this research project focuses only on the integration process of the immigrants themselves, without attempting to analyze the trajectories of their descendants. This is due fundamentally to our interest in observing the process of constructing integration strategies within the generation that undertakes the migration, strategies that are not comparable with those of the next generations. Although all the generations form parts of the same families, their integration follows different logics.

CHAPTER 2

Mexican Immigration and the Development of the Los Angeles Metropolitan Area

Mexicans have the dubious honor of constituting both the largest group of legal immigrants and the largest group of undocumented immigrants living in the United States. One out of every ten people born in Mexico resides in the United States temporarily or permanently, and the majority are in that country without documents, which means they face the daily fear of being deported. The rest are naturalized citizens, legal permanent residents, persons granted political asylum, or persons whose temporary stay is authorized by particular types of visas such as those for students, professionals (TN or H-1B), or agricultural workers (H-2A) reprising the work done by their grandparents under the Bracero Program.

In 2008 there were an estimated 11.6 million Mexican immigrants in the United States, of whom seven million were undocumented. In March of that year, the total undocumented US population reached an estimated 11.9 million, including the seven million Mexicans who made up 59 percent of that total.[1] The Mexican immigrant population has grown rapidly over recent decades. In 1970, only 760,000 people living in the United States had been born in Mexico. During the 1990s, this population increased, on average, by nearly a half-million people per year. This dizzying growth has been driven primarily by undocumented migration.[2]

The undocumented population grew rapidly in the opening years of the 2000s, then slowed in 2005–2008. The flow of undocumented

TABLE I   LEGAL PERMANENT RESIDENTS ADMITTED TO THE UNITED STATES,
2005: TOTAL VOLUME AND THOSE ADMITTED FOR EMPLOYMENT REASONS, BY
COUNTRY OF BIRTH

	Total immigrants	Admitted for employment reasons	For employment as % of total
Mexico	161,445	16,347	10.1
India	84,681	47,705	56.3
China	69,967	20,626	29.5
Philippines	60,748	18,322	30.2
Cuba	36,261	18	0.05
Vietnam	32,784	304	0.9
Dominican Republic	27,504	444	1.6
All countries	1,122,373	246,877	22

SOURCE: US Department of Homeland Security, 2006, "Office of Immigration Statistics" (Table 10).

immigrants reached an estimated annual average of eight hundred thousand between 2000 and 2004, declining to five hundred thousand between 2005 and 2008, with a diminishing tendency year by year.[3] This decline in the rate of undocumented immigration stemmed mainly from the impact of the global economic recession that began in the United States in 2008.

Affirming the fact that Mexico contributes the largest share of legal immigrants to the United States, data from the US Department of Homeland Security show that Mexicans received the highest proportion (14.4 percent) of the 1,122,373 immigrant visas issued by the US government in 2005.[4] The 161,445 immigrant visas issued to Mexicans were almost double the number received by immigrants from India and outranked the totals received by immigrants from China, the Philippines, Cuba, Vietnam, and the Dominican Republic by still higher ratios (see table 1).

As table 1 shows, while Mexicans received a total of 161,445 immigrant visas, only 16,347 of those (10.1 percent) were awarded for employment reasons under the quota or preference system. The remaining 145,098 (89.9%) were awarded for family reunification under the quota or preference system or for being immediate family members (parents, spouses, or minor children) of US citizens.

In contrast to Mexico's very low 10.1 percent of visas being issued under the system of employment preferences, India and Philippines saw high shares of their visas being awarded in this way—56.3 percent and 30.2 percent, respectively. This demonstrates that most Mexican immigrants admitted as permanent residents in 2005 were offered that status because of family ties, not job skills.

In 2005, the metropolitan area comprising Los Angeles/Long Beach/ Santa Ana was the place of residence of 8.8 percent of the 1,122,373 immigrants admitted by the United States that year. This area was surpassed only by the New York/Northern New Jersey/Long Island area, with 15.4 percent, and was followed by Miami/Fort Lauderdale/Miami Beach, with 7.1 percent.[5]

HISTORICAL PERSPECTIVE ON MEXICAN IMMIGRATION AND LOS ANGELES ECONOMIC DEVELOPMENT

Mexicans constitute the largest immigrant group in metropolitan Los Angeles, an area of Southern California made up of Los Angeles, Orange, San Bernardino, Riverside, and Ventura Counties. Map 1 shows the main cities in this sun-drenched region marked by a giant shadow of urban sprawl. According to data from the American Community Survey, in 2007 metropolitan Los Angeles had a population of 17.7 million inhabitants, of whom 5.7 million had been born outside the United States. Of that immigrant population, 2.6 million had been born in Mexico, constituting 14 percent of the total area population and almost half (45 percent) of the immigrant population, far outweighing other immigrant groups such as Asians, Central Americans, Europeans, and Africans.

Ivan Light[6] notes that in spite of the numerical superiority of Mexican immigrants in Los Angeles, the five-county area redirected Mexican immigrants to other parts of the United States between 1980 and 2000, as can be seen from the drop over that twenty-year period in the share of the Mexican immigrant population in the United States that resided in metropolitan Los Angeles—from 31.7 percent to 16.7 percent. If this region had maintained the proportion of all Mexican immigrants that it had in 1980, they would have totaled 2,491,068 in 2000, instead of the 1,530,280 officially reported.

Light[7] argues that metropolitan Los Angeles redirected these Mexicans to other destinations through a combination of lower immigrant wages, rising rents, and the application of a policy of poverty intolerance. This urban policy, while progressive in principle, reduced Mexican immigrant employment by impeding the functioning of informal workplaces. In the same way, restrictions on the use of the irregular housing units to which Mexican immigrants have recourse has contributed to the rising rents they must pay.

Ethnic diversity in metropolitan Los Angeles is exemplified by the concentration of ethnic communities in the interior of Los Angeles, which Camille Charles[8] depicts as one of the world's most racially, ethnically, and culturally diverse cities. The African American community is concentrated in Watts and South Central, made world-famous by the social disturbances of 1965 and 1992. Better-off African Americans live in Ladera Heights, Baldwin Hills (the "black Beverly Hills"), Inglewood, and Carson. Los Angeles is home to the largest Latino population in the United States, with the subset having access to greater resources living in Pico-Union and East Los Angeles. Among Asian immigrants, the largest Korean community in the United States lives in Los Angeles, with its businesses concentrated in Koreatown. Monterrey Park is a middle-class suburb for Chinese and Japanese residents. The white population, for its part, is concentrated in the expensive neighborhoods of Brentwood, Bel Air, Beverly Hills, Hollywood, Malibu, and Burbank.[9]

The predominance of Mexicans in comparison to other immigrant groups may be explained by Los Angeles having been a Mexican city before the 1847 war between Mexico and the United States, when Mexico lost a large part of its territory, including the Pueblo de Nuestra Señora la Reina de Los Ángeles de Porciúncula, which had been founded at the end of the eighteenth century and would later be known as the city of Los Angeles. This city, as Mike Davis[10] points out, is both the utopia and the anti-utopia of advanced capitalism.

Over time, the Los Angeles economy began to exercise a growing attraction for Mexican workers, and US immigration policies began, at various points, to encourage the settlement of a new Mexican population in the region—both documented and undocumented. As a result Los Angeles became the city with the fourth largest Mexican population in the world after Mexico City, Guadalajara, and Monterrey.[11] The movement of Mexican migrants has also been facilitated by geographic proximity. The city of Los Angeles lies approximately 125 miles from the border city of Tijuana in Mexico.

The metropolitan Los Angeles economy in which Mexican immigrants have found employment has gone through a variety of structural changes over time. Until the mid-nineteenth century, its agriculture-based economy experienced slow growth. The heavy industrial base, according to Roger Waldinger and Mehdi Bozorgmehr,[12] came into being in the 1930s with the founding of branch factories for the production of steel, tires, and automobiles by the large firms dominating this sector. With the coming of the Second World War, the aerospace industry of the

MAP 1. Los Angeles Metropolitan Area.

East Coast moved to the West Coast. Then the Cold War contributed to the growth of a high-technology industrial complex belonging almost entirely to the Department of Defense. Natural resources, tourism, and the Hollywood entertainment industry also contributed to Los Angeles developing the greatest concentration of manufacturing employment in the United States. However, this industrial base began to deteriorate in the 1970s, while more labor-intensive sectors grew rapidly, offering jobs that paid terribly low wages.[13] Mike Davis[14] argues that Los Angeles has developed under the stimulus of financial, real estate, and military interests, but unlike other US cities that benefited from comparative advantages such as location, ports, capital, or manufacturing centers, Los Angeles has been a creation of real estate capital whose promoters have subdivided and sold the western region of the United States.

In describing the participation of Mexican immigrants in Los Angeles's economic development, we will make use of the periodization of Edward Soja,[15] who identifies five different stages of population, urban, and economic development in the region. In the first period, from 1870 to 1900, according to Soja, the "WASPization" of Los Angeles took place with the arrival of a white population—Anglo-Saxon, Protestant, and largely from the Midwest. During this period, agricultural production was the basis of the local economy. According to Richard Griswold del Castillo,[16] of the Mexican heads of family who lived in the city in 1844, twelve remained until at least 1888, long after the 1846–48 war between Mexico and the United States. Most of the Mexicans who arrived in Los Angeles before 1852 were from Sonora and other states in the north of Mexico, and so the section where Spanish speakers lived became known as Sonora Town. For the three decades after the war, the Mexican population experienced great instability due to continuous movement.

In the Regressive-Progressive era—from 1900 to 1920, according to Soja[17]—the new century opened with a boom in which, increasingly, industrial development made Los Angeles an auxiliary extension of the manufacturing belt of the Northeast. George Sánchez[18] reports that between 1910 and 1930 the city's population quadrupled, from 319,000 to 1.24 million, and that as a result, "what was left of California's nineteenth-century Mexican life and culture was completely transformed in the face of rapid American settlement and urbanization."

During the First World War came a great campaign to "Americanize" the immigrants of Los Angeles, which began in the schools in 1916 and was extended to women in the home through mothers' classes, home teaching, and the provision of special library services. In addition, adult night schools offered English and citizenship classes, and there were theatrical works dramatizing "the democratic and cosmopolitan spirit of America." This campaign, however, did not prevent the Los Angeles school district from continuing its practice of operating separate schools for Mexican children under the premise that they had special needs.[19]

In the third period, between the First and Second World Wars, came the boom of urban and economic development when the aeronautic industry financed by the Department of Defense became the motor of industrial development in the region. Mexican immigration to Los Angeles grew during this period, but in the Great Depression, and more specifically between 1929 and 1935, approximately 415,000 Mexicans were deported from the United States, including many US citizens of Mexican descent. That figure does not include those who were repatriated to Mexico of their own volition or by the Mexican government. The deportations took place in a tumultuous operation in which the city authorities of Los Angeles played a central role.[20]

It was not until the early 1940s, with US entry into World War II, that Mexican migration to Los Angeles resumed its previous course. In 1942, in the context of the war, the governments of Mexico and the United States signed an agreement creating two contract-labor programs for massive recruitment of Mexican workers. The first was designed for agriculture, under which 4.6 million contracts were issued; it lasted from 1942 to 1964.[21] The second was established to maintain the railway lines; sixty-nine thousand contracts were issued from 1943 to 1945.[22]

During the fourth era, from 1940 to 1970, when, according to Soja,[23] the "Big Orange" exploded, a major industrial transformation took place, led by the aerospace industry and an extensive network of manufacturing and service industries. Between 1940 and 1970, the regional population tripled, reaching ten million inhabitants. Meanwhile, in the context of the US civil rights movement, the mid-1960s brought a radical change in immigration policy at the federal level. Ironically, while African Americans were rebelling in Watts, the new Immigration and Nationality Act of 1965 suppressed the restrictive system of national-origins quotas established in 1921, eliminating national origin, race, and ancestry as immigration criteria. That led to a more diversified universe of legal immigrants based on the criteria of family reunification and job skills.[24]

This reform radically changed immigration into the United States, and the Los Angeles region in particular. It brought a decline in the participation of Europeans, and massive immigration by Asians and Latin Americans, among whom Mexicans began to predominate. Through the "front door" opened by the 1965 law came skilled Asian immigrants, and through the "back door" came the Mexicans and Central Americans, who swelled the ranks of undocumented immigrants.[25]

The fifth and last stage of the development of Los Angeles came between 1970 and 2000. Soja[26] calls this the era of New Urbanization. Although the process of industrial and population growth was slower than in earlier years, in absolute terms Los Angeles still led all US metropolitan areas. The region's economic restructuring, as in the rest of the United States, has been based on de-industrialization. As a result, the Fordist manufacturing industries have virtually disappeared, but both labor-intensive and knowledge-based industries continued growing until the 1980s. In ethnic makeup, between 1970 and 1990 Los Angeles County shifted from being 60 percent Anglo to 60 percent non-Anglo. This population growth led to a re-Mexicanization of Los Angeles.

The US processes of de-industrialization and decline of manufacturing beginning in the 1970s paralleled the appearance of new forms of production in regions without previous industrial traditions, and the rise of new forms of regional development that did not rely on the Fordist system of mass production.[27] Piore and Sabel[28] argue that the model of industrial development based on mass production, the use of machines designed for a single purpose, and the employment of semi-skilled workers who produce standardized products is in decay, faced with the rise of an industrial system of flexible specialization. Labor relations have become more flexible as well. Companies have fragmented, outsourced some of their production processes, and made growing use of non-union, temporary workers. For the workers, this situation means job insecurity and lower wages; for employers, it implies a high degree of labor rotation.[29]

In 1990, more than half of all adults who had arrived in Los Angeles after 1965 were from Mexico, as well as from El Salvador and Guatemala. These immigrants were mostly undocumented. Asian immigration also accelerated thanks to migration from China, the Philippines, Korea, Vietnam, and India.[30] The Latin American population continued to grow at a rapid pace during this decade. As Rafael Alarcón[31] notes, a 1997 *Los Angeles Times* article reported that in 1996, for the first time in the history of Los Angeles, a Spanish-language radio station, the romantic KLVE-FM, had become the most-listened-to in the metropolis.

The arrival of new immigrants from Latin America and Asia brought a rapid ethnic transformation of Los Angeles County. While the immigrant population in 1980 was 22 percent, by 2000 it had risen to 33 percent. According to Camille Charles,[32] this change in overall numbers was accompanied by changes in ethnic geographical distribution, with the growth of the Latino population in South Central (historic home of the black population) and a small increase in the black population to the north of Pasadena. Latinos, besides dominating East Los Angeles, have spread eastward to Downey, to the south of Los Angeles, and to the San Fernando Valley. Charles[33] further observes that although the change in ethnic geographical distribution has brought conflict between African Americans and Latinos, Asians have not experienced this type of confrontation because their population has grown in the San Gabriel Valley and in areas near Orange and San Bernardino Counties.

The industrial restructuring of Los Angeles has been accompanied by worsening conditions of employment and the rapid growth of an informal sector in which Mexican immigrants participate to an important degree. Many men and a few women work as urban day laborers, or *"esquineros"* (street corner men), gathering on corners, vacant lots, and the parking lots of large building-supply chains such as Home Depot to seek work at least for a day. Abel Valenzuela,[34] in a study carried out in metropolitan Los Angeles in 1999 with a random sample of 481 *esquineros,* found that almost all (98.7 percent) were immigrants, most of them from Mexico (77.5 percent), and that 84 percent were undocumented. More than a third had attended school for between nine and twelve years, and almost a quarter (23.4 percent) had lived in the United States for more than ten years.

Within this growing informal sector, Mexican immigrants also work as gardeners, domestics, and street vendors, among other activities.[35] Pierrette Hondagneu-Sotelo[36] notes that since the 1970s, hundreds of thousands of women from Mexico, El Salvador, and Guatemala have found paid domestic work in Los Angeles, often undocumented, in three different categories: as nannies and domestic workers living full-time with the employing family, as nannies and domestics working five or six days a week but living in their own homes, or as housecleaners with multiple employers and generally not doing childcare. All told, the Los Angeles economy now requires a labor force that is flexible, low skilled, and low paid, which is supplied by workers from Latin American countries, especially Mexico.[37]

With the goal of "regaining control of its borders" and solving the "problem" of undocumented migration, the US Congress in 1986 passed the Immigration Reform and Control Act (IRCA), which had three main elements: an amnesty for undocumented workers; sanctions against employers who knowingly hired undocumented workers; and increased border enforcement. The implementation of this law has been fragmented. While the amnesty was implemented according to plan, employer sanctions have never moved beyond a symbolic level, and a real border enforcement occurred only in 1993, when the Clinton administration decided to take that step.

The amnesty was administered under two programs: the "general amnesty" and the special program for agricultural workers (Special Agricultural Workers, SAW), which resulted in three million people regularizing their immigration status. Of these, 2.3 million were from Mexico.[38] The greater part of these individuals obtained legal permanent residence in the late 1980s and early 1990s.

The most important effect of IRCA was a vigorous process in the late eighties and early nineties in which both documented and undocumented immigrants settled in the United States and reunified families. The family reunification aspect of the law brought about the presence in various parts of the country, but most especially in Los Angeles, of families with mixed immigration status—including among their members US citizens, legal permanent residents, and undocumented persons. Also, in Los Angeles, as has been noted above, communities of Mexican and Central American immigrants began to grow up in areas such as South Central that had historically been home to African Americans, creating serious friction between the different groups.

Finally, at the end of 1993, the Clinton administration, returning to the provisions of IRCA, decided to strengthen US vigilance of the border with Mexico so as to stanch the flow of undocumented migrants. The means to this end were a substantial increase in the budget for what is now called the Department of Homeland Security, and the concentration of resources for the installation of walls and electronic surveillance equipment on the border routes traditionally used by migrants.

This has provoked the emergence of a fortified border, which has in turn compelled those crossing without documents to venture into more rugged and dangerous areas, where many have died. It has been documented that more than five thousand people have died in attempts to cross the border since 1994.[39] The tightening of border surveillance has also led to a drop in the circular movements of undocumented migrants, who no longer dare re-cross the border once they are inside the United States. Border control took on a new dimension in 2001, after the attacks of September 11, when the Patriot Act was passed and immigration into the United States became a matter of national security.

In a parallel trend, in 2002 the number of deportations from the interior of the United States began to grow, as the government applied section 287(g) of the Illegal Immigration Reform and Immigrant Responsibility Act (IIRIRA) of 1996. This law allows the Department of Homeland Security to establish agreements with city and county police departments to train local officers as immigration agents. This intensification of deportations from the US interior is carried out by Immigration and Customs Enforcement (ICE), an agency that, like the Border Patrol, belongs to the giant Department of Homeland Security. ICE has more staff than any other division of Homeland Security and administers a variety of programs that directly affect Mexican undocumented migrants, such as the Secure Communities Program and the National Fugitive Operations Program.

IMMIGRANTS FROM ZACATECAS, OAXACA, AND VERACRUZ IN LOS ANGELES

The ninety Mexican immigrants living in the Los Angeles Metropolitan Area whom we interviewed in 2008 came originally from the states of Zacatecas, Oaxaca, and Veracruz. They have been influenced by differing economic contexts, inherited distinct political cultures and migratory traditions, and for the most part arrived in Los Angeles at different times.

Mexican migration to the United States became a very important social process at the end of the nineteenth century, when two independent processes converged. One was the passage of the 1882 Chinese Exclusion Act. The other was the 1884 opening of the Central Railway, connecting Mexico City with Ciudad Juárez on the Texas border. From the beginning, Mexico's west-central region has stood out as the place of origin of the greatest share of migrant workers.

In the 1920s, Manuel Gamio[40] found that the majority of Mexicans living in the United States came from the states of Michoacán, Guanajuato, and Jalisco, with migrants from those states responsible for more than half (54.3 percent) of the 23,846 money orders sent back to Mexico in July and August of 1926. Zacatecas appeared in seventh place among thirty-one states, with 1,140 money orders (4.8 percent). Veracruz figured in twenty-second place with fifty-four money orders (0.2 percent) and Oaxaca in twenty-fourth with forty-eight (0.2 percent).

Five decades later, the Mexico's national survey on emigration to the northern border area and the United States (Spanish initials ENEF-NEU), undertaken throughout the country between December 1978 and January 1979 under the direction of the Secretariat of Labor and Social Welfare, revealed the continuity of this spatial distribution of migration to the United States, with a continued predominance of the west-central region.[41]

That household survey, based on a national sample, found that in 1978 there were a total of 990,719 migrants of fifteen or more years of age, of whom 519,301 (52.4 percent) were in the United States working or looking for work during the time of the survey; 471,418 (47.6 percent) had worked in the United States for at least one day during the past five years though they were living in Mexico at the time of the survey.

To analyze the distribution of migrants by Mexican state of origin, the country was divided into five regions. The survey results for the two groups of migrants showed that 60 percent were from the regions labeled #2 and #3, which included primarily the west-central states, Zacatecas among them. Region #5, labeled "southeast" and including Oaxaca and Veracruz, provided 10.4 percent of the migrants.

Mexico's National Population Council,[42] in its analysis of the index of migration intensity for the year 2000, reconfirmed the substantial differences between the international migratory processes from Zacatecas, Oaxaca, and Veracruz. The index of migratory intensity used by CONAPO[43] is based on a sample of 10 percent of the Twelfth Census of Population and Housing 2000. The index combines into a single metric the following indicators of international migration: (1) households receiving remittances; (2) households with emigrants during the five-year period 1995–2000 who were in the United States at the time of the census; (3) households with emigrants between 1995 and 2000 who returned to the country during that five-year period; and (4) households with members who lived in the United States in 1995 and returned to live in Mexico before the census.

The results reveal that while Zacatecas had the country's highest index of migratory intensity (2.58), followed by the states of Michoacán, Guanajuato, Nayarit, and Durango, the states of Oaxaca and Veracruz had medium (-0.26) and low (-0.70) indices, respectively.

The ninety immigrants we interviewed in 2008, who came from Zacatecas, Oaxaca, and Veracruz, settled in metropolitan Los Angeles at different times and in different historical contexts. Table 2 displays several types of statistical measurements of their years of arrival in the metropolis.

Table 2 shows that the average year of the Zacatecans' arrival was 1979, during what Jorge Durand and Douglas Massey[44] call the "undocu-

TABLE 2   YEAR OF ARRIVAL IN METROPOLITAN LOS ANGELES OF THE NINETY
INTERVIEWEES FROM ZACATECAS, OAXACA, AND VERACRUZ, 2008

	Zacatecas	Oaxaca	Veracruz
Average	1979.6	1985.3	1991
Median	1977	1986	1990
Mode	1972	1988	1999

SOURCE: Interviews with ninety Mexican immigrants in the Los Angeles Metropolitan Area, 2008.

mented era," which began in 1965, after the end of the Bracero Program, and ended in 1986 with the passage of IRCA. The Oaxacans arrived, on average, in 1985, the year before the period when IRCA had its greatest impact (1986–1993). The Veracruzans arrived on average in 1991, when the IRCA amnesty was no longer accessible to them, and two years before the launching of Operation Hold the Line in El Paso, Texas, in 1993 and Operation Gatekeeper in San Diego in 1994. Those operations opened the period in which the US government decided to tighten its border control and surveillance, making undocumented crossing much more dangerous. In the pages that follow, we will analyze the migration to the United States from each of these three states.

Zacatecans: Migrants of the Undocumented Era

The immigrants originally from the state of Zacatecas are emblematic of the traditional sending region to the United States; Zacatecas has a century-long history of such migration. In 2005, according to census data from the Conteo de Población y Vivienda (Count of Population and Housing) of that year, Zacatecas had a population of 1,367,692 inhabitants, with an annual average growth rate from 2000 to 2005 of 1.3 percent (slightly higher than the national rate of 1.0 percent). The state's tendency to generate primarily male emigration is reflected in the fact that in 2005, Zacatecas had 93.1 men for every 100 women.

According to the CONAPO[45] decennial census data referred to above, Zacatecas in 2000 was the state with the highest migratory intensity. Its 306,882 households reported higher percentages of all the US-bound migration indicators than any other Mexican state: the highest share of households receiving remittances (13.03 percent); the highest share of those with emigrants to the United States during 1995–2000 who were still there (12.18 percent); the highest share of those with emigrants during 1995–2000 who returned to Mexico during that time

(3.31 percent); and the highest share of those who were living in the United States in 1995 and returned to live in Mexico before the census (2.55 percent).[46]

Delgado, Márquez, and Rodríguez[47] assert that there are more Zacatecans living in the United States than in Zacatecas; they estimate 2.1 million US residents of Zacatecan origin, a figure well above the population of the state, which is only 1.4 million. Zacatecan communities in the United States have been developing throughout the past century, and this massive migration has led to the depopulation of some areas, such as the so-called Zacatecan high-emigration zone, an area of thirty-one municipalities showing negative population growth, which contrasts with the rest of the state.

Since the 1980s, Zacatecan state government administrations have tried to establish strong ties with their population residing in the United States. Although the Federation of Zacatecan Clubs of Southern California, the most important Mexican migrant organization outside of Mexico, was founded in 1965, its institutionalization came in the 1980s thanks to support from then-governor Genaro Borrego (1986–1992). In 1986 the federation and the state government signed an agreement for the state to match donations from the migrant organization to carry out public works and social projects, an endeavor that came to be known as the Two for One Program. Later, with participation of municipal governments as well, this became Three for One, which has spread throughout the country and is internationally recognized. In 1999, the Federation of Zacatecan Clubs of Southern California affiliated with the larger Confederation of Zacatecan Clubs, which also included groupings in Oxnard (California), Chicago, Denver, Dallas, Houston, Las Vegas, and Atlanta—all told, approximately 120 associations with some forty thousand members.[48] In 1998, the Federation of Zacatecan Clubs of Southern California was made up of thirty-nine migrants' associations, which by 2001 had risen to forty-seven.[49] In 2006, the number of migrants' associations had risen to seventy-four, distributed across forty-one cities of the Los Angeles Metropolitan Area.[50]

The main destination of the Zacatecan migrants has been California, especially metropolitan Los Angeles. The majority of our Zacatecan interviewees live in the cities of East Los Angeles, Wilmington, and San Fernando. Other studies, however, have found other California destinations. Richard Mines,[51] in his research in the late 1970s, found that the migrants from Las Ánimas in the municipality of Nochistlán de Mejía were concentrated in the metropolitan Los Angeles cities of Santa

TABLE 3   INDICES AND DEGREES OF MARGINALIZATION AND MIGRATORY
INTENSITY IN THREE MUNICIPALITIES AND THE STATE OF ZACATECAS, 2005

Community	Marginalization index	Degree of marginalization	Index of migratory intensity	Degree of migratory intensity
Jerez	–1.22783	Very low	1.60	High
Nochistlán de Mejía	–0.82451	Low	2.58	Very high
Tepechitlán	–0.61791	Medium	2.34	Very high
Zacatecas			2.58	Very high

SOURCE: Estimates by CONAPO, 2002, "Índices de intensidad migratoria, México-Estados Unidos, 2000," based on 10 percent sample of the XII Censo General de Población y Vivienda, 2000.

Ana-Artesia, East Los Angeles, and San Fernando, as well as in South San Francisco, Escondido, Bell Gardens, Reedley-Sanger, and Watsonville. Sandra Nichols[52] reports a migratory circle connecting the municipality of Jerez to Napa, California, and Miguel Moctezuma[53] finds a similar relationship between the municipality of Sain Alto and the city of Oakland, California.

For our study, we selected the following three Zacatecas municipalities with a significant part of the population living in metropolitan Los Angeles: Jerez, Nochistlán de Mejía, and Tepechitlán. In 2005, according to the Conteo de Población y Vivienda, these three localities had quite differently sized populations: the city of Jerez was by far the largest, with 52,594 inhabitants, followed by Nochistlán de Mejía with 26,195, and Tepechitlán with only 7,965.

As can be seen in table 3, the three localities have degrees of marginalization that fall between medium and very low, and degrees of migratory intensity between high and very high, which demonstrates their inhabitants' high level of participation in migration to the United States. The municipality of Nochistlán de Mejía, in fact, has the same migratory intensity index as Zacatecas as a whole.

The three municipalities chosen for our Los Angeles study are located in the so-called Zacatecan high-emigration area.[54] Their emigrants' significant presence in the Los Angeles area is also reflected by the presence of their clubs. In 2006, there were three clubs of Jerez emigrants in the region: Club Jomulquillo, Familias Unidas por Jalpa, and Club Social Hermandad Jalpense. Nochistlán de Mejía had four clubs: Fraternidad Las Ánimas, Club Las Ánimas, Club Social Estancia Nochistlán, and

Club Social Nochistlense. Finally, Tepechitlán had two clubs: Club Tepechitlán and Club Familias Unidas de Tepechitlán.[55]

The *matrícula consular* is a form of official identification issued by Mexican consulates in the United States, mostly at the request of undocumented migrants. This identification is very useful for undocumented individuals who, in some US states, may apply for driver's licenses and open bank accounts, among other things. Of the 37,863 *matrículas consulares* issued in 2006 to Zacatecan migrants in the forty-three Mexican consular offices in the United States, 9,520 (25.1 percent) were issued by the consulates in Los Angeles, San Bernardino, and Santa Ana, which shows the high concentration of Zacatecan migrants in metropolitan Los Angeles. The next-highest percentages of *matrículas consulares* for Zacatecans were issued by the consulates in Dallas and Chicago, at 12.9 percent and 11.7 percent, respectively.

In the Los Angeles region, the three consulates named above issued 1,064 *matrículas* for migrants from Jerez, 513 for Nochistlán de Mejía, and 171 for Tepechitlán; the total of 1,748 amounts to 18.4 percent of all matrículas issued to Zacatecans in metropolitan Los Angeles in 2006.[56]

Based on conversations with our ninety interviewees, in the second part of this book we will examine in depth the life experiences of Zacatecan migrants in the United States. Still, it is important to mention here that the son of one couple among our Zacatecan interviewees has already done a part of that work, with great success, in print. In *Orange County: A Personal History,* Gustavo Arellano[57] humorously portrays his experience living in Orange County as the child of Mexican immigrants. Gustavo Arellano is also the author of the syndicated column "Ask a Mexican!" published in thirty-nine newspapers in the United States.

Oaxacans: Migrants of the Amnesty

The immigrants from the state of Oaxaca form part of a later wave of migration to the United States than the one from western central Mexico. Though there are traces of Oaxacan migration in the first half of the twentieth century, Oaxacans began to come in large numbers in the 1980s and 1990s, making their way to a variety of locations but especially metropolitan Los Angeles.

The state of Oaxaca, located in the southern part of Mexico, has 3,509,821 inhabitants according to the 2005 Conteo de Población y Vivienda. It is the most culturally and ethnically fragmented Mexican state, home to about 20 percent of the country's indigenous population, who in turn belong to sixteen different groups of which the Mixtec and Zapotec populations are the largest. Oaxaca's inhabitants are distributed among 570 municipalities grouped into eight geographic regions.

When the process of Oaxacan emigration began in the 1930s, the main destinations were the city of Oaxaca, the state of Veracruz, and Mexico City. Later, Oaxacan emigrants joined the Bracero Program, and they also sought work in the agribusinesses of northern Mexico as a result of intensified recruiting by labor contractors from that industry. Thus they settled in the valley of Culiacán in Sinaloa and especially in the valley of San Quintín in Baja California.

In the 1980s, as a result of economic crises affecting Mexico, the Oaxacan migration pattern turned toward the United States, first to California and later to Oregon, Washington, Florida, North Carolina, New York, and New Jersey.[58] California, though, became the major destination of Oaxacan migration, which reached massive proportions in the 1990s, with networks established in the agricultural valleys of the north and central parts of the state, in metropolitan Los Angeles, and in San Diego County—that is to say, Oaxacan migrants have sought out the most important agricultural regions and the service sector of the large urban centers.[59] Though some pioneer Oaxacans had settled in the Los Angeles region in the years before the Bracero Program, they made up only a very small share of Mexican immigrants. By the 1990s, however, their migratory wave had reached the neighborhoods of Koreatown, Pico Union, South Central, Venice, Santa Monica, Lynwood, and South Gate.[60]

A key factor in the accelerated Oaxacan migration to California was the implementation of IRCA in 1986, which enabled many Mexican immigrants to regularize their immigration status and thus gain access to better jobs.[61] Meanwhile, thousands of Oaxacan immigrants, especially those of Mixtec origin, found agricultural work in California,[62] and similar numbers of Oaxacans of Zapotec origin took service-sector jobs in Los Angeles.[63]

In spite of their relatively recent arrival, their dispersion to different parts of the United States, their ethnic and social status, and their incorporation into the lowest rungs of employment in the rural regions and urban centers of California, the migrants of Oaxaca have formed a wide range of binational communities and organizations that have been extensively documented in the academic realm[64] and have given rise to the concept of "Oaxacalifornia."[65]

The three communities of Oaxacan migrants selected for this study come from two municipalities that, according to the Conteo de Población y Vivienda, had less than a thousand inhabitants each in 2005—San Pablo Macuiltianguis, with only 956 inhabitants, and San Lorenzo Victoria, with 948—and from the much larger third municipality of Tlacolula de Matamoros, with a population of 16,510.

The inhabitants of San Pablo Macuiltianguis, located in the Ixtlán de Juárez district of the Sierra Norte region, belong to the Zapotec group. Their small numbers are typical of many Oaxacan municipalities, severely fragmented because of the large number of localities. Over the years, however, they have created a migratory circuit to and from the Los Angeles region. Some studies have documented the presence of Macuiltianguins in Los Angeles since the Bracero Program, which eventually led to the formation of migration networks linking the two sites.[66] By the 1990s, migrants from the Sierra Norte in general and from the communities of the Macuiltianguis municipality in particular had settled in various parts of the Los Angeles region.[67]

The bulk of the San Pablo Macuiltianguis emigrants whom we interviewed arrived in metropolitan Los Angeles in the 1980s. While practically all were undocumented when they arrived, by now practically all have obtained legal permanent residence or US citizenship. They are concentrated mostly in the cities of San Gabriel, El Monte, Reseda, El Sereno, and North Hollywood.

One of the central aspects of the lives of Macuiltianguins is their transnationalism. Since they maintain constant communication with neighbors and friends in Oaxaca, they stay informed about events in their communities in both countries. This communication and sense of community are reinforced by cultural events organized by a Macuiltianguin association. This has also meant, however, that a political confrontation in Oaxaca was reproduced in California, causing a rift in the Los Angeles community that has only recently begun to heal.

Macuiltianguin migrants have a notable participation in school PTAs, church associations, unions, and organizations created by the migrants themselves. Their main such organization is OPAM, the Organización para la Ayuda a Macuiltianguis, which has been in existence for approximately two decades.

The municipality of Tlacolula de Matamoros, located in the central valleys of Oaxaca in the district of Tlacolula, has about sixteen thousand inhabitants, also primarily Zapotec. This is a larger town, located in a geographically more welcoming and prosperous region that also includes the city of Oaxaca. Like other Oaxacan migrants of Zapotec origin, the Tlacolulans joined the migratory flow by way of some pioneer migrants

TABLE 4   INDICES AND DEGREES OF MARGINALIZATION AND MIGRATORY
INTENSITY IN THREE MUNICIPALITIES AND THE STATE OF OAXACA, 2005

Community	Marginalization index	Degree of marginalization	Index of migratory intensity	Degree of migratory intensity
San Pablo Macuiltianguis	0.16	High	0.60	Medium
Tlacolula de Matamoros	–0.68	Medium	0.62	Medium
San Lorenzo Victoria	–0.01	High	2.07	Very high
Oaxaca			–0.26	Medium

SOURCE: Estimates by CONAPO, 2002, "Índices de intensidad migratoria, México-Estados Unidos, 2000," based on 10 percent sample of the XII Censo General de Población y Vivienda, 2000.

who settled in the cities of Santa Monica and Los Angeles in the 1970s or before. By the 1990s they had spread throughout the city of Los Angeles.[68]

The cultural dimension also plays a key role in the Tlacolulan community, whose members have cultivated a variety of forms of artistic expression, including music and dance. The celebration of the day of El Señor de Tlacolula, the town's patron saint, brings together Tlacolulan migrants in Los Angeles, and associations have formed to foster both religious celebrations and cultural preservation. However, as in the case of Macuiltianguins, divisions have appeared within the community that are tied to internal divisions in the community of origin or to relationships with authorities there.

Finally, the municipality of San Lorenzo Victoria lies in the Mixtec region, in the Silacayoapan district, and has fewer than a thousand inhabitants. Unlike the migrants from the other two selected municipalities, this population of Mixtec origin has settled in a more concentrated fashion in an outlying area of the Los Angeles region. The first migrants from San Lorenzo Victoria arrived in the 1970s and settled in the city of San Bernardino. Like the members of the other Oaxacan communities, they carry on an active community life. The center of this life is the celebration of fiestas attached to patron saints, but the community's strength is also evident in social events like baptisms, *quinceañeras,* and sports, especially basketball games.

Table 4 shows that the Oaxacan municipalities selected for our study have high or medium degrees of marginalization, and migratory intensity at a medium level, like that of the state of Oaxaca as a whole. Only San Lorenzo Victoria has a very high migratory intensity.

Of the forty-three consular offices, the Los Angeles one has granted far and away the most *matrículas consulares* to Oaxacan migrants, a total of 8,223. If we add in those issued by the consulates in San

Bernardino and Santa Ana, the resulting total of 11,566 constitutes 22.6 percent of all *matrículas* issued to Oaxacan migrants in the United States in 2006.[69] Of the *matrículas consulares* issued in metropolitan Los Angeles specifically to migrants from our three selected Oaxacan communities, the number for those from Tlacolula de Morelos stands out (1,951, or 17 percent of the total to Oaxacans in the region), reflecting the municipality's much larger population.

Veracruzans: Migrants of the Increased Border Enforcement

Unlike the cases of Zacatecas and Oaxaca, migration from Veracruz to the United States is a very recent phenomenon. According to the Mexican census of 1990, international emigration from Veracruz remained very low as of that date. However, in part because of its large population (7,110,214 according to the 2005 Conteo de Población y Vivienda), Veracruz leaped in a single decade to ninth on the list of Mexican states with greatest participation in the migratory flow to the United States.[70]

This does not mean there was a complete absence of early migration, including some Veracruzan participants in the Bracero Program, but those movements did not create permanent networks that would affect future flows.[71] The intensification of Veracruzan migration to the United States coincided with the period of tightened control of the US-Mexican border that began toward the end of 1993. Therefore, Veracruzans had to confront much more difficult conditions in their undocumented crossing. Also, since the Veracruzan migration originated after the amnesty set in motion by IRCA, a high proportion of the migrants have not been able to obtain legal permanent residence.

A range of authors, including Mestries,[72] Rosas,[73] and Córdova, Núñez, and Skerritt,[74] agree that what sparked the emigration flow from Veracruz was a crisis in the agricultural sector, especially a fall in the prices of coffee and sugar, the state's two major farm products. A significant proportion of the municipalities with the highest indices of emigration lie either in the sugarcane-growing region in the south of the state or in the coffee-producing region in the center.

Undertaking the journey to the United States is viewed as an extreme measure but one that may make it possible to earn extra money to pay off debts, buy livestock, or preserve ownership of family parcels of land.[75] This is why, among these "migrants of the coffee crisis," the cause of migration is linked to goals rooted in their communities.[76] At first, the flow was made up of men of prime working age, including a high number of heads of families who sought in the US labor market a way to amass the resources they needed to overcome the crisis and return home.[77] By the year 2000, one out of every three households in the municipality of Landero y Coss had family members in the United States. Remittances began to represent a key source of income in municipalities like Yanga, where at least one out of every five households received this type of income.[78]

Despite its short history, Veracruzan migration has already passed through "eras" that took decades in the cases of other Mexican contingents. For instance, Pérez[79] shows how the migration networks in the central part of Veracruz developed a significant degree of organization within a period of only five years. Also, only a few years after the men's migration pattern solidified, women began to migrate as well, giving rise to the establishment of families north of the border, which in turn accelerated the formation of communities.[80]

Thus, after only a bit more than a decade, the migrants from Veracruz have succeeded in creating dozens of associations and a federation.[81] Currently they have at least two clubs in the Los Angeles area: La Fundación Yanga and El Club Porteños, as well as the Federación Veracruzana U.S.A. Among the reasons why the Veracruzan migration has developed so rapidly is the need to stay in the United States due to the high cost and high risk of border crossings, which make periodic trips back to Mexico impossible. Another important aspect is the re-creation of ties with the "pioneer" emigrants who were already established in the United States. An additional element that contributes to explaining the rapid organization of the Veracruzan community is the formation of ties with the most structured organizations of Mexican migrants from other regions. For example, the Fundación Yanga, in California, enjoyed the support of Casa Guanajuato.

Also, as Mestries[82] points out, the Veracruzan migration began at a time when communications media were significantly more advanced. Thus Veracruz soon became dotted with internet cafes, "travel agencies" that specialized in transportation to the border, and money-transfer agencies. An additional characteristic of the Veracruzan migration is its heterogeneity,[83] both in terms of its many destinations[84] and in terms of the wide range in migratory intensity among the sending municipalities and the diversity in the demographic profiles of their migrants. While migrants from rural areas characterized the first stage of the process, Veracruzans from the main urban centers of the state have more recently joined them.

TABLE 5 INDICES AND DEGREES OF MARGINALIZATION AND MIGRATORY
INTENSITY IN THREE MUNICIPALITIES AND THE STATE OF VERACRUZ, 2005

Community	Marginalization index	Degree of marginalization	Index of migratory intensity	Degree of migratory intensity
Yanga	-0.38801	Medium	2.08	Very high
Orizaba	-1.72663	Very low	-0.56	Low
Playa Vicente	0.35123	High	0.16	Medium
Veracruz			-0.70	Low/very low

SOURCE: Estimates by CONAPO, 2002, "Índices de intensidad migratoria, México-Estados Unidos, 2000," based on 10 percent sample of the XII Censo General de Población y Vivienda, 2000.

According to data from the Survey of Migration to the Northern Border of Mexico (Spanish initials EMIF), the number one destination of emigrants from Veracruz is Texas, followed by California, Florida, and North Carolina, and then in smaller proportions by Arizona, Louisiana, Virginia, Georgia, Michigan, Oregon, Kansas, and Minnesota.[85] Another survey estimates that 22 percent of the rural migrants from the central region go to California, while 17 percent go to Illinois, 11 percent to Texas, and 7 percent to Georgia.[86]

To study the integration processes of Veracruzans living in Los Angeles, we chose three municipalities that could represent the heterogeneity of this population: Orizaba, Yanga, and Playa Vicente. All three, according to the 2005 Conteo de Población y Vivienda, had much larger populations than most of the Zacatecan and Oaxacan municipalities in the study: 117,289 inhabitants in Orizaba, 15,447 in Yanga, and 38,125 in Playa Vicente. Among these three municipalities, there are large differences in terms of marginalization and migratory intensity (see table 5). Yanga stands out with a very high degree of migratory intensity.

Yanga is one of the two municipalities with the highest migratory intensity indices in the state of Veracruz and exemplify the regions in which the exodus to El Norte appears to be directly related to the fall in sugar prices. Another distinctive characteristic of Yanga is the historical importance of its black population. Yanga's people like to describe their home as "the first free town in America" because it was founded and freed by Afro-Mexicans. Some migrants from Yanga settled in metropolitan Los Angeles in the early 1980s. Now, they reside principally in the cities of Placentia and Fullerton in Orange County.

Looking at the community of migrants from Orizaba, on the other hand, allows for analysis of the experience of urban Veracruzans with more formal education. Although there is no organization specifically for those from Orizaba, they are very visible in the Federación Veracruzana U.S.A. In the Los Angeles area, natives of Orizaba and neighboring Río Blanco live mainly in the city of Lynwood, in Los Angeles County.

If we look again at the issuance of *matrículas consulares* in the year 2006, we find that in spite of Veracruzans' dispersion to many different US states, 15 percent of their *matrículas* were issued by the Los Angeles area consulates as compared to 12 percent for Chicago, 8 percent for Raleigh, and 6 percent each for Atlanta and Indianapolis.

Los Angeles area consular records also show that although the majority of the Veracruzan migration to metropolitan Los Angeles is male (61 percent), there is an important presence of women (39 percent). Of the municipalities of origin most represented in the Los Angeles area consulates, three are important urban centers (Veracruz [city], Orizaba, and Córdoba), but there is also a strong presence from Playa Vicente at the Los Angeles consulate and from Maltrata and Mariano Escobedo at the Santa Ana one. All the regions of Veracruz are represented somewhere in metropolitan Los Angeles; in terms of municipalities, more than 80 percent of the 212 municipalities of Veracruz have migrants registered in the three consulates of the Los Angeles area. Migrants from Orizaba, Yanga, and Playa Vicente received 831 *matrículas consulares* issued by those three consulates, or 14 percent of the total awarded to Veracruzan migrants. Surprisingly, those from Playa Vicente received a large share of those documents in spite of the small population of that municipality.

CHAPTER 3

Statistical Analysis of Mexican Immigrants' Integration in the Metropolitan Los Angeles Area

Born as a Spanish colonial city, Los Angeles has become an emblematic immigrants' metropolis. For the purposes of our study, the Los Angeles Metropolitan Area consists of five Southern California counties: Los Angeles, Orange, San Bernardino, Riverside, and Ventura.[1] According to our analysis of the American Community Survey data, this region's 2007 population totaled 17,755,837 inhabitants, of whom 5,570,377 were born outside the United States. Of that immigrant population, 2,608,054 were born in Mexico. Adding the population of Mexican origin born in the United States, that figure slightly surpasses five million.

Mexican immigrants make up 14 percent of total metropolitan Los Angeles residents and almost half (45 percent) of the immigrant population, a much higher share than any other immigrant group. The 1,681,120 Asian immigrants make up 29 percent of the immigrant population, followed by 630,663 Central Americans (11 percent), 471,218 Europeans (8 percent), 227,128 from South America and the Caribbean (4 percent), 72,849 Africans (1 percent), and 9,345 born in countries not included in those categories (see table 6).

The object of this chapter is to examine the Mexican immigrants' economic and social integration on the basis of data from the American Community Survey of 2007. First we will examine basic sociodemographic characteristics in comparison with those of the native-born population and of the three next-largest immigrant groups—Asians, Central Americans, and Europeans. Then we will present a comparative analysis of the degree of economic and social integration of the Mexican

TABLE 6 NATIVE AND IMMIGRANT POPULATION IN METROPOLITAN LOS ANGELES, BY
SEX AND REGION OF BIRTH, 2007

Region of origin	Total	%	Male	% male	Female	% female	Ratio male:female
Native	12,055,460	100	5,998,367	49.8	6,057,093	50.2	99.0
Europe	471,218	100	210,040	44.6	261,178	55.4	80.4
Latin America	3,465,845	100	1,797,500	51.9	1,668,345	48.1	107.7
Mexico	2,608,054	100	1,385,083	53.1	1,222,971	46.9	113.3
Central America	630,663	100	305,016	48.4	325,647	51.6	93.7
S. Amer. and Caribbean	227,128	100	107,401	47.3	119,727	52.7	89.7
Asia	1,681,120	100	783,482	46.6	897,638	53.4	87.3
Africa	72,849	100	38,054	52.2	34,795	47.8	109.4
Other	9,345	100	4,074	43.6	5,271	56.4	77.3
Total	17,755,837	100	8,831,517	49.7	8,924,320	50.3	99.0

SOURCE: Authors' calculations based on US Census Bureau, "American Community Survey."

immigrants, making use of the following indicators: (1) level of educational attainment, (2) English proficiency, (3) naturalization, (4) occupation, and (5) home ownership.

MEXICAN IMMIGRANTS: PREDOMINANCE
OF MEN OF WORKING AGE

A first point to consider in analyzing the integration of Mexican immigrants is the composition of their population according to age and sex, which allows for constructing a profile for purposes of comparison with native-born and other immigrant populations in metropolitan Los Angeles. The data in table 6 reveal that the ratio of men to women among Mexican immigrants is almost the inverse of that among the other immigrant groups. Among Mexicans there are 113 men to every 100 women, whereas for most of the other immigrants groups (including Europeans, Asians, and Central Americans) there are more women than men. The higher concentration of Mexican men may be explained by the nature of their migration, which has historically been undertaken for reasons of employment.

In terms of age distribution, both Mexican and Central American immigrants tend to be quite young, with median ages of thirty-eight and forty, respectively. In a breakdown by age groups, Mexicans are concentrated in the groups between twenty and forty-five years old, the ages with highest labor force participation. The same pattern appears in the other immigrant groups except for the Europeans, who are much older (see figure 1).

The presence of men in the most economically active age groups is stronger among Mexicans and Central Americans than among other immigrant groups, as can be seen in figure 1. The native-born population, on the other hand, shows an almost inverse age structure, with a large presence of children and smaller proportions at working ages. The native-born population also shows equilibrium between the sexes, with ninety-nine men per every hundred women. The much stronger presence of children and adolescents among the native-born population may be explained by an important share of these young people being the children of immigrant residents in the area.

ECONOMIC AND SOCIAL INTEGRATION OF MEXICAN IMMIGRANTS

Our comparative analysis of Mexican immigrants' social and economic integration vis-à-vis that of the native-born population and the three next-most numerous groups of immigrants (Asians, Central Americans, and Europeans) will be carried out, as noted above, through observation of five indicators: educational attainment, English proficiency, naturalization, occupation, and home ownership. Some of these indicators, in turn, will be analyzed over time, through four historical periods of Mexican immigration to the United States defined according to the impact of US immigration policy.[2] The first period culminates with the end of the Bracero Program in 1964. The second, which we will call the period of "undocumented migration," begins in 1965 and ends in 1986 with passage of the Immigration Reform and Control Act (IRCA).[3] The third period, from 1987 to 1994, is characterized by the impact of that legislation on Mexican migration. The fourth period, from 1995 to 2007, covers the years in which the US government has tightened control and surveillance of its border with Mexico, has made immigration a matter of national security, and has maintained a firm policy of deporting noncitizens from the interior of the United States.

EDUCATIONAL ATTAINMENT

From the perspective of assimilation theory, level of school completion is considered (along with mastery of the language of the receiving

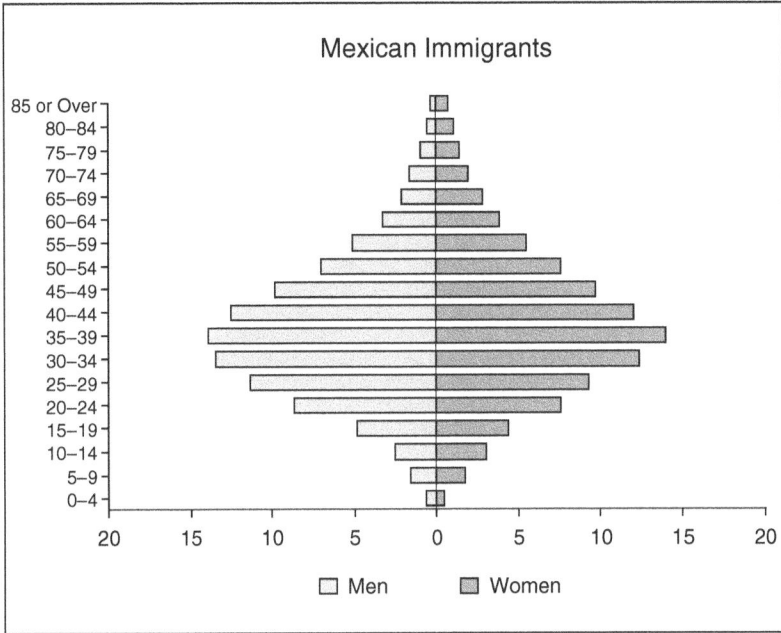

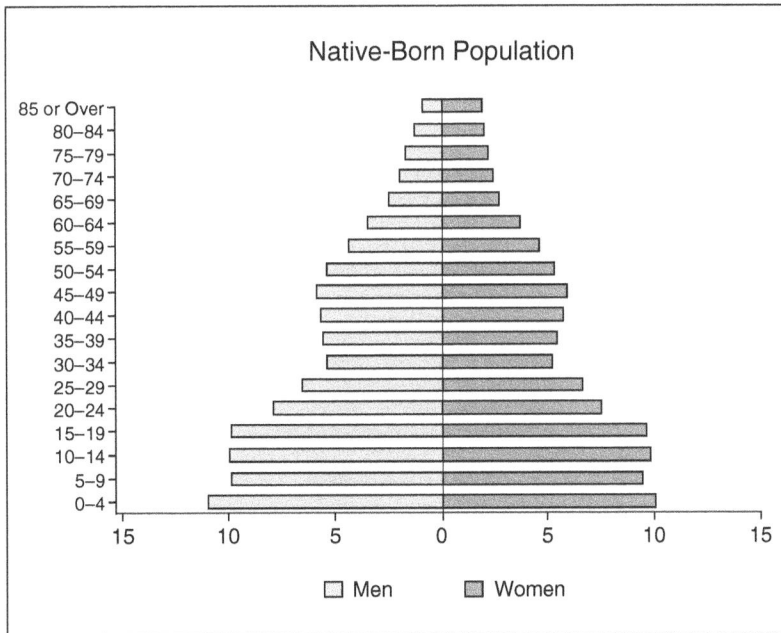

FIGURE 1. Age pyramids of native-born and immigrant populations, Los Angeles Metropolitan Area, 2007. Authors' calculations based on US Census Bureau, "American Community Survey."

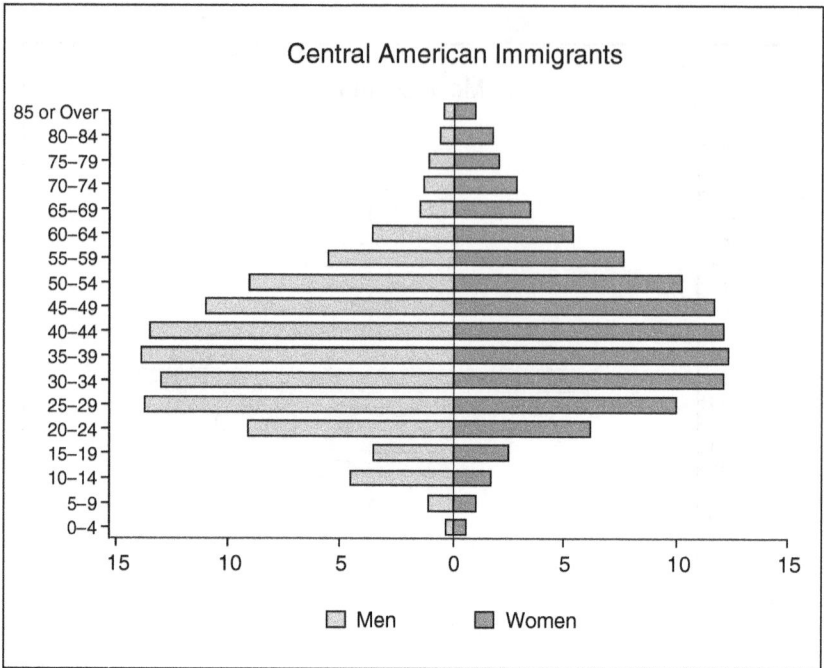

Central American Immigrants

Age	Men	Women

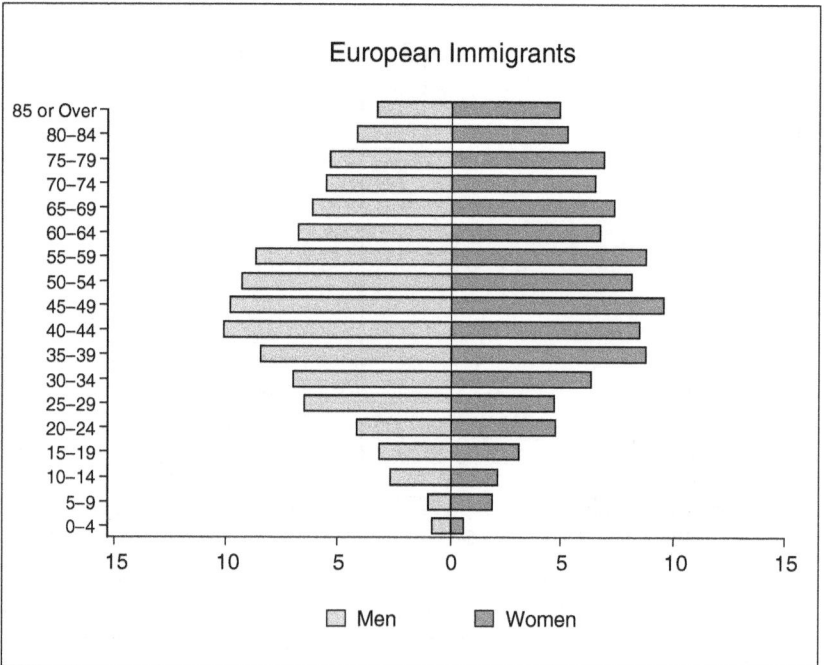

European Immigrants

FIGURE 1. *(continued)*

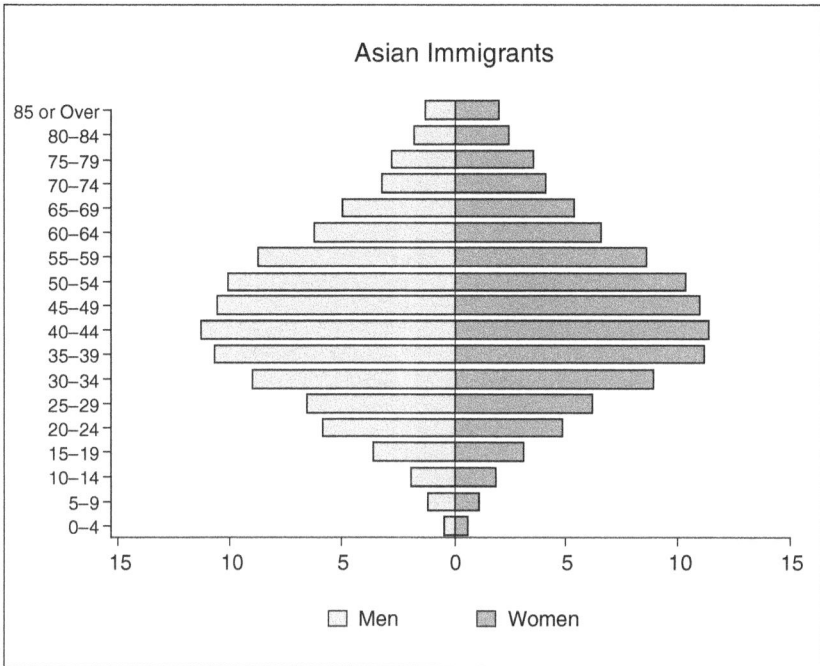

Asian Immigrants

FIGURE I. *(continued)*

society) one of the most important factors in immigrants' economic and social integration.[4] Edward Telles and Vilma Ortiz[5] characterize education as the variable that most determines life opportunities in the United States and propels individuals toward other dimensions of assimilation. A key milestone in this process is acquisition of a high school diploma. The lack of this credential, according to Elaine Levine,[6] is a predictor of poverty and low-skilled jobs. The average annual income for a person in the United States who has not finished high school is nearly $20,000, while it is nearly $30,000 for those with high school degrees. Those with college or postgraduate degrees earn, on average, 2.3 times as much as those with only high school degrees.[7] In fact, among the arguments used by Huntington[8] to question the integration of Mexicans and their descendants in the United States is the high proportion of the Mexican immigrant population that lacked a high school diploma between 1989 and 1990 (69.9%); for the second generation, that statistic was 51.5 percent.

Data from the 2007 ACS support Huntington's claims in the sense that Mexican immigrants in metropolitan Los Angeles had educational

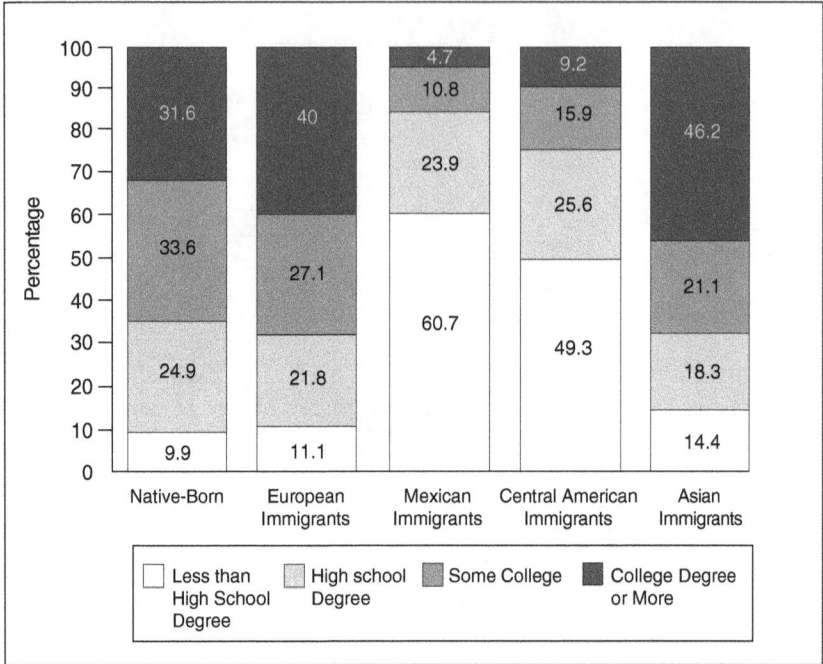

FIGURE 2. Percent distribution of the native-born and immigrant populations, age twenty-five and over, by level of education and ethnic origin, Los Angeles Metropolitan Area, 2007. Authors' calculations based on US Census Bureau, "American Community Survey."

levels much lower than those of the native-born population or other immigrants. As can be seen in figure 2, only 39.3 percent of Mexicans twenty-five or older residing in the Los Angeles area had finished high school, and only 4.7 percent had finished college. By contrast, among the native-born, 90.1 percent had high school diplomas, and three out of ten had at least an undergraduate college degree. Similar results are evident for Asian and European immigrants, among whom approximately four of every ten had college degrees or higher. Central American immigrants had educational levels lower than natives, Asians, and Europeans, but slightly higher than Mexicans.

The data in table 7 reveal that in comparison to the native-born and to other immigrant groups, Mexican and Central American immigrant men and women had the lowest levels of basic education as measured by high school graduation rates. The data also show that Mexican female immigrants have slightly higher levels of college and postgraduate study than their male counterparts.

TABLE 7   PERCENT DISTRIBUTION OF NATIVE-BORN AND IMMIGRANT
POPULATION TWENTY-FIVE OR OLDER, BY SEX, ETHNICITY, AND EDUCATIONAL
LEVEL, LOS ANGELES METROPOLITAN AREA, 2007

Educational level	Natives	Europeans	Mexicans	Central Americans	Asians
Men					
No education	0.4	0.7	5.2	4.3	1.5
Less than high school	9.6	9.4	55.2	43.2	9.8
Finished high school	24.6	20.0	24.7	27.0	17.1
1–3 years college	31.5	25.5	10.2	15.9	21.3
College graduate	33.9	44.5	4.6	9.6	50.2
Total	100.0	100.0	100.0	100.0	100.0
Women					
No education	0.4	0.6	6.0	6.6	3.7
Less than high school	9.3	11.4	54.9	44.4	13.3
Finished high school	25.2	23.2	22.9	24.2	19.2
1–3 years college	35.6	28.5	11.3	15.9	20.8
College graduate	29.5	36.3	4.9	8.9	43.0
Total	100.0	100.0	100.0	100.0	100.0

SOURCE: Authors' calculations based on US Census Bureau, "American Community Survey."

The low educational attainment of Mexican immigrants living in metropolitan Los Angeles is hardly surprising, given that the nature of their migration involves obtaining lower-skilled jobs. Alejandro Portes and Ruben Rumbaut[9] have argued that the high volume of Mexican immigrants in the United States, the proximity of the two countries, and the demand from employers has led these immigrants to confront less selectivity in comparison to some Asian immigrant groups, such as those from India. In any case, the low educational level of Mexican immigrants translates into difficulties in integration into the labor market and an obstacle to upward mobility.

ENGLISH PROFICIENCY

Assimilation theory holds that adoption of the host language is one of the fundamental aspects of the process of social integration into the receiving society. Linguistic assimilation is expected not only for instrumental reasons but also for symbolic ones, given that language figures at the center of national identities and ethnic solidarities.[10] From this point of view, it follows that acquisition of the language of the dominant culture is the first step in the immigrant's integration into the new society. Linguistic competence not only serves as a catalyst for everyday tactical communication but also can contribute to strengthening communication between natives and immigrants and to positive insertion in employment and educational spheres.[11] Immigrants' English acquisition depends on a number of factors, including age at arrival, schooling, and length of residence in the United States.[12]

Several studies undertaken in the United States report that although less so than other immigrants, Mexicans and their offspring try to learn English because they judge it to be an indispensable element for success in that country.[13] However, Samuel Huntington[14] argues that Mexicans and other Latino immigrants have not assimilated the majority culture of the United States, but instead have formed their own political and linguistic enclaves and rejected the Anglo-Protestant values that, he claims, built the American Dream. Alba,[15] on the other hand, asserts that in 1990 a bit more than 60 percent of the members of the third generation of Mexican origin spoke only English at home, and in 2000 this figure rose to around 70 percent.

The American Community Survey data show that Mexicans have less English-speaking ability than other groups. Table 8 reveals that a bit more than half (51.1 percent) of Mexican immigrants do not speak English well or do not speak it at all. This figure contrasts with those found for Europeans and Asians (11.5 percent and 24.1 percent, respectively). Central Americans show levels similar to the Mexicans. In contrast, while 44.3 percent of European immigrants and 9.9 percent of Asian ones speak only English, only 2.5 percent of those born in Mexico do so, and 4.2% of Central Americans. Table 8 also shows that the percentage of immigrant Mexican women who do not speak English is notably greater than that of Mexican men (24.8 percent and 17.8 percent, respectively).

The high residential concentration of Mexican immigrants in California, the proximity of the Mexican border, and their strong social networks all influence the delay in English acquisition. However, English competence is a characteristic of the majority of US immigrants after ten years.[16] Not all the Hispanic immigrants in the United States retain their Spanish, and linguistic assimilation (defined as monolingualism in English) tends to increase with the immigrants' length of residence and becomes dominant in the third generation.[17]

Observing the distribution of the Mexican immigrant population's English abilities according to arrival cohort, it can be seen that longer

TABLE 8 PERCENT DISTRIBUTION OF NATIVE-BORN AND IMMIGRANT POPULATION
FIVE OR OLDER BY ENGLISH PROFICIENCY AND ACCORDING TO ETHNICITY AND SEX,
LOS ANGELES METROPOLITAN AREA, 2007

Ethnic origin and sex	Total	Speak English only	Speak English very well	Speak English well	Do not speak English well	No English
Native	*100*	*72.2*	*23.3*	*3.4*	*1.0*	*0.2*
Men	100	72.2	23.1	3.6	1.0	0.1
Women	100	72.2	23.4	3.2	1.0	0.2
European	*100*	*44.3*	*31.4*	*12.8*	*7.8*	*3.7*
Men	100	45.6	31.1	12.9	7.5	2.9
Women	100	43.3	31.6	12.7	8.1	4.4
Mexican	*100*	*2.5*	*24.3*	*22.2*	*30.0*	*21.1*
Men	100	2.4	24.3	25.2	30.4	17.8
Women	100	2.7	24.3	18.7	29.5	24.8
Central American	*100*	*4.2*	*26.7*	*22.5*	*28.0*	*18.5*
Men	100	3.7	27.5	24.7	27.8	16.3
Women	100	4.7	25.9	20.4	28.3	20.6
Asian	*100*	*9.9*	*40.8*	*25.2*	*18.2*	*5.9*
Men	100	10.1	43.2	26.1	16.4	4.2
Women	100	9.7	38.7	24.4	19.9	7.4

SOURCE: Authors' calculations based on US Census Bureau, "American Community Survey."

residence facilitates a greater mastery of English (see table 9). Among Mexicans who arrived before 1965, 63 percent were concentrated in the categories "speak English only," "speak English very well," and "speak English well" by 2007. This percentage diminishes consistently in the cohorts that arrived in later periods; at the other extreme, among those who arrived between 1995 and 2007, only 38.7 percent had those levels of English proficiency. When English proficiency among Mexicans is compared to that of Europeans and Asians, we see that even in the older cohorts, the Mexicans are the group with the lowest percentage speaking only English or speaking it very well or well. This same pattern is true for Central American immigrants.

There are other factors that affect Mexican immigrants' difficulties in acquiring English. Fix and Passel[18] point to a study of the education of Latinos in the southwestern United States indicating that a lack of trained English-as-a-second-language teachers was the most significant problem. Data from the 2002 National Survey of Latinos carried out by the Pew Hispanic Center and Kaiser Family Foundation[19] indicate that

TABLE 9 PERCENT DISTRIBUTION OF THE IMMIGRANT POPULATION FIVE OR
OLDER BY ENGLISH PROFICIENCY, ACCORDING TO IMMIGRANT GROUP AND PERIOD
OF ARRIVAL IN THE UNITED STATES, LOS ANGELES METROPOLITAN AREA, 2007

Immigrant group and arrival year	Total	Speak English only	Speak English very well	Speak English well	Do not speak English well	No English
European	*100*	*44.3*	*31.4*	*12.8*	*7.8*	*3.7*
Before 1965	100	65.0	23.1	8.3	2.9	0.7
1965 to 1986	100	51.0	30.6	11.3	6.4	—
1987 to 1994	100	26.3	41	14.6	10.4	7.6
1995 to 2007	100	31.6	33	17.0	11.8	6.5
Mexican	*100*	*2.5*	*24.3*	*22.2*	*30.0*	*21.1*
Before 1965	100	7.1	34.9	21.1	21.8	15.1
1965 to 1986	100	3.3	27.6	24.8	28.7	15.6
1987 to 1994	100	1.8	24.8	23.6	30.9	18.8
1995 to 2007	100	1.6	18.8	18.3	31.8	29.5
Central American	*100*	*4.2*	*26.7*	*22.5*	*28.0*	*18.5*
Before 1965	100	14.4	43.7	15.8	18.7	7.4
1965 to 1986	100	5.4	31.9	26.5	25.1	11.2
1987 to 1994	100	3.0	28.2	24.3	29.1	15.5
1995 to 2007	100	2.9	16.7	15.8	32.2	32.5
Asian	*100*	*9.9*	*40.8*	*25.2*	*18.2*	*5.9*
Before 1965	100	34.3	37.2	16.6	9.1	2.9
1965 to 1986	100	12.1	44.6	23.6	15.4	4.2
1987 to 1994	100	8.0	38.8	24.9	19.9	8.4
1995 to 2007	100	6.3	37.8	28.0	21.3	6.6

SOURCE: Authors' calculations based on US Census Bureau, "American Community Survey."

although English proficiency can lead to greater economic benefits for Latin American immigrants, it does not necessarily reduce discrimination; a significant portion of the interviewees who spoke the language well reported having been the objects of discrimination in their workplace because of their appearance.

NATURALIZATION

Naturalization is a key factor in immigrants' integration. As the world's leading destination of immigration, the United States has designed complex laws and huge institutions to manage the admission of foreigners and the offer of citizenship. The US approach is guided by the principle of Jus Soli, under which citizenship is conferred on all persons born within the territory, even if their parents are undocumented, which is not the case in European countries, generally governed by Jus Sanguinis. A foreigner who has been admitted as a legal permanent resident may request naturalization after five years if she or he meets certain requisites, such as not having a criminal record. Spouses of US citizens may apply for naturalization after three years of legal permanent residency.

Until the end of the 1990s, Mexican immigrants had low levels of naturalization owing to a combination of nationalism and the Mexican government's requirement that they renounce Mexican nationality when taking on US citizenship. However, at the end of that decade, Mexican immigrants changed their attitude toward naturalization because of the Illegal Immigration Reform and Immigrant Responsibility Act (IIRIRA), approved by the US Congress in 1996, which drastically limited permanent legal residents' access to many social benefits. For its part, the Mexican Congress approved a constitutional reform in 1997 allowing those who decided to adopt another citizenship to also retain Mexican nationality, thus making Mexican nationality an irreversible right. The combination of those two processes caused an unprecedented increase in the number of naturalizations of Mexican immigrants, many of whom had become legal permanent residents thanks to passage of IRCA in 1986, including its broad amnesty for the undocumented.

In spite of the recent increase in naturalizations, according to the 2007 Current Population Survey,[20] the population born in Mexico and resident in the United States presents percentages of naturalization much lower than those of other immigrant groups. While approximately one out of five Mexicans has US citizenship, nearly one out of three immigrants from other Latin American countries has been naturalized, and one out of every two Asians and Europeans.

In metropolitan Los Angeles, according to 2007 American Community Survey data, only 28.3 percent of Mexican residents has US citizenship, as compared to a very high percentage of the Asian and European population, approximately 63 percent (see figure 3). After the Mexicans, the next lowest percentage belongs to the Central Americans. Also, if one compares the citizenship status of Mexican immigrants by period of arrival, the low degree of citizenship among the most recent arrivals stands out. While 7.6 percent of the Mexican population that arrived between 1995 and 2007 had US citizenship by the close of that period, 24.5 percent of the Asians who arrived in the same period were citizens.

If we examine citizenship status among Mexicans according to sex, we see that among Mexican women the percentage with citizenship is

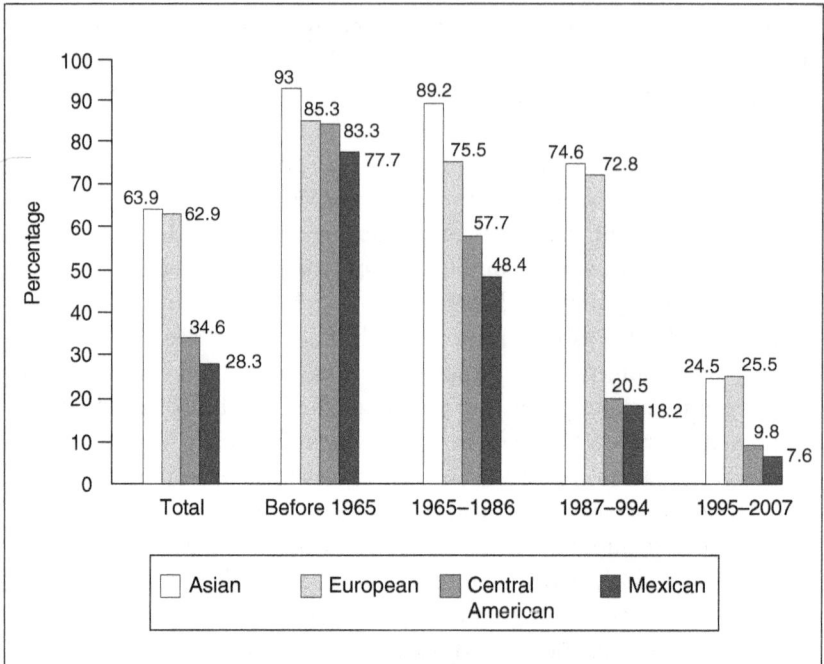

FIGURE 3. Percent distribution of the immigrant population with US citizenship by immigrant group and period of arrival to the United States, Los Angeles Metropolitan Area, 2007. Authors' calculations based on US Census Bureau, "American Community Survey."

30.6, while for men it is 26.2 (see table 10). For Central Americans, the percentage of women with US citizenship is also higher than that among men, while among Asian and European immigrants there is almost no difference according to sex.

Michael Fix and his coauthors[21] argue that what prevents many of the Latino immigrants who might aspire to become US citizens from doing so is the requirements set by the US government. Once an immigrant has achieved legal permanent residence, he or she must wait at least five years to apply for citizenship, pay high fees associated with this process, and demonstrate mastery of English, which as we have shown is very low among Mexican immigrants.

OCCUPATION

Although Mexican immigrants have high levels of labor force participation, they work mostly in low-skilled and low-paid occupations. The

TABLE 10   PERCENT DISTRIBUTION OF THE IMMIGRANT POPULATION BY US
CITIZENSHIP STATUS, ACCORDING TO IMMIGRANT GROUP AND SEX, LOS ANGELES
METROPOLITAN AREA, 2007

Immigrant group and sex	Total	Citizen	Noncitizen
European	*100*	*62.9*	*37.1*
Men	100	62.7	37.3
Women	100	63.0	37.0
Mexican	*100*	*28.3*	*71.7*
Men	100	26.2	73.8
Women	100	30.6	69.4
Central American	*100*	*34.6*	*65.4*
Men	100	29.4	70.6
Women	100	39.4	60.6
Asian	*100*	*63.9*	*36.1*
Men	100	64.1	35.9
Women	100	63.7	36.3

SOURCE: Authors' calculations based on US Census Bureau, "American Community Survey."

ACS data show that out of all Mexican immigrants of working age (sixteen or over), 2.4 million were part of the economically active population of metropolitan Los Angeles in 2007. This figure represents a labor force participation rate of 68.7 percent, slightly lower than that reported by Central American immigrants, but higher than those of other immigrant groups or the native-born.

A first approximation of the structure of Mexican immigrants' workforce participation can be gained by observing their concentrations in the various occupations of the metropolitan Los Angeles labor market. Table 11 shows the percent of different ethnic groups in each occupational category in the region in 2007. Four labor market niches stand out in that Mexicans occupy more than 40 percent of the jobs in each: (1) agriculture, forestry, and fishing; (2) production; (3) food preparation and building cleaning; and (4) construction and extraction.

The main geographical areas in which Mexican immigrants make up the majority of farmworkers are the outlying parts of San Bernardino, Riverside, and Ventura Counties. Although the absolute numbers of these workers have been declining rapidly, the occupation is completely dominated by Mexicans. The category of production workers refers to those in the manufacturing sector, where the most important subsector is clothing production, which employs both men and women. Many Mexican men

TABLE 11 PERCENT DISTRIBUTION OF THE NATIVE-BORN AND IMMIGRANT
POPULATION SIXTEEN OR OLDER BY IMMIGRANT GROUP, ACCORDING TO MAJOR
OCCUPATIONAL CATEGORIES, LOS ANGELES METROPOLITAN AREA, 2007

Occupation	Native	European	Mexican	Central American	Asian	Other
Professional and specialized occupations	70.0	4.3	5.7	2.3	15.1	2.6
Food preparation and building cleaning	34.5	1.3	44.5	11.4	6.7	1.6
Sales and administration	67.9	3.0	11.9	3.3	11.8	2.3
Personal services	53.9	3.2	16.9	6.9	16.7	2.3
Agriculture, forestry, and fishing	16.7	0.4	75.4	3.1	3.1	1.3
Construction and extraction	41.1	1.6	43.3	8.6	3.6	1.8
Production	28.1	1.8	47.0	9.4	11.9	1.7
Installation, maintenance, and repair	53.7	2.4	27.1	6.3	8.5	2.0
Transportation and materials transport	47.3	1.3	35.3	9.2	4.9	2.0
Military occupations	81.9	0.9	3.5	2.8	9.4	1.5

SOURCE: Authors' calculations based on US Census Bureau, "American Community Survey."

and women also work in restaurants (serving all sorts of national cuisines) and as cleaning workers in buildings. Finally, Mexicans make up a substantial share of construction workers, a labor niche they had been coming to dominate over the years but that grew much less stable with the beginning of the world economic crisis in 2008. Although Mexicans' presence in the transportation sector is smaller, it is still an important one.

However, it is necessary to note that Mexican immigrants' predominance within certain labor niches is also the result of a victory of employers over labor unions. For example, employers in construction, cleaning services, and transportation began in the 1980s to hire non-union workers through subcontractors, and for that reason have employed more recent immigrants.[22] In the second part of this book, we will discuss in detail the experiences of our interviewees from Zacatecas, Oaxaca, and Veracruz who work in these niches.

Table 11 also reveals that native-born workers have a very large share (70 percent) of the jobs in professional and specialized occupations, which are better paid and require more education. Natives are followed by Asian immigrants, as a distant second, while Mexicans display a low rate of participation. Native-born workers also dominate in military occupations, again distantly followed by Asian immigrants.

Table 12 shows the distribution of jobs within ethnic groups, by the various occupational categories. While 68.5 percent of Mexican immigrants are employed in food preparation and building cleaning, production, sales and administration, construction and extraction, native-born workers show strong concentrations in professional occupations and in sales and administration.

Mexicans' limited participation in professional occupations contrasts sharply with that of natives, Asians, and Europeans. Almost half (47.9 percent) of Asian immigrants are employed in these occupations, in contrast with 10.8 percent of Mexican ones. These data depict a labor market polarized according to region of origin, where Mexicans and Central Americans respond to the demand in lower-skilled and generally lower-paid occupations, while European and Asian immigrants find entry into skilled occupations with higher salaries.

The two lower panels of table 12 further break down immigrants' occupational distribution according to whether or not they have acquired US citizenship, in order to analyze differences caused by immigration status. US citizens are all fully documented while the non-naturalized immigrants include both documented and undocumented individuals. It can be seen that a higher percentage of Mexicans who have US citizenship are employed in higher-skilled occupations than those who do not. Thus, for example, while 19.4 percent of Mexican immigrant workers with US citizenship are employed in professional and specialized occupations, this is true of only 7 percent of the noncitizens. Inversely, the proportion of Mexican naturalized citizens employed in low-skilled occupations (food production and building cleaning) is much less than the proportion of those without that status.

Nonetheless, on comparing Mexican immigrants' occupations to those of the native-born population and other immigrants, the data reaffirm that the Mexican immigrant population, with or without US citizenship, is concentrated in occupations that require fewer skills. Still, it is important to note that while the difference in professional occupations between the naturalized and the non-naturalized is twelve percentage points among Mexicans and seventeen percentage points among the Central Americans, the same is not true for European and Asian immigrants, who have almost the same percentage shares among naturalized and non-naturalized workers in these occupations. This suggests the effect of the greater concentration of the undocumented

TABLE 12 PERCENT DISTRIBUTION OF THE NATIVE-BORN AND IMMIGRANT
POPULATION SIXTEEN OR OLDER BY MAJOR OCCUPATIONAL CATEGORIES,
ACCORDING TO ETHNIC ORIGIN AND US CITIZENSHIP STATUS, LOS ANGELES
METROPOLITAN AREA, 2007

Occupation and citizenship status	Native	European	Mexican	Central American	Asian
Total	*100*	*100*	*100*	*100*	*100*
Professional and specialized occupations	44.1	52.7	10.8	16.7	47.9
Food preparation and building cleaning	5.7	4.1	22.1	21.8	5.5
Sales and administration	30.9	26.5	16.3	17.4	27.1
Personal services	3.5	4.1	3.4	5.3	5.6
Agriculture, forestry, and fishing	0.1	0.1	1.6	0.3	0.1
Construction and extraction	4.3	3.2	13.7	10.5	1.9
Production	3.2	4.1	16.4	12.7	6.9
Installation, maintenance, and repair	2.9	2.6	4.5	4.0	2.4
Transportation and materials transport	5.3	2.7	11.2	11.2	2.6
US citizens	*100*	*100*	*100*	*100*	*100*
Professional and specialized occupations	44.1	52.0	19.4	27.7	49.3
Food preparation and building cleaning	5.7	3.7	14.4	16.5	3.8
Sales and administration	30.9	28.0	23.3	21.8	28.1
Personal services	3.5	3.5	4.6	6.5	4.9
Agriculture, forestry, and fishing	0.1	0.0	0.8	0.0	0.1
Construction and extraction	4.3	2.6	8.5	3.3	1.8
Production	3.2	4.7	13.6	9.8	6.9
Installation, maintenance, and repair	2.9	2.7	4.6	4.6	2.6
Transportation and materials transport	5.3	2.8	10.9	9.8	2.5
Noncitizens		*100*	*100*	*100*	*100*
Professional and specialized occupations		54.4	7.0	10.9	43.2
Food preparation and building cleaning		4.8	24.9	24.3	9.6
Sales and administration		23.8	13.5	15.1	25.5
Personal services		4.7	3.0	4.7	6.9
Agriculture, forestry, and fishing		0.1	2.0	0.5	0.1
Construction and extraction		4.1	16.1	14.7	2.3
Production		3.3	17.7	14.0	7.5
Installation, maintenance, and repair		2.2	4.3	3.6	1.8
Transportation and materials transport		2.6	11.4	12.2	3.3

SOURCE: Authors' calculations based on US Census Bureau, "American Community Survey."

NOTE: This table does not include military occupations, which have a very low percentage.

among Mexicans and Central Americans: their immigration status keeps them from getting professional jobs.

Meanwhile, limited education and less English proficiency contribute to a pattern of segregation that principally affects Mexicans and Central Americans, who, even if they have US citizenship, are largely employed in low-skilled jobs in comparison with native and naturalized immigrants from Asia and Europe. For example, 14.4 percent of naturalized Mexicans and 16.5 percent of naturalized Central Americans work in areas related to food production and building cleaning, as compared to 3.7 percent of Europeans and 3.8 percent of Asians.

The concentration of Mexican immigrants in low-skilled jobs in turn expresses itself in a wage differential with respect to natives and European and Asian immigrants. About half (46 percent) of the native population has earned income of $40,000 a year or more. Fifty-four percent of European immigrants are in that income group, as are 48 percent of Asians. Only 17 percent of Mexicans, however, have this level of income. Among them, and also among Central Americans, around 70 percent make less than $30,000 a year. The large earnings gap between Mexican immigrants and US natives, European immigrants, and Asian immigrants clearly demonstrates the Mexicans' difficulty in achieving successful economic integration (see figure 4).

HOME OWNERSHIP

Home ownership is a key indicator for use in the analysis of immigrant integration, not only because it suggests permanent settlement within the United States but also because it represents a fundamental economic investment on the immigrant's part. Therefore the purchase of a home is an important symbol of membership in the middle class and of residential assimilation.[23]

In the specific case of Mexican immigrants living in metropolitan Los Angeles, the American Community Survey data show that a little more than 45 percent live in households that include the owners of the home. This is less than the 60 percent figure for European and Asian immigrants, but a bit higher than the 42 percent for Central Americans.

Several studies find that immigrant home ownership is a sign of commitment to the host society, since it manifests a desire to remain in the country.[24] These same studies also find that immigrants' legal status plays a discriminatory role that affects the rates of home ownership for different ethnic groups. The data in figure 5 seem to corroborate this

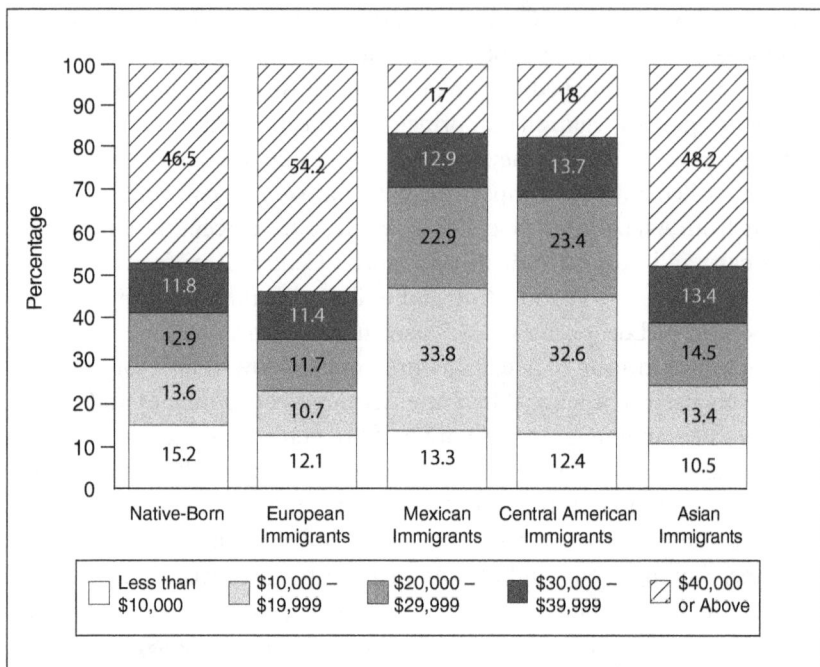

FIGURE 4. Percent distribution of the native-born and immigrant population, age sixteen and over, by earned annual income group (in dollars) and ethnic origin, Los Angeles Metropolitan Area, 2007. Authors' calculations based on US Census Bureau, "American Community Survey."

hypothesis, given that seven out of every ten Mexican immigrants with US citizenship reside in an owner-occupied home, as compared to only three out of every ten for the noncitizens. Naturalized Mexican immigrants' home ownership percentage (about 68 percent) is similar to that of their Asian and European counterparts, which suggests that documented status comes accompanied by economic and social mobility.

Duration of residence in the United States is another factor that affects home ownership among the immigrant population. The longer they have lived in the United States, the higher the share of immigrants who are homeowners, as is shown in table 13 for all the groups considered in this analysis.

FINAL CONSIDERATIONS

Our analysis of Mexican immigrants' economic and social integration in metropolitan Los Angeles, as based on American Community Survey

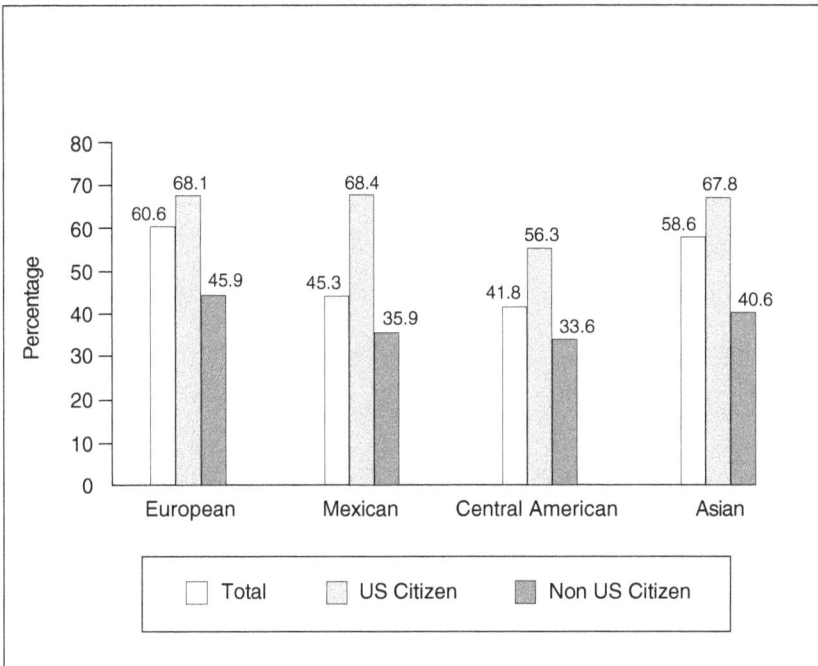

FIGURE 5. Percent distribution of the immigrant population living in an owner-occupied home, by naturalization status, Los Angeles Metropolitan Area, 2007. Authors' calculations based on US Census Bureau, "American Community Survey."

data from 2007, shows that they are undertaking the process of integration in conditions of disadvantage compared to other immigrants groups such as Europeans and Asians, and in conditions very similar to those faced by Central Americans. The data reflect lower levels of educational attainment, English proficiency, naturalization, labor force participation in skilled occupations, and home ownership.

Only 39.4 percent of Mexican immigrants twenty-five or older have completed high school, and only 4.7 have finished college or undertaken any graduate study—very low percentages in comparison to those of other immigrant groups or the native-born. In relation to English proficiency, Mexican immigrants show comparatively less ability to communicate in that language, since more than half do not speak it well or do not speak it at all. However, the analysis of English-speaking ability according to cohort of arrival in the United States shows that longer residence in the country does contribute to greater mastery of the language.

In spite of being the largest immigrant group in the Los Angeles region and having the longest immigration history there, only one out

TABLE 13   PERCENT DISTRIBUTION OF THE IMMIGRANT POPULATION BY HOME
OWNERSHIP, ACCORDING TO IMMIGRANT GROUP AND PERIOD OF ARRIVAL IN THE
UNITED STATES, LOS ANGELES METROPOLITAN AREA, 2007

Region of origin	Arrival before 1965	Arrival 1965–1986	Arrival 1987–1994	Arrival 1995–2007
Europe	100	100	100	100
Owner	82.9	73.2	51.2	36.5
Non-owner	17.1	26.8	48.8	63.5
Mexico	100	100	100	100
Owner	74.3	60.9	42.9	26.7
Non-owner	25.7	39.1	57.1	73.3
Central America	100	100	100	100
Owner	74.4	51.3	40.4	26.8
Non-owner	25.6	48.7	59.6	73.2
Asia	100	100	100	100
Owner	82.5	71.8	60.6	39.9
Non-owner	17.5	28.2	39.4	60.1

SOURCE: Authors' calculations based on US Census Bureau, "American Community Survey."

of every four Mexicans has acquired US citizenship. Nonetheless it is important to mention that the low incidence of citizenship results primarily from the high proportion of undocumented persons, a high proportion that is continuously regenerated by the arrival of new immigrants with that status.

In the labor market, Mexican immigrants are concentrated in occupations with low skill levels. Approximately seven out of ten are active in occupations related to food preparation, building cleaning, production jobs in manufacturing, administrative support, sales, and construction. The Mexicans seem to have conquered labor niches in sectors not desired by other workers, whether native or immigrant, but it is possible that such niches in manufacturing sectors exclude some other workers—for instance, African Americans—who suffer a process of discrimination more severe than that of the Mexicans.[25]

In terms of homeownership, the study results show that slightly more than 45 percent of Mexican immigrants live in a household that includes the owners of the home. This is a low proportion in comparison to the 60 percent among European and Asian immigrants. However, it shows that an important percentage of Mexican immigrants, by being homeowners, are strongly integrated into the Los Angeles economy and society.

Analysis of the impact of legal immigration status on occupation and homeownership shows, through comparison of the experiences of those who are and are not naturalized, that Mexicans who have US citizenship work in more highly skilled occupations than those who do not have US citizenship. Similarly, a higher percentage of Mexican immigrants with US citizenship reside in owner-occupied households. The analysis of homeownership by cohort of arrival also shows that, in general, a longer period of residence in the country brings a higher likelihood of home ownership. Given these results, it can be argued that legal immigration status and long period of residence have led to more successful economic and social integration for Mexican immigrants in the Los Angeles Metropolitan Area.

This chapter has shown that Mexican immigrants are integrating into the economy of metropolitan Los Angeles in a disadvantageous manner in comparison to other immigrants, such as Europeans and Asians. In this sense, our indicators agree with those cited by Huntington,[26] but we argue that the Mexicans do demonstrate strong integration into the Los Angeles economy because they have inserted themselves in the formal and informal labor markets of this metropolis as it has gone through a difficult process of economic restructuring in recent decades.

This profound economic restructuring of metropolitan Los Angeles has brought a decline in its manufacturing base and a growing expansion of its informal economy, which offers many jobs that require few skills, are unstable, do not provide benefits, and are subject to systems of subcontracting and other forms of poor labor conditions. Many of these jobs have been filled by Mexican immigrants.

PART TWO

Dimensions of Integration among Immigrants from Zacatecas, Oaxaca, and Veracruz

CHAPTER 4

Economic Integration

Mobility, Labor Niches, and Low-End Jobs

In Los Angeles, learning to drive is more important than
learning English.

—Adelaida, interviewee from Veracruz

Since the city's founding at the end of the eighteenth century, metropolitan Los Angeles has experienced economic growth—sometimes
very rapid—that has integrated immigrants from all corners of the
world, but in different ways. As discussed in chapter 1, analyzing such
economic integration involves comparative examination of immigrants'
patterns of economic mobility through their insertion in the labor market, self-employment, business formation, and investment in real estate
both in the country of destination and in that of origin. In this study we
specifically include analysis of businesses formation and property acquisition in the United States and Mexico, rejecting the "methodological
nationalism" that considers only processes in the destination country to
be of importance.[1]

Mexican immigrants have access to certain occupational niches built
over the course of many years via relationships with employers, niches
that can also limit native-born workers' and other immigrants' access to
those jobs.[2] In addition, given the context of economic restructuring
marked by increasingly flexible and insecure terms of employment, a
key issue for understanding immigrant labor integration today is the
informal economy. Although we do not try in this work to resolve the
question put forward by Saskia Sassen[3] about whether the growth of
the informal economy in industrialized countries is a consequence of
advanced capitalism or the result of immigration, we will analyze the
mechanisms of access to informal economic activity, which, according

to Manuel Castells and Alejandro Portes,[4] is not illegal but exists at the margins of state regulation.

The central objective of this chapter is to analyze the economic integration of our ninety interviewees from the states of Zacatecas, Oaxaca, and Veracruz, all of whom resided in metropolitan Los Angeles in 2008 when the interviews were carried out. To examine their upward or downward occupational mobility through insertion in both formal and informal sectors of the economy, we will look at the changes between the first jobs they obtained in the United States—usually in Los Angeles—and their jobs at the time of the interviews. We will include the economic integration experiences of both the skilled and unskilled immigrants from Zacatecas, Oaxaca, and Veracruz. The majority of our interviewees do not have high skills in the sense that they have not completed college.[5] According to the American Community Survey of 2007, only 4.7 percent of all Mexican immigrants twenty-five or older in metropolitan Los Angeles received undergraduate degrees or undertook any postgraduate study.

This chapter also examines the formation of small businesses in the formal and informal sectors and their possible functional ties with Mexico, since in recent decades an accelerated growth of immigrant-owned business has been observed in cities such as New York, Los Angeles, and Miami, with Chinese, Korean, and Cuban immigrants displaying high participation rates, suggesting an alternative route of economic mobility with respect to employment.[6] Since metropolitan Los Angeles is the principal destination of Mexican immigrants, it is crucial to analyze the degree to which our interviewees, whether through formal or informal businesses, are participating in the construction of a Mexican ethnic economy.

Finally, a fundamental indicator of economic integration is investment in the purchase of a home in the United States, something that would demonstrate our interviewees' commitment and intent to stay in that country and entrance, at least symbolically, into the US middle class and the "American Dream."[7] Our interviews took place in 2008, when the global economic recession had already begun. One of its fundamental causes was the "housing bubble" that finally burst, plunging many homeowners with mortgages into turbulent waters. It is important to note that in the pre-recession period, undocumented immigrants in the United States could easily get mortgages, which shows that banks were more concerned with documents demonstrating good credit history than with those certifying legal immigration status.

The following sections will examine the experiences of our interviewees from Zacatecas, Oaxaca, and Veracruz in relation to labor force insertion and business formation. The second part of this chapter is devoted to real estate investment in the United States and Mexico.

ZACATECANS AND RELATIVE UPWARD LABOR MOBILITY

As has been pointed out before, of the three groups of immigrants that we interviewed, Zacatecans have the longest tradition of migrating to Los Angeles; their average year of arrival was 1979. One of our interviewees, Lázaro, was seventy-three at the time of the interview and had retired after thirty-five years of work in an aluminum foundry. He arrived in Los Angeles in 1953, when the city still had some farming activity. Lázaro, who is a naturalized citizen, is originally from Las Ánimas, Zacatecas, and came to Los Angeles to work on a cattle ranch. Later he worked for a firm that repaired clutches and then went to work in the aluminum foundry, from which he eventually retired. For many years, that company has employed many of his fellow towners.

Our Zacatecan interviewees who arrived in Los Angeles in the 1960s and 1970s were mostly undocumented. Although they entered a solid regional economy supported by a manufacturing base that offered plentiful permanent, well-paid, unionized jobs, the interviewees' first jobs tended to be in worse-paid occupations with poor working conditions. The majority of the men worked as restaurant dishwashers, garment factory workers, or farm laborers. The women worked in fruit and vegetable canneries or garment factories.

Abelardo is a naturalized citizen, married, who has worked in restaurants ever since arriving in Los Angeles in 1977. At that time, restaurant work was the Zacatecan occupational niche, and the job ladder began with dishwashing:

> I started out washing dishes in a restaurant, that was almost a requirement, you arrived and you had to start at the bottom . . . later you moved on to assistant waiter or to cleaning the restaurant either daytimes or nighttimes . . . in those days there wasn't any construction work, just dishwashing, and if you managed to work your way up to cook, that was pretty good.

Among women finding jobs in canneries processing fruits and other foodstuffs, Marcia worked in a fish-canning plant for more than three decades. But it was not easy for her to get this job in 1966:

I went every day with my husband, at four in the morning, to a room where everyone who wanted to work had to sit and wait . . . until we got work, and then we stayed put where we got it . . . we spent thirty-six years working there. My husband died and I kept on working to keep going. . . . When I left, in 2001, I was making $6.75 an hour. We never got ahead in there.

Marcia is a US citizen, never was undocumented, and is now collecting retirement income. Jacinta, on the other hand, was born on a ranch in Jerez, Zacatecas, and arrived in Los Angeles in 1973 after an undocumented crossing in Tijuana with the aid of a *coyote*. She was married and crossed the border with her five children. Her sixth was born the next year, in Los Angeles. Her husband had already worked in Los Angeles; Jacinta started working as a strawberry picker. Then she got a job in a clothing factory. Over time, she acquired US citizenship and Social Security income for her years of work.

Ponciano, now married and a US citizen, came to Los Angeles in 1973. Since he was a good baseball player in Las Ánimas, other Zacatecans who had a team invited him to join as a pitcher. "That was how I first connected with people from my town, and then another man on the team told me they were hiring in his factory . . . a clothing factory where they made pleated skirts, and they taught me how, and I stayed, starting out with a wage of $1.75 an hour."

Since Ponciano wanted to advance, he went to school to learn English and, although he still had many limitations in his use of the language, he got a chance to work in a company that produced clutches. His first task involved use of an air compressor and, with his limited English, he did not know how to carry out his orders, but a workmate from Hawaii spent those first eight days showing him what to do. "He didn't speak a single word of Spanish and I didn't speak a single word of English . . . but [I learned how to do the work] thanks to that Hawaiian who taught me."

In spite of their difficult beginning in the 1960s and 1970s, our Zacatecan interviewees began to acquire work experience, learn English, make contacts with employers, and regularize their immigration status. For that reason, as table 14 shows, their 2008 occupations reveal important changes in the course of their labor trajectories.

In general, the table shows a relative occupational mobility linked to the very high percentage who became naturalized citizens or legal permanent residents. Among the eighteen men interviewed, thirteen are naturalized citizens, four are legal permanent residents, and there is one undocumented migrant. Among the twelve women, eight are naturalized citizens, three are legal permanent residents, and only one is undocumented (table 14).

The relative occupational mobility is notable especially among the men, most of whom became small business owners or moved into professional or technical occupations between their first job and their job at the time of the interview. Because of the aging process, some are now collecting retirement income after long years of work.

Of our interviewees, only René was unemployed in 2008; after three decades working in a neon sign factory he was laid off along with 150 other workers. He is married, a naturalized citizen, and receiving job retraining. For twenty-six years he was the foreman in the metal section of the factory, until it shut down due to a combination of poor management and competition from other firms. René still laments the loss of this job:

> I never thought they were going to close. . . . well, at first I thought God will keep me in this job till I can retire; I'm going to work here till I'm at least sixty-two or sixty-five. . . . My wife is the one who encourages me. At first I couldn't believe this had happened, and still there are times when I wake up at midnight and have to tell myself I can no longer rely on that company.

Ricardo illustrates the experience of a skilled Zacatecan migrant who has been successful in the labor market. He is married, a US citizen, and all his children have professional careers. He first came to Los Angeles, where his brothers already lived, in 1977 while he was a university student. After graduating with a degree in electrical engineering from the Universidad de Zacatecas, he began working in a US-owned company in Mexico City and then, after a few years, was reassigned to their Los Angeles plant. Since then, Ricardo has taken further professional development courses in engineering, has had his own business, and for the past twenty-three years has worked as an engineer in a company owned by European immigrants that manufactures and maintains motors for ships and oil refineries.

Mariana is another skilled immigrant. Now a US citizen, she was brought to Los Angeles as a child, undocumented, when her parents came in the mid-1970s. She attended college in California and then continued her study of human rights in Europe. Although she has worked in various occupations, she defines herself as a community activist.

A significant group of women have retired after their working years or have returned to unpaid household work in their homes. Still others are the owners of formal businesses or carry out informal freelance activities. Among the business owners, Rafaela stands out. She arrived in Los Angeles in 1988, is a naturalized citizen, and is married with children born in the United States. In Zacatecas she was a cosmetologist and, although she didn't want to keep working in this field, she needed to do so and later became the owner of a beauty salon:

> I never really liked cosmetology. I did it because my mother told me I had to learn a trade. In Los Angeles, I wanted to work as something else, but talking with other women in laundromats and with my neighbors, they told me they were making $3.75 an hour. I said, I'm not working for $3.75, no way . . . some of them worked in restaurants, others in factories, one woman packed candles, another one sewed in a clothing factory where they paid her five cents per piece . . . my husband made $3.75 an hour too, which was the minimum wage in those days.

Rafaela tells how she found her first job: "I saw a beauty parlor with a sign that said '*se habla español*,' so I went in and told the owner—a Salvadoran, twenty-one years old—I was a cosmetologist in Mexico and I wanted to work. 'I've got five years' experience,' I said." During the interview the owner asked Rafaela to cut the hair of three young men from Jalisco, and her work was good enough to get her hired right away. "That was Thursday, and by Sunday I had $70 in tips and $430 in pay because I got 60 percent of what I took in." In 2008, twenty years after her arrival in Los Angeles, she owned a salon and had four employees.

Jairo's trajectory illustrates the experience of a worker who began in Los Angeles in 1963 as a dishwasher, then rose to assistant waiter, cook, and restaurant manager, then opened his own refrigeration and air-conditioning business, and finally retired. "When I opened my own shop I saw the difference between having your own business and working for someone else. That year I made $130,000." Over time, Jairo became a US citizen, brought his two sons to work for him in the company, and after a number of years began to have back problems, at which point he followed his doctor's advice and retired. "My house is paid for, thank God, I get $1,600 a month from Social Security and a pension of $400. There are workers right now who don't make $500 a week, and I'm making that sitting home taking care of my grandchildren."

Another immigrant who became a successful businessman is Hilario. He is married, a naturalized citizen, and has three children; one of them, a daughter, is a lawyer. Hilario arrived in Los Angeles in 1972 and went to work in a series of garment factories. The last of those made caps, scrubs, and gowns for surgeons. When he was let go by that factory,

TABLE 14   FIRST AND CURRENT OCCUPATIONS OF THE ZACATECAN INTERVIEWEES
IN THE LOS ANGELES METROPOLITAN AREA, BY SEX, YEAR OF ARRIVAL, AND
IMMIGRATION STATUS, 2008

Sex	Year of arrival	First US occupation	2008 L.A. occupation	2008 immigration status*
M	1974	Restaurant employee	Building contractor	NC
M	1977	Restaurant employee	Engineer in motor factory	NC
M	1963	Restaurant employee	Retiree	NC
M	1977	Restaurant employee	Restaurant employee	NC
M	1986	Restaurant employee	Administrative employee, environmental field	NC
M	1978	Restaurant employee	Unemployed	NC
M	1972	Clothing factory worker	Factory owner, surgical gowns	NC
M	1973	Clothing factory worker	Sales employee	NC
M	1967	Carpet factory worker	Driver	NC
M	1984	Factory worker	Mechanical workshop owner	NC
M	1987	Construction worker	Trucking company owner	NC
M	1972	Farmworker	Sales employee	NC
M	1953	Farmworker	Retiree	NC
F	1976	Teacher's assistant	Assistant in law firm	NC
F	1972	Clothing factory worker	Personal care, self-employed	NC
F	1979	Vegetable-packing worker	Restaurant owner	NC
F	1966	Vegetable-packing worker	Retiree	NC
F	1973	Farmworker	Retiree	NC
F	1988	Beauty parlor worker	Beauty parlor owner	NC
F	1992	Personal care, self-employed	Personal care, self-employed	NC
F	1996	Homemaker	Homemaker	NC
M	2003	Teacher's assistant	High school teacher	LPR
M	1966	Farmworker	Mariachi singer	LPR
M	1964	Restaurant employee	Gardener	LPR
M	1996	Retiree	Retiree	LPR
F	1974	Clothing factory worker	Homemaker	LPR
F	1993	Homemaker	Personal care, self-employed	LPR
F	2001	Homemaker	Homemaker	LPR
M	1997	Sales employee	Sales manager	UND
F	1990	Sales employee	Homemaker	UND

SOURCE: Interviews with ninety Mexican immigrants in the Los Angeles Metropolitan Area, 2008.

*NC = naturalized citizen; LPR = legal permanent resident; UND = undocumented.

Hilario decided to produce hospital garments on his own. "I left there and in two months I'd bought two old sewing machines, and a woman I had worked with all my life helped me out. . . . I set up a garage workshop, put up walls, and that's where we did the sewing; later we got up to having six machines." Eventually, Hilario rented a larger space with the support of a financial partner; he later opened a workshop in Zacatecas, which had to close because of, as he put it, taxation and labor "terrorism."

OAXACANS AND RESTAURANT WORK

The state of Oaxaca is located in southern Mexico and, as explained above, is characterized by the large size and wide diversity of its indigenous population. Its history of migration to the United States is more recent than that of Zacatecas; the average year of arrival of our Oaxacan interviewees is 1985. The male interviewees found their first jobs in restaurants, which constituted their labor market niche. As table 15 shows, eight of the seventeen male interviewees found their first jobs in that field, working as dishwashers, cleaners, assistant waiters, and cooks. Others worked in agriculture or construction, or in self-employment as gardeners, popsicle vendors, or car washers. The women found their first jobs as factory workers, sales workers, housecleaners, or personal care attendants.

Jonathan Fox and Gaspar Rivera-Salgado[8] point out that the majority of Mixtec workers from Oaxaca have concentrated in agricultural work in the Fresno Valley and in the Napa Valley in Northern California. Two of our interviewees, Carmela and Eduardo, recount how they came first to Parlier and Madera, in Fresno Valley, to work in agriculture by way of Mixtec social networks. Over time, and primarily thanks to the amnesty included in the Immigration Reform and Control Act, they decided to move to Los Angeles because urban jobs were easier and better paid than farmwork.

Carmela tells how her first job in agriculture was picking peaches, squash, and grapes in Fresno: "Frankly, I didn't like it because we had to get up at three in the morning, and if we were late we couldn't get in because the agents of *la migra* would be posted on the highway to arrest people without documents." Eduardo says that he went to work in Parlier first because it was easier and quicker to find employment in the fruit harvest there. Later, relatives in Los Angeles found him work in a restaurant in the city.

TABLE 15   FIRST AND CURRENT OCCUPATIONS OF THE OAXACAN INTERVIEWEES
IN THE LOS ANGELES METROPOLITAN AREA, BY SEX, YEAR OF ARRIVAL, AND
IMMIGRATION STATUS, 2008

Sex	Year of arrival	First US occupation	2008 L.A. occupation	2008 immigration status*
M	1977	Restaurant employee	Restaurant employee	NC
M	1985	Restaurant employee	Sales manager	NC
M	1979	Restaurant employee	Sales employee	NC
M	1986	Restaurant employee	Driver	NC
M	1988	Farmworker	Carpentry worker	NC
M	1987	Restaurant employee	Gardener, self-employed	NC
M	1988	Construction worker	Maintenance worker	NC
M	1989	Farmworker	Construction worker	NC
M	1988	Gardener, self-employed	Painter, self-employed	NC
M	1970	Car wash employee	Restaurant employee	NC
F	1986	Clothing factory worker	Restaurant employee	NC
F	1978	Clothing factory worker	Cosmetic sales, self-employed	NC
F	1980	Toy factory worker	Restaurant owner	NC
F	1986	Vegetable-packing worker	Housecleaner, with agency	NC
F	1989	Personal care, self-employed	Food sales, self-employed	NC
M	1976	Restaurant employee	Store owner	LPR
M	1979	Farmworker	Out of labor force	LPR
M	1985	Popsicle vendor, self-employed	Driver	LPR
M	1996	Car washing, self-employed	Construction, self-employed	LPR
F	1988	Restaurant employee	Restaurant owner	LPR
F	1984	Sales employee	Homemaker	LPR
F	1982	Housecleaner, self-employed	Restaurant employee	LPR
F	1971	Housecleaner, self-employed	Restaurant employee	LPR
F	1989	Housecleaner, with agency	Housecleaner, with company	LPR
F	2000	Personal care, self-employed	Sales worker	LPR
M	1990	Restaurant employee	Restaurant employee	UND
M	1983	Restaurant employee	Painter, self-employed	UND
M	1992	Personal care, self-employed	Gardener, self-employed	UND
F	2000	Sales worker	Restaurant employee	UND
F	1988	Sales worker	Homemaker	UND

SOURCE: Interviews with ninety Mexican immigrants in the Los Angeles Metropolitan Area, 2008.
*NC = naturalized citizen; LPR = legal permanent resident; UND = undocumented.

Elías was undocumented when he got his first job in a Los Angeles restaurant, under very adverse conditions, and he later went to work in agriculture to get legalized by way of IRCA:

> My first job was as a dishwasher. I found a cousin who was working in a restaurant on the west side of Los Angeles and he told me they needed somebody there, but only nights, from six P.M. to three A.M., and since I was in a tight spot and wanted to get ahead [I took the job] . . . the only problem with night work is there's no transportation . . . so when I left work I'd go sleep under the stairs of a building, from three A.M. until daybreak so I could get a bus and go to where I was living, which was about fifteen miles away.

Elías arrived in Los Angeles in 1985, is married, and currently is a US citizen. He explains how he became a legal permanent resident:

> When I came, they had the amnesty law and it gave a chance to those who went to work in agriculture. . . . Some friends who worked in the countryside told me to come and work with them in Madera, California, which I did. There, somebody told me that on that farm they were giving amnesty letters, so I went and they gave me a work letter . . . and I came back to Los Angeles and someone steered me to a notary public, who told me, if you've got the letter, let's use it. So we sent it in, we did all the paperwork, and I became part of the amnesty.

Mariela is a legal permanent resident, married, with children born in the United States. She got her first job as a domestic worker through a temporary agency. Several of our interviewees, especially from Oaxaca and Veracruz, say they got their first jobs taking care of children and cleaning houses through such agencies, which provide employees for their clients for limited amounts of time. The number of temporary agencies in the United States rose from 23,552 in 1997 to 31,711 in 2007, accounting for slightly more than three million workers.[9]

Mariela tells how she got her first job in Los Angeles: "A friend took me around to the agencies with her and I got a job. I lived in the house of the people I worked for and had the weekends off." Later she worked in restaurants, in a toy factory, cleaning homes and offices, and taking care of sick people. At the time of the interview, Mariela, like the majority of our interviewees, worked very long hours, seven days a week, because she not only worked for a housecleaning company but also did the same work on her own.

The intensity of work for women carrying out simultaneous occupations is well illustrated by the case of Azhálea, who because of the economic crisis unleashed in 2008 suffered a loss of working hours in her job as a waitress. "For the past year, they've only given me part-time work and to survive I've had to clean houses and condominiums, whatever I can find. I made up business cards, I work as a waitress, bartender, I make food for small buffets, I keep afloat by working all the time." Azhálea works so much that she has undertaken jobs usually reserved for men, such as roofing. Currently she is a legal permanent resident, is single, and has two children.

At the time of the interviews in 2008, among our seventeen male Oaxacan interviewees, there were ten naturalized citizens, six permanent residents, and only two undocumented. Yet our Oaxacan interviewees' regularization of their immigration status has not brought any important change in their occupations, but only allowed them to move within the spectrum of low-end jobs. Some men leave restaurant work to become self-employed gardeners, painters, carpenters, or construction workers. Others stay in the restaurant business but move up from dishwasher to cook or barman. The ones who manage to leave these sorts of work are those who, as a result of studying, have come to work in maintenance for a school district or become tractor-trailer drivers, salesmen, or business owners.

Israel has a small gardening business that he started in 1992; it involves creating gardens with the help of workers from his hometown. Married, a US citizen, and with daughters born in the United States, Israel always had the dream of becoming an electrician, so he studied for two years in a technical school in Sinaloa as well as taking several English and electricity courses in Los Angeles.

His first job in the United States was as an assistant cook, in his case in a Korean restaurant. After obtaining legal permanent residence through IRCA, Israel worked in home construction. He continued to study English, and he began to work in a greenhouse with five white workers who did not speak Spanish. Later he moved to another greenhouse, owned by a Swiss immigrant, at a starting wage of $8 an hour. "I stayed there for about four years . . . that was where I learned a lot more about plants . . . it was a science to me, and it interested me." With his boss's permission he began to offer services at customers' home gardens, but over time he began to have so much freelance work in advising customers and creating and maintaining gardens that he decided to work independently. He formed his own company, which came to employ ten workers.

Helen Ramírez and Pierrette Hondagneu-Sotelo[10] view gardening work, a generally male activity, as the counterpart of the domestic work done primarily by women. In Los Angeles, this occupational niche now dominated by Mexicans was originated by Japanese immigrants. The occupation includes a series of levels, with entrants generally beginning under the supervision of a fellow countryman who has a route, pickup truck, and the necessary machinery. Over time, some become freelancers on their own.

As in the case of the Zacatecans, a new option for documented Oaxacan immigrants is in the transportation sector, as drivers of tractor-trailers and other freight-hauling trucks. Misael is a naturalized citizen, married with two children born in the United States, who worked for ten years as a retail cashier. Needing to increase his earnings, he enrolled in a truck-driving school and got his license. He began to drive a tractor-trailer in the port of San Pedro and has done so for seven years, earning around $1,000 a week. However, he gets no fringe benefits because he is a contract worker rather than an employee.

The Oaxacan women, to judge by their 2008 employment, seem to take on the jobs vacated by men who leave the restaurants. Quite a number of our Oaxacan female interviewees ended in up in the restaurant sector after having begun in other occupations. The sample also includes two women who became restaurant owners. The majority of the other Oaxacan women work in sales, in self-employment, or at home.

Sometimes self-employment as food sellers is a last resort. Since 1967, Verónica has been selling bread she bakes at home when she is not working as a restaurant cook. Carmela, who came to the United States in 1978 and is a naturalized citizen, found herself forced to sell food in the street when her husband left her:

> I became a single mother when my youngest son was seven months old. I had to be both father and mother to bring up my kids; I cleaned two houses each day . . . and I started selling corn on the cob. I had a big metal container full of ears of corn; it weighed so much I felt ashamed to see my little kid so bent over trying to help his mom.

Aurora started her food business by selling from house to house:

> With the amnesty, I went to Oaxaca and began to bring back a little gold to sell to Oaxacans in L.A. But the people here didn't just want gold; they wanted things to eat. In 1987 nobody was selling things to eat here, so I went to Oaxaca and started bringing back *mole,* tortillas, bread, and cheese. In 1991 my husband lost his job and so I got the idea of opening a little restaurant, where we now have two employees.

Currently Aurora is a naturalized citizen and has four children born in the United States.

Fausto, who is a legal permanent resident, has a store in which he and his wife sell handicrafts. He arrived in Los Angeles in 1976 and found his first job in a restaurant. Later he worked for sixteen years in a laundry, where he started out sweeping floors but ended up as a supervisor. In 1990, his wife opened the business selling Mexican handicrafts, which has grown to include items from other countries. Then Fausto, who is an artist, began to produce his own pieces, such as copper crosses and palm-leaf masks. A museum in Los Angeles County invited him to do a show there and bought a collection of his masks. Fausto became acquainted with other artists in Los Angeles and Oaxaca, and he aspires to devote himself full-time to artistic work. "What I'd most like is to go to New York, to the big galleries or the Museo del Barrio, where they present most of the Latino artists."

VERACRUZANS AND LOW-END JOBS

Out of the more than seven million inhabitants of the populous state of Veracruz, only recently have large numbers decided to seek employment in the United States. Our Veracruzan interviewees' average year of arrival is 1991, when it was no longer possible to make use of the IRCA amnesty, and only two years before heightened border enforcement began making undocumented crossings significantly more dangerous. Therefore, the Veracruzans have confronted much more adverse conditions than the two previously discussed groups.

Although our interviewees do not constitute a random sample, their immigration status shows their vulnerability, since the majority are undocumented. At the time of the interviews in 2008, there were only four naturalized US citizens among the seventeen male interviewees, along with one legal permanent resident and twelve undocumented persons. The majority of the thirteen women interviewed were also undocumented; two were naturalized citizens, two more were legal permanent residents, and the remaining nine had no immigration papers.

As a result, the Veracruzan interviewees—both men and women— have entered the labor market in lower-end niches. Among the men, the most common first occupations were as garment factory workers or restaurant employees (dishwashers or assistant waiters). To a lesser degree, they found work as freelancers in the informal sector. Women found their first jobs in the formal sector as garment factory workers, restaurant and hotel employees, or sales workers, and in the informal sector as housecleaners or childcare workers (see table 16).

The Veracruzan men we interviewed have established strong social networks with employers in the garment factories. For example, Fernando found a job because his sister was working in a garment factory whose owner was from Veracruz. Mari Luz arrived in Los Angeles in 1985 and is undocumented, married, with three children born in the United States. Since her arrival she has been a seamstress, a very unstable job.

> In the factory where we worked, we were sewing regular pants, but then they switched to running pants and we couldn't make ends meet so we had to look for something else. I worked in another company for about nine years making pants and then about three years ago I left there and went to another place for six months . . . [in the factory where I am now] I've been working about two years.

This job also pays by the piece, but Mari Luz says she's guaranteed at least minimum wage, though she gets no fringe benefits.

Leonardo, who came to Los Angeles in 1986, is married, has three children, is a naturalized citizen, and has had a more successful career. When he arrived, an uncle found him a job sewing pants and jackets, and now he is a foreman in a factory owned by Oaxacans. Leonardo makes $12 an hour at that job, and in his free time he washes cars on his own. He thinks the economic crisis is hurting the garment industry: "Work has been very bad, very low the last two years. . . . They've laid off like a hundred people in this factory. There are a lot of people out of work, and others working just four hours a day." Leonardo thinks that being a supervisor is hard: "I liked working the machines better. I don't like being a foreman because you've got a lot of responsibility—you have to make sure everything goes well. If it goes badly, the boss will dress you down because you aren't looking out for the quality of the work."

The Los Angeles clothing industry was built by old and new immigrants who have participated as both employers and workers. In 1990, an estimated 93 percent of the workforce was immigrant, and its many Asian proprietors were hiring Latino workers to make up for a lack of Asian ones.[11]

Veracruzans from Orizaba have created a special niche in restaurants, as Oscar explains: "I know a lot of people who clean restaurant kitchens . . . it's night work, hard work . . . I know a lot of people from Orizaba doing that, especially in Hollywood."

Our Veracruzan interviewees agree with the Zacatecans that restaurants have a job hierarchy that begins with dishwasher, then waiter's assistant, then cook's assistant, cook, assistant manager, and finally

TABLE 16 FIRST AND CURRENT OCCUPATIONS OF THE VERACRUZAN INTERVIEWEES IN
THE LOS ANGELES METROPOLITAN AREA, BY SEX, YEAR OF ARRIVAL, AND
IMMIGRATION STATUS, 2008

Sex	Year of arrival	First US occupation	2008 L.A. occupation	2008 immigration status*
M	1986	Clothing factory worker	Clothing factory manager	NC
M	1986	Restaurant employee	Medical instrument factory worker	NC
M	1986	Restaurant employee	Worker in family-owned entertainment business	NC
M	1987	Restaurant employee	Sales employee	NC
F	1971	Clothing factory worker	Homemaker	NC
F	1969	Housecleaner, self-employed	Retiree	NC
M	1993	Gardener, self-employed	Cleaning worker	LPR
F	1999	Silk-screening factory worker	Hotel employee	LPR
F	1990	Personal care, self-employed	Housecleaning, self-employed	LPR
M	1988	Clothing factory worker	Sales supervisor, tiles	UND
M	1988	Clothing factory worker	Clothing factory worker	UND
M	1995	Clothing factory worker	Clothing factory worker	UND
M	2001	Clothing factory worker	Clothing factory worker	UND
M	1992	Clothing factory worker	Restaurant employee	UND
M	2004	Bag factory worker	Sales employee	UND
M	2003	Sales employee	Worker in anti-pollution company	UND
M	1999	Sales employee	Sales employee	UND
M	1990	Restaurant employee	Owner, handicraft sales company	UND
M	1985	Restaurant employee	Cardboard factory worker	UND
M	1999	Painter, self-employed	Restaurant employee	UND
M	1988	Recycling collector, self-employed	Car sales employee	UND
F	1990	Sales employee	Folk dancer	UND
F	1985	Clothing factory worker	Clothing factory worker	UND
F	1989	Sales employee	Food sales, self-employed	UND
F	1992	Sales employee	Vitamin sales, self-employed	UND
F	1999	Restaurant employee	Personal care, self-employed	UND
F	1992	Personal care, for agency	Unemployed	UND
F	1989	Housecleaning, self-employed	Food sales, self-employed	UND
F	2000	Housecleaning, self-employed	Unemployed	UND
F	1995	Homemaker	Homemaker	UND

SOURCE: Interviews with ninety Mexican immigrants in the Los Angeles Metropolitan Area, 2008.

* NC = naturalized citizen; LPR = legal permanent resident; UND = undocumented.

manager. The problems in restaurant work are illustrated by Baltazar, who is undocumented, arrived in Los Angeles in 1992, and lives with his wife and two US-born children. He started out as a cleaner. "Then I got to be a sandwich man and . . . I talked with the owner, who was from Hawaii, and I asked her for a chance. She told me, 'We'll switch you to the sandwiches but only if you find us another dishwasher.'" Baltazar invited a friend to come work as dishwasher, and he moved up to the sandwich job, which he kept for five years.

Some Veracruz women got their first jobs in the informal sector selling food, cleaning houses, and caring for children. Such was the case for Catarina, who takes care of two children and gets paid $20 a day for each. Amalia reports that many women who do this work find it prestigious to work in Beverly Hills, but she herself had a disagreeable experience there that leads her to conclude that "most of the people who live there are more 'slavedrivers' than in other places; the women there are more sticklers than the rest."

Petra, who attended college in Veracruz without completing her degree, came to Los Angeles in 1989, is married, has two children, and is undocumented. She worked delivering phone books with her husband until they decided to try selling Mexican food.

> We started by making one pot of *tamales,* which we'd take out in the morning to sell at car-repair shops. We sold the *tamales* and earned more than we'd been making with the telephone books. We had to get up very early, but by noon we'd made between $80 and $100.

Finally, Rita, who works cleaning houses three days a week as well as selling *tamales* and the hot drink called *champurrado,* told us: "This past Friday my daughter took ninety *tamales* out to sell and we made $135. She had to work very hard, though." Rita is undocumented, arrived in Los Angeles in 1989, and is married. Two of her daughters live in Los Angeles as well.

Zaira, who is sixty, arrived in Los Angeles in 2000. She is undocumented and currently unemployed. She prefers to work through temporary agencies rather than seek jobs through other means such as *Penny Saver,* a free magazine distributed in supermarkets: "The people who look for workers in *Penny Saver* are very racist. There are lots of agencies; I worked with one that was very good where they treated me with respect and give me a lot of support." Amalia, by contrast, has a very negative view of the employment agencies: "They're more into ripping you off; the first paycheck goes right into their pockets and then, after eight days, if the lady [who has contracted for a domestic worker] likes you, then you start to make money . . . no way I'll work through an agency . . . the slick people live off the people in dire straits, you know."

The system of subcontracting through temporary employment agencies is also common in other sectors, such as sales, so employers can avoid the laws against hiring undocumented workers directly. This is Osvaldo's case. "I started dropping by a furniture store and making friends with the salespeople . . . and the owner told me I couldn't be hired by the company but he'd hire me through an agency." Nonetheless, the same owner later told him it was very expensive to hire through the agency, which charged the employer $100 for every $500 the worker made.

The Veracruzan interviewees' undocumented status seems to be the primary factor causing the majority of them to start out in low-level jobs and to still be in those types of positions in 2008. Naturalized citizens of both sexes have better jobs, but this is not so clearly true for legal permanent residents. The undocumented have no choice but to remain on the lowest rungs, with the exception of the possibility, for some, of creating informal businesses, particularly cooking and selling Mexican food. Emir Estrada and Pierrette Hondagneu-Sotelo[12] argue that although street vending is illegal in Los Angeles, the enforcement of the law is selective. They report that in 1999, MacArthur Park was briefly a main site for such activity, but since then the activity has grown rapidly in L.A.'s Latino neighborhoods.

The case of Vidal shows that not all the Veracruzans have insecure or poorly paid jobs, yet his experience also shows that many skilled Mexican immigrants do not get jobs that match their education. As a young man, Vidal moved to Mexico City to study medicine, graduating as a general practitioner. Returning to Veracruz to pursue his career, he came to own a small clinic with ten beds, an operating room, and a pharmacy. But the economic crisis of the early 1980s made it hard for him to continue, so he decided to emigrate to the United States with his wife and children. Entering the country in 1986 on a tourist visa, he got his first job as a dishwasher, without papers. "I worked in a hamburger place, washing dishes, and within two weeks I was in front grilling hamburgers . . . later they made me assistant supervisor, but one day I lost my temper, and they got rid of me." For the next thirteen years he worked as a medical assistant, in two clinics. He has never been able to work as a physician, since he has not been able to have his degree recertified, although he does dispense medical advice through a store that sells herbs and supplements. Vidal has acquired US citizenship, is married, and has adult children born in Mexico and in the United States. He currently works in his son's business in the entertainment sector.

Adelaida is another immigrant with a university background, a legal permanent resident who came to Los Angeles in 1999. She works in a hotel as a chambermaid and supervisor, does freelance cleaning on the side, and volunteers in a nonprofit that promotes art and culture among Veracruzan immigrants. Always motivated to study, she majored in philosophy for a year and then transferred to sociology at the Universidad Veracruzana, where she fulfilled all the major requirements but did not graduate.

In spite of her professional skills, Adelaida has not had any professional jobs. When she first arrived in Los Angeles she worked in a silk-screening shop, later took care of children and seniors, and still later began working in hotels. The reason she now makes $12 an hour, she says, is that the workers in that hotel are unionized: "Very few workplaces have unions, but those that do have good rights and compensation, including insurance. Unions are useful for some things, but there's also a lot of resistance. People would rather not [go to union meetings]."

REAL ESTATE INVESTMENTS IN LOS ANGELES AND MEXICO

Homeownership is a very important indicator of immigrant integration, since it not only suggests permanent settlement in the United States but also constitutes a fundamental economic investment. According to Myers and Woo,[13] for immigrants to the United States owning a home is an important symbol of membership in the middle class and of residential assimilation. As discussed in chapter 3, the 2007 American Community Survey data demonstrate that slightly more than 45 percent of Mexican immigrants in metropolitan Los Angeles live in an owner-occupied home. This is a lower percentage than for European and Asian immigrants, among whom 60 percent are homeowners, and a bit higher than for Central Americans (42 percent).

The first important finding about the homes owned by our interviewees is that more than half (57 percent) are in Los Angeles and 43 percent are in Mexico, which suggests that the majority of our interviewees have decided to stay in Los Angeles (see figure 6).

One of our Zacatecan interviewees reports his decision to stay and invest in Los Angeles, where he lives with his family, this way: "We have a house in Zacatecas, but it's in very bad shape. My grandparents' house was sold, and I have land in Jerez but I'm not going to invest $15,000 or $20,000 there; it's better to invest that money here. I'm investing about $350,000, always improving the house. Recently I decided to add a second story; I've got eight bedrooms and six baths." On the other hand, another Zacatecan immigrant tells how his family bought a house in Zacatecas when they arrived in Los Angeles, "because we thought we'd go back after five years, but this never happened. Now we're here, our children are grown up, and we can't go."

However, the issue of investing in Mexico and the expectation of returning can generate conflicts within couples. One interviewee from Zacatecas says:

> We're still paying for this house because we had another one in Long Beach and my husband sold it. When he did that, I signed on the condition that the money would go toward buying another house in Los Angeles . . . he wanted to invest the money in Mexico, but I told him, if you don't put the money into a house right here, I won't sign.

A Veracruzan immigrant recounts, with a sense of humor, how he is in the early stages of paying off a thirty-year mortgage: "We're paying for the house, maybe so far only the front door lock is mine, but that's something." The same interviewee describes how he also has a house in Veracruz that he inherited from his parents, which he rents out to tenants.

Among our interviewees, the naturalized citizens and legal permanent residents have a higher percentage of homeownership than the undocumented ones. Still, it is very important to point out that ten houses in metropolitan Los Angeles were bought by our undocumented interviewees in spite of their immigration status. Such is the case of an immigrant from Oaxaca who bought a house while he was undocumented: "I bought a house in 1998 thanks to a woman who helped me a lot, because at that time I didn't have papers, and between her and the fake Social Security number I was using at work, I was able to qualify and I bought this house. Last year we bought a second one."

Figure 6 shows how immigration legal status plays a discriminatory role, given that naturalized citizens and legal permanent residents make up a larger share of the homeowners than the undocumented. As a result of that condition and also their more successful economic trajectories, the Zacatecans have the highest proportion of homeownership, followed by the Oaxacans, with the Veracruzans coming last (see figure 6).

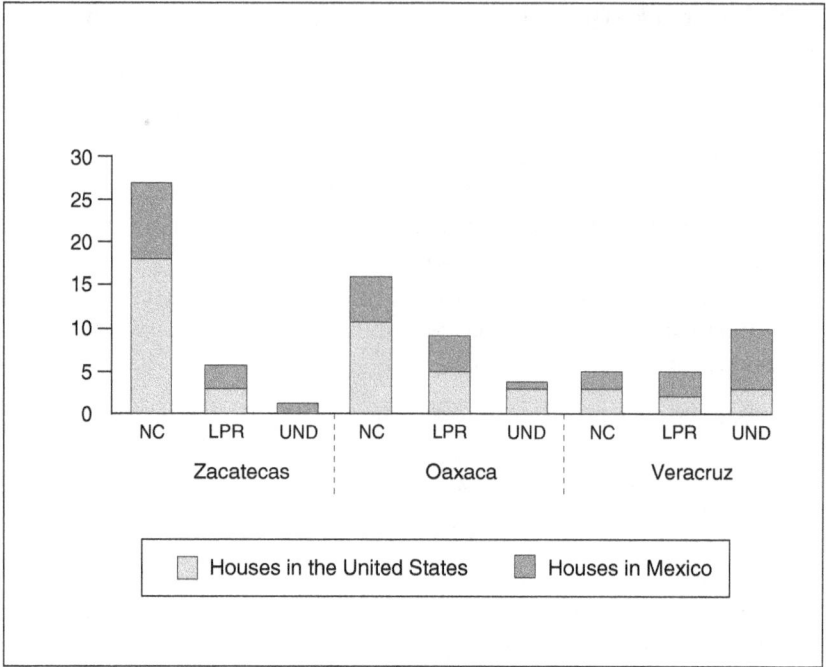

FIGURE 6. Number of houses in the United States and Mexico owned by interviewees from Zacatecas, Oaxaca, and Veracruz, by immigration status, 2008. NC = naturalized citizen; LPR = legal permanent resident; UNC = undocumented. Authors' interviews with 90 Mexican immigrants in the Los Angeles Metropolitan Area, 2008.

Eileen Diaz McConnell and Enrico A. Marcelli,[14] in their study of Los Angeles homeownership, argue that because of changes in the mortgage market and in financial institution practices in the 1990s, undocumented status did not prevent Mexican immigrants from becoming homeowners until recently. They point to, for instance, banks' acceptance of *matrículas consulares* and other documents as forms of identification for undocumented clients. From 2004 on, Washington Mutual, Bank of America, and Wells Fargo were the leading providers of mortgage credit to Latinos in Los Angeles.

As for the houses located in Mexico, many are owned by our interviewees because of inheritance. Some are rented out, but most are occupied by relatives or kept to be used when the immigrants visit their hometowns. Importantly, all the houses in Los Angeles have been bought—not inherited—by their owners, which implies a significant economic investment.

One couple, however, differ from all the rest of our interviewees in that they have decided not to buy a home in Los Angeles but instead to invest in their children's education, with the plan of returning to live in Mexico in retirement. This is a family from Tlacolula, Oaxaca. The wife says, "We don't have a house in Los Angeles. All we have is the satisfaction of paying for college for our children, because that has used up the little we've been able to save. . . . we do have a house in Tlacolula, just a few small rooms. My husband says now it's time to think about ourselves, so we'll start to save for our old age and have somewhere to live when we decide it's time to go back there and take it easy."

A final issue to consider about homeownership in the United States is the impact of the world economic crisis that began in 2008 and burst the "housing bubble." Home prices began to decline and, especially for mortgages with increasing payment schedules, foreclosures became common. Some of our interviewees spoke of difficulties making their payments. Given the Zacatecan immigrants' long presence in Los Angeles, many of them had already paid off their thirty-year mortgages—unlike the case for most Oaxacan and Veracruzan interviewees, who were still paying.

A Oaxacan immigrant describes the impact of the crisis this way:

> We ended up with the house where we live almost by obligation, because my wife had signed for her cousin, and then the cousin couldn't keep up with the payments. The mortgage was $2,400 a month and the cousin couldn't pay it, so we didn't have any choice but to protect my wife's credit, or else she would have been ruined. We had to pay about $12,000 to get the payments up to date, and we moved in there and started renting our old house to a nephew.

An immigrant from Yanga in Veracruz tells how he sold his properties there to buy his house in Los Angeles, which he is now at risk of losing:

> I had a house and land in Yanga and had the 'great idea' of investing in a house in Los Angeles two years ago. In the end I lost my house in Yanga because of how the house here dropped in value. Now I'm in the process they call mortgage modification, to try and save my house here, but I don't know whether the bank will agree.

FINAL CONSIDERATIONS

This analysis of the economic integration of our interviewees in metropolitan Los Angeles shows that they are going through that process in conditions of disadvantage. Most of the men and women are participating in labor niches with low salaries and deplorable working conditions.

In spite of the solid regional economy of the 1960s and 1970s, the Zacatecan men and women began with insecure and low-paid jobs in restaurants, garment factories, agriculture, and canneries. Still, because of their extended presence in Los Angeles and their high percentage of naturalization or legal residency, the Zacatecan men show a relatively upward occupational trend, given that by the time of the 2008 interviews some of them had become business owners, worked in professional and technical occupations, or had retirement income after long working lives in the formal economy. Some women, too, had retirement income or had returned to homemaking.

Our male Oaxacan interviewees found their main initial occupational niche in the restaurants of Los Angeles. The women, meanwhile, found their first jobs as factory workers, sales workers, or self-employed housecleaners or personal care workers. Although the majority of these interviewees have regularized their immigration status, their responses about their 2008 employment do not show upward occupational mobility, but rather horizontal circulation among lower-end jobs. Some men leave restaurant work for self-employment, while women, in turn, move into the restaurant jobs. The Oaxacan men and women who achieve a small degree of upward mobility do so working as drivers or in sales, or by creating a small business.

The Veracruzan interviewees, the last to arrive in Los Angeles, have filled low-end jobs as both their initial and 2008 employment, due fundamentally to their undocumented status. Many of the undocumented men worked first in garment factories. Also, both men and women work in restaurants, sales, and to a lesser degree in the informal sector. Some women in this sector depend on temporary employment agencies. One path of economic mobility for the Veracruzans is to start informal food businesses.

These findings allow us to state that in general, the Mexican immigrants we interviewed are integrated into the Los Angeles labor market in spite of their undocumented immigration status, low levels of education, and limited mastery of English. The majority of them do find work, whether in the formal or informal sector. The integration occurs within conditions of disadvantage as compared to other immigrant groups. But, ironically, their situation represents an advance with respect to their employment conditions in Mexico.

As for the location of the businesses that our interviewees currently operate, we found that most of them are in the Los Angeles region. However, the case of the clothing workshop in Zacatecas, which is connected to a Los Angeles factory for surgical wear owned by one of the interviewees, suggests the possibility of this kind of transnational economic tie with Mexico.

Our interviewees are integrated into the Los Angeles economy because they meet the demand from the degraded manufacturing sector (e.g., clothing production), from restaurants serving all types of international cuisines, and from the large number of labor-intensive service industries (such as housecleaning, childcare, and caring for the old and the sick). Similarly, the Mexican ethnic economy that has developed alongside the growth in the Mexican population, which requires many products and services like Mexican regional foods, promotes the expansion of the informal economy.

As we will analyze in detail in chapter 8, the governments of the city and county of Los Angeles have enacted laws, regulations, and municipal ordinances to improve the situation of workers in the informal sector, the majority of whom are Mexican. In this sense, there is an attempt to protect the labor rights of domestic workers, *esquineros,* and car washers. In the specific case of street food vendors, the Asociación de Loncheros Familias Unidas de California has won important legal battles to enable the vendors to carry out their work. This struggle was begun by the lunch vendors of Anaheim, who won the court case *Barajas v. City of Anaheim* in 1993.

The Immigration Reform and Control Act of 1986, which led to the legalization of 2.3 million undocumented Mexican immigrants, has been key to the longer term immigrant communities winning better jobs. This is particularly true for the Zacatecans, whose earlier arrival in the Los Angeles region made them eligible for the legalization of their immigration status, and to lesser degree for the Oaxacans. Most of the Veracruzans, because of their later arrival in Los Angeles, were excluded from this immigration regularization and thus from the opportunity to move on to better jobs. As has been reported more generally by other researchers,[15] some of our interviewees who acquired legal permanent residency through the special program for farmworkers that was part of IRCA did so without actually meeting all the requirements.

The longer term presence of the Zacatecans in Los Angeles, their significant numbers, high percentage of legal permanent residents and naturalized citizens, solid social networks, and level of organization have been key to their currently demonstrating more successful economic integration. Nonetheless, all these factors are connected to their having arrived in Los Angeles when the metropolitan area had a solid economy supported by a manufacturing base that offered many permanent, well-paid, and unionized jobs. In contrast, the more recent immigrants, who have come since the late 1980s, like the Veracruzans, have arrived in the context of a degraded economy.

In this regard, it can be argued that even the recent immigrants from Zacatecas confront fewer difficulties in crossing the border without documents and in finding jobs in Los Angeles because of the dense migratory social networks that their predecessors developed over several decades. Not only do Zacatecans have contacts with many employers in the region, but many of them have become business owners themselves and so have the ability to hire undocumented fellow Zacatecans.

There is a segmentation in the market for Mexican immigrant labor that depends in part on immigration status. Legal permanent residents and naturalized citizens have more opportunities to find permanent jobs, better paid and more stable, or to start successful businesses, than do undocumented immigrants. Nonetheless the Oaxacans, with their high proportion of documented persons, still have not achieved noteworthy upward mobility.

Mexicans seem to have conquered occupational niches in sectors that are not desired by other workers, whether native-born or immigrant. However, it is possible the labor niches of Mexican immigrants in some sectors of manufacturing do exclude, for instance, African American workers, who face a longer and deeper process of discrimination. Since the mid-1990s, Roger Waldinger[16] argues, poor black workers in Los Angeles have been displaced from low-level jobs as domestic workers, cleaning workers, and sewing machine operators due to the expansion of Mexican and Central American occupational niches, which also include furniture making and the garment industry.

The majority of our interviewees work in lower-skilled jobs because of their lack of education and because of the sectors in which they work. Although some of our skilled interviewees do have professional jobs, others find themselves in the situation of "wasted brain power" because they have been doing work that does not match their education.

Our interviewees' investment in buying homes in Los Angeles reaffirms their decisions to integrate themselves and stay in the region. In general, immigration legal status plays a discriminatory role, given that naturalized citizens and legal permanent residents include a higher proportion of homeowners than do the undocumented. Houses in Mexico, many of them inherited, are used as investments, vacation homes, or with a view toward a return after retirement, which in many cases turns out not to be feasible because of the presence of descendants in Los Angeles.

In conclusion, analysis of the economic integration of our interviewees in metropolitan Los Angeles—through examination of their employment histories, small business formation, and homeownership—suggests that legal immigration status and a long period of residence lead to more successful economic integration.

CHAPTER 5

Social Integration

Building a Family, a Community, and a Life

The Los Angeles region provides an ideal case study for applying the range of perspectives on immigrants' social integration in general and that of Mexican immigrants in particular. Several analysts have stressed the importance of understanding and strengthening that process. For example, Fix, Laglagaron, et al. and Fix, McHugh, et al.[1] have emphasized the centrality of understanding and addressing both the changes undertaken by immigrants so as to insert themselves into the new environment (in this case, the Los Angeles region) and the changes implemented by society with respect to the presence of those same immigrants. Pastor and Ortiz,[2] after gathering the opinions of multiple social actors in the Los Angeles region, conclude there is an urgent necessity to devote more attention and resources to promoting the effective social integration of immigrants, toward the goal of improving the region's social and economic conditions in comparison to those of the rest of the United States and the world of the future.

In chapter 3 we presented some fundamental indicators that provided a first approximation of the degree of social integration of Mexican immigrants in the Los Angeles region. According to the 2007 American Community Survey data, Mexicans form the largest immigrant group in this region. However, in spite of the size of their population, their English proficiency and their educational attainment lag behind those of other immigrant groups. At the same time, they have the lowest naturalization rate. These indicators demonstrate clear structural limitations to their social integration.

However, it would be an error to imagine that those quantitative data provide a complete panorama of the social integration process of Mexican immigrants in the Los Angeles region. Developing a more detailed understanding of the dynamics of this process—that is, what the Mexican migrants do or fail to do to integrate themselves into the society into which they have moved—requires an analysis of the perceptions and practices of the immigrants themselves. In this chapter we will present and analyze a detailed selection from their testimonies so as to highlight the efforts and strategies implemented by Mexican immigrants, their families, and their communities to integrate into the society of the Los Angeles region (that is, their integration "into" the receiving society). In a later chapter, we will examine the existence and limitations of policies and services intended to promote their more effective social integration (that is, integration "by" the society). We will examine the following social dimensions that are involved in the potential integration of Mexican immigrants in the region: (1) immigration status; (2) family networks; (3) access to health-care services; and (4) access to educational and language services. Following this examination, we will consider the influence of the immigrants' possible transnational ties and their participation in associations.

IMMIGRATION STATUS

Having or not having legal immigration status is a key factor that shapes the actions of Mexican immigrants in their pursuit of social and occupational integration. In the case of our ninety interviewees, the majority are naturalized citizens, legal permanent residents, or in the process of seeking such status, while slightly under a third are undocumented. The information supplied by our interviewees matches the trends in both Los Angeles County and the rest of the United States: more members of the documented population have lived for longer periods in the United States, while those with shorter stays in the country are more likely to lack legal documents. The interviewees' legal status profile also matches the general pattern of the immigrant population in Los Angeles County, where the proportion of undocumented to documented immigrants has remained relatively stable in recent years, in contrast to the rest of the United States, where the proportion of the undocumented has increased.[3]

However, the above profile also reflects the presence of families whose immigration status is not homogeneous. In the case of our Zacatecan immigrant interviewees, almost all the family members (spouses and children) had documented status, while the predominant trend among the Veracruzan immigrant families is that at least one spouse is undocumented. The majority of Oaxacan immigrant family members are documented, but there are cases of undocumented spouses or children. All families with mixed status face the fear of separation as a result of possible deportation of those members without documents, in particular given the growing prevalence of such separations throughout the United States. Fitzgerald and Alarcón[4] and Passel, Cohn, and Gonzalez-Barrera[5] point out the devastating effect that the growing wave of deportations from the interior of the United States is having on immigrant families. According to their sources, around 3.3 million children live in families with at least one undocumented member, and another 1.1 million children are themselves undocumented and therefore potentially deportable. Clearly, this situation constitutes a serious obstacle to the potential social integration of the Mexican immigrant population in the United States.

More specifically, our interviewees offer a variety of comments on their immigration status and how it affects their social integration process. For example, an immigrant from Zacatecas describes how he experienced the sharp difference between undocumented and documented status:

> Before having my papers, yes, I felt that pressure—"oh, you're undocumented"—and I remember I had a lot of nightmares. I always dreamed I was going to Zacatecas but I was never at ease there, always worrying about how I was going to get back [across the border again]; that was my recurring nightmare. And once I got my resident status, then the nightmares went away.

The perception of a "before" and an "after" with respect to a change in immigration status was a constant among the interviewees who had experienced such a change. Those who were still undocumented, meanwhile, described their status as one more difficulty they had to confront as immigrants, a difficulty faced with resignation. A Veracruzan immigrant pointed out that living in Los Angeles as an undocumented person was "like living in a cage where you fly and fly but you feel you're drowning; you've got work, you make money, but you don't have any credit and you see how you're being discriminated against."

Although for some of our interviewees naturalization presents a problem in terms of identity, for others it is seen as a natural decision within the integration process, as a means to get access to civic participation. Some are even critical of Mexico and thus justify their decision to become US citizens. A Oaxacan immigrant who became a citizen in 1997 says that her husband criticized her for this choice:

> He said that you can't betray your homeland and who-knows-what but I'd tell him, "But that's why we left Mexico, because our homeland hasn't given us what we need and so we had to leave it." And since they were giving dual citizenship by that time we said, "We're not losing anything—we're getting two countries."

Since differences in immigration status among our interviewees are associated in many cases with the number of years of residence in the United States, and thus with more or less consolidated relations with the destination society, it might seem that this status is the variable that signifies eventual social integration. However, as we shall see over the course of this chapter, having or not having legal immigration status does not seem to be determinant of our interviewees' ability to cope with or function in Los Angeles.

FORMATION OF FAMILIES AND KINSHIP NETWORKS

While some of our interviewees report that one or several members of their families live only in Mexico, and others report family members in both countries, most say that the majority of their close relatives—especially within the nuclear family—live in the United States. This is particularly important in terms of the social integration of Mexican immigrants in the Los Angeles region because, as we will discuss below, the growth of family networks implies gradual involvement in activities that are part of the social fabric of the new environment.

In a number of cases, we can observe the maintenance of family ties that link the places of origin and destination, and sometimes members of the immigrant's family circulate between the two countries in spite of heightening border enforcement. However, in the majority of cases, the tendency is toward settling in Los Angeles. Cecilio, an immigrant from the city of Zacatecas, notes how this process includes both concentration and dispersion in various parts of the United States. "There are ten of us, five men and five women; all the men are here in Los Angeles—well, one has since gone to Idaho—and there's one sister here and one in Idaho, and three sisters in Mexico." In other cases, the dispersion is limited to different parts of the Los Angeles region.

In all these cases, we see the functioning of social networks in that one pioneer immigrant's successful establishment in Los Angeles is followed by the gradual arrival and eventual settling of other relatives and neighbors. This mechanism is key to increasing the migrants' chances of arriving safely from their places of origin and surviving in the new location, both of which depend on arrangements made by the earlier members of the network. Thus such networks, especially family ones, tend to be the best means of access to the destination society. As Rodrigo, a Zacatecan immigrant, put it, "Normally, since so many people have left their hometowns by now, everyone has relatives in Los Angeles, so they get here with a cousin ahead of them, or a brother, and that's how they get work."

Thus, the continued growth of immigrant families in Los Angeles allows for the gradual formation of social networks that many times overlap networks of other sorts (especially those defined by friendship or locality of origin) and improve opportunities for successful settlement in Los Angeles. As several of our interviewees pointed out, these networks are fundamental not only for border crossings, initial financial support, and access to jobs, but also as sources of information that promotes incorporation into the new society. Therefore the nature of such supports based on the immigrants' hometowns eventually translates into different degrees of social integration in their places of arrival. As Rodrigo observed,

> I think leaving the family there in Mexico, especially my mother, every time we went there and then had to come back it was very hard; my family has been the hardest thing to leave behind, but with time you get used to the fact that you live here [in Los Angeles] and you go there to visit. I used to go more often, up to two or three times a year, even four, but now the bills, the debts you take on, they don't allow it, although you want to go, but you know how much you're going to owe every month, and that limits you.

Such observations show that despite the immigrants' multiple ties with Mexico, incorporation in Los Angeles eventually becomes central to their lives. In other words, although transnational relationships are strong, it gets harder and harder to keep them up. Rodrigo's recognition of the imperatives of the US economic and social realms—such as having to work to pay expenses, debts, and bills—illustrates how, while many immigrants maintain their family networks in Mexico to one degree or another, this ceases to signify the prevalence of the transnationalism in a broad sense, with intense flows of persons between the two countries, for the reasons we have explained in previous chapters.

Many of our interviewees' observations about family networks center on marriage ties. In the majority of cases, they either married someone from their own community of origin and later migrated to the United States, or they got married in the United States to someone from their original community. For example, Josefa from Zacatecas reports, "I came with my children and my husband who is also from Jerez; we got married there and came here together. We crossed the border with a *coyote* back in about 1975; later we got papers in '85." Joel from Zacatecas said his wife "was my neighbor, on the same street, but she got here [California] first because her sisters brought her in '61 . . . and we got married here."

Nonetheless, some interviewees' marriages diverge from this classic pattern and can be considered mixed in the sense that one of the spouses is from a different Mexican state than the interviewee, or even from a different country. Although, as noted, our interviewees are not a representative sample of the Mexican immigrant population in the Los Angeles region, still it is suggestive that twenty of the eighty married interviewees report this type of marriage. Among the married Zacatecan interviewees, five out of twenty-eight have this type of mixed marriage; three spouses are from Veracruz, Jalisco, and Baja California, while two are from El Salvador and Guatemala. Among the Oaxacans' marriages, eight out of twenty-six are mixed; five spouses are from other Mexican states (one each from Baja California Sur, Mexico City, Baja California, and two from Puebla) and three from the United States (of Mexican origin). Finally, in the cases of the twenty-six married Veracruzans, seven spouses are from other parts of Mexico (one each from Zacatecas and Michoacán, two from Jalisco, and three from Mexico City) and two are from the United States (again of Mexican background).

This information pertains to each interviewee's most recent marriage, and so it is possible that some cases of marriage to US citizens could involve spouses who have been naturalized. Still, the number of mixed marriages is suggestive to the extent that it shows the interviewees tending to conform to the pattern of Mexican migration to the United States that followed the passage of IRCA in 1986. This is important because, as Durand and Martínez[6] point out, earlier Mexican immigrants traditionally showed a strong tendency to choose spouses from their hometowns. Such endogamous ties were facilitated by the prevalence of social networks strongly anchored in these towns, and immigrants from the same locality eventually became neighbors or workmates in the new country. Thus, a degree of exogamy could be found only in the descendants in the second or third generation.

Nonetheless, and continuing to follow Durand and Martínez,[7] the importance of the presence of mixed marriages with respect to the process of social integration lies in these marriages denoting "the existence of a process of the migrants' establishment and integration" in the destination society. All of our interviewees in this situation met and married their spouses in the United States, and it did not seem to matter to them whether or not the spouse came from the same place of origin. For example, in Amalia of Veracruz's account of meeting her husband, "He was playing a mariachi band where I was working as a hostess, and then while we were dancing he paid me a lot of compliments and we started going out and then we got married. That [rapid courtship and marriage] made me kind of nervous—and guess what, he's a Mexican too, from Zacatecas."

The presence of mixed marriages appears significant to us in part because, while these do not account for the majority of our interviewees, they are also not isolated cases. Above all, their significance lies in the fact that none of the interviewees refer to such ties with concern or with any suggestion that they constitute a social disadvantage. Thus this new attitude "has to do with the fact, finally or fatalistically accepted, that the couples now live and will remain outside their original localities, the fact that they will build their lives in the United States."[8] This seems to be the case among several of our interviewees in mixed marriages. For example, Ramón, from Oaxaca, says in respect to his possible return to Mexico, "Mostly I'd rather stay here, though in the future, I don't know. My wife is from here, my children are from here, and I don't think they could get used to life in Mexico."

These perceptions suggest the progress made in the realm of social integration by Mexican immigrants in regions like Los Angeles, as seen through the traditional indicator of intermarriage among first-generation immigrants. As such, they are consistent with what other analyses have found. In fact, Telles[9] has shown the growing presence, over time, of marital ties between Mexican immigrants and spouses from outside their ethnic group.

ACCESS TO HEALTH SERVICES

Although the state of California offers more benefits for immigrants than other US states, particularly in areas such a health care, nutrition, and economic compensation,[10] still the degree of true access to such services is an indicator of the destination society's disposition to promote the integration of immigrant communities. The case of health services is particularly illustrative. Access to these services among Mexican immigrants in the Los Angeles region varies widely across different situations, as a result of many structural transformations, including those in the labor market and in political decision making. Such differences translate, on the one hand, into guaranteed access to services among the minority of immigrants who have both legal immigration status and stable jobs. On the other hand, for many others they represent restricted and selective access, requiring the immigrants to adopt a variety of strategies to obtain at least a minimum degree of medical care. Some analysts[11] refer to the "adaptation mechanisms" of immigrant communities faced with deficiencies in public health coverage in their societies of arrival.

Some of our interviewees spoke of satisfaction with their access to medical services in the Los Angeles region, thanks to their having jobs offering this type of access as a fringe benefit through their employer or union. For the majority, however, medical insurance must be paid for out of pocket. For example, Verónica, a Oaxacan immigrant, says, "I had to buy private medical insurance, because I have diabetes. Without health insurance you don't know what might happen and it's better to have insurance even though it's expensive, because there's no other way." Among families with minor children, we frequently found mixed access to medical services, where the minors receive coverage through the state.

Also, for a number of interviewees, private medical insurance means policies with very restricted coverage, often applicable only to large medical expenses, which makes it a mechanism of last resort. Carmen, from Veracruz, synthesizes this as follows:

> That's the problem; when you're sick you just have to get through it, because if you go to a doctor that's $60 for the visit, and the medicine is expensive too. And if you can't stand it anymore, then you go to the emergency room, which is why the emergency rooms are overloaded.

Finally, there are those who lose their jobs and thus their access to medical insurance, and from then on they must pay for all care themselves.

In that sense, the perceptions about access to medical services among the interviewed immigrants reveal the limitations of a public health system that falls short of universal coverage and emphasis on prevention. That predicament is particularly difficult for those interviewees in the informal sector or unemployed.

Another common strategy for getting access to health services—for those interviewees encountering restrictions in the Los Angeles region because of legal immigration status, their job situation, or both—is the use of such services in Mexico, particularly in the city of Tijuana on the California border. Use of this option also derives, in part, from cultural perceptions about the medical services of the two countries. For many Mexican immigrants, "good medicine" and "good doctors" are those in Mexico, in contrast to what might be found in the United States. That explains their inclination to consider this possibility if they have the immigration status that allows them to go and come back. But even among those who don't have such status, some regard access to Mexican medicine as a serious option, as Valente, an undocumented Veracruzan, explains: "Here medical care is very expensive, so often you send a letter or talk with someone who is going to Mexico and you say, 'send me a pile of medications.' That's what I do so I'll have my medications and I can self-prescribe them—which isn't good, but it's necessary."

At the same time, several of the interviewees emphasize that a lack of knowledge about how the public health system works can often mean lack of access to medical services or access at very high cost, especially if they are undocumented. A Veracruzan immigrant, Lucas, points out: "We've always worked with phony papers—that's how things are, and no, we didn't have insurance, we just worked, and so if I get sick, I have to pay out of my pocket." In another case, an interviewee from Oaxaca reflected on his perception of his undocumented status and the resulting fear of making use of any kind of public service. "I remember I told my kids, when they got to Los Angeles, 'Here it's very hard to get well; if you get sick you just have to bear it, because there aren't any doctors for us and if we do go they'll grab us and send us back to Mexico.'"

In sum, our interviewees' comments demonstrate differential access to health services. While in some cases they have maintained stable access, the large majority have been forced to turn to other arrangements and options in their attempt to preserve their health, whether because they are undocumented or because of the types of jobs they have. These comments are consistent with the findings of Portes, Fernández-Kelly, and Light[12] about the prevalence of "systematic contradictions" in a society that has a sustained demand for an immigrant labor force but simultaneously lacks an immigration policy that envisions providing basic living conditions for that population, such as access to health services. Thus, and in accord with the observations of our interviewees in terms of social integration, it is clear that although the Mexican immigrant population has sought to advance in this area, there have been structural factors, especially public health policies, that have limited greater advances in social integration.

ACCESS TO EDUCATIONAL SERVICES AND
LANGUAGE PROFICIENCY

The educational profile of our interviewees presents diverse characteristics that resemble the rest of the Mexican immigrant population in the Los Angeles region. On the one hand, only two out of the ninety interviewees have no formal schooling; thirteen have finished primary school; eighteen have finished junior high; and eleven have high school diplomas. On the other hand, only eight have college degrees or higher. In this sense, the profile resembles what we have described in chapter 3, since existing sociodemographic data show Mexican immigrants having low levels of school completion, especially as compared to other immigrant groups or to US natives. According to the American Community Survey,[13] 60.7 percent of Mexican immigrants over twenty-five years of age have less than a high school education, in contrast to 9.9 percent of natives. In addition, only 4.7 percent of Mexican immigrants have college-level study, as compared to 31.6 percent among natives, 40 percent among European immigrants, and 46.2 percent among Asian immigrants.

In spite of this panorama, one finding common to all the interviewees is that they have done some kind of studying in the United States, whether in English-language classes, technical schools, high schools, or universities. In some cases, this results from the importance assigned to additional education in order to achieve any kind of upward social mobility, even for those who already had some schooling in Mexico. Equally, many are convinced of the importance of studying, especially learning English, as an element fundamental to integration.

Nonetheless, for the majority of our interviewees, the demands of the Los Angeles labor market, along with family responsibilities, end up frustrating any aspirations or interest in education. This is consistent with the sociodemographic indicators for the Mexican immigrant population in the Los Angeles region that we presented in chapter 3. The focus on getting jobs implies giving up school and makes returning to it later more difficult.

The degree of English proficiency has been one of the key indicators used to assess immigrants' degree of integration in the United States. For Mexican immigrants, as demonstrated by the indicators presented in previous chapters, competence in this area has been low, especially compared to that of other groups of immigrants. According to the 2007 American Community Survey data,[14] slightly more than half (51.1 percent) did not speak English well or at all, compared to 24.1 percent among Asian immigrants and 11.5 percent among European ones.

This situation seems to be replicated in the lives of our interviewees. When asked to define their degree of English proficiency, only some estimated to have full ability, while others say that although they could describe themselves as having some proficiency, they can also point to some limitations in speaking, comprehension, or writing. Finally, some of the interviewees judge themselves to have serious limitations, meaning they know some words and understand only a little. In this sense, the majority of our interviewees consider that their mastery of English is at a level between intermediate or very limited, which is consistent with our observations in chapter 3.

This first approximation is rendered more complex by further comments our interviewees offer about linguistic competence. For the majority, their initial experience with English was difficult, which presented a serious obstacle to their achieving more successful social integration. As a result, their accounts of the initial stages of their lives in the Los Angeles region inevitably involve the limitations stemming from lack of knowledge of the language and resulting experiences. As a Oaxacan immigrant recalls, "It was very hard not knowing the language; I despaired about it. You feel powerless when you don't know; we went somewhere and didn't know anything." Another Oaxacan, Marco, recalls that on his arrival in the United States, "English was very complicated for me; I found it tremendously difficult to adapt to the language. English has always been very hard."

And yet, a positive valuation of learning English clearly prevails. Facility in the language is systematically associated with the opportunity to get better jobs. An immigrant from Zacatecas, Mario, synthesizes this perception as follows:

> In this country you have to speak English one hundred percent. I really believe that Mexicans, if they don't speak English, won't get more opportunities, will stagnate in one job. In fact I now have many nephews and nieces who, with the economic crisis, by the fact of not speaking English are unemployed here. Although people will say that more Spanish than English is spoken around here, that's not true for work—for work, there's nothing more important than speaking English.

This positive assessment of English is especially widespread among members of the second generation. For instance, Gilberto, a Veracruzan immigrant, says: "If you're a parent and you are in the United States, your children need to know English one hundred percent."

Our interviewees' responses show that lack of facility in English has been an obstacle in the process of social integration of Mexican immigrants in the Los Angeles region. Although the great majority had acquired some notions about the United States while still in Mexico, their initial contact with US culture was particularly difficult because of their lack of knowledge of the language. Its acquisition is seen as something necessary for accessing better job opportunities—and an accompanying full social integration—as well as to increase such opportunities for their children.

One clear factor accounting for limited language acquisition among Mexican immigrants in the Los Angeles region lies in the marked difficulties of attending English classes. While all the interviewees knew of the existence of at least one location offering free classes (as part of the English as a Second Language system), the great majority referred to obstacles presented by long work days, which made it hard to attend. For instance, according to an immigrant couple from Oaxaca, "It's hard for all of us who come from Mexico [because] the work interferes a lot with going to school, or the type of work one does is very exhausting, and you come home so tired."

Another key factor limiting the opportunity to attend classes is family obligations. An immigrant from Oaxaca, Sergio, says, "When I went to the English language school I was doing pretty well there, but when my family came, I stopped going to school." Another Oaxacan, Gretel, offers a similar opinion. "I can't go to school with the kids. You want with all your heart to go, but you can't because of children and work— we have to work to pay the rent, to feed the children."

One additional obstacle cited by a large share of our interviewees is the prevalence of daily-life environments in which Spanish predominates. A Zacatecan immigrant says, about living in the Los Angeles region, "You can pretend you're in Mexico, the way it's all Spanish all the time. You go to the store and nothing but Spanish—you pretend you're in Guadalajara." Similarly, a Veracruzan concludes, "I don't know whether this is for better or for worse, but where we're working it's all Latinos, and that's why we don't learn English."

Thus in spite of a positive evaluation of English and a general interest in learning it, the Mexican immigrants we interviewed confront structural obstacles to this pursuit, including not only family obligations but also long workdays, the contexts in which they live, and their low level of education. Nonetheless, as Telles has confirmed,[15] the positive valuation of English by the first generation of Mexican immigrants becomes, in the next, full mastery of the language. By the fourth generation, only 5 percent still use Spanish to communicate with their children. This linear integration pattern is very similar to that of other immigrant groups in the history of the United States, in spite of the observations made by critics of Mexican immigrants with respect to supposed low levels of social integration.

At the same time, almost all our interviewees offer very positive valuations of preserving knowledge of Spanish—among themselves as first-generation immigrants, among their children, and even among their grandchildren. A Zacatecan who said she has full English proficiency comments, "Spanish—there's no way they can pull it out of my heart, because there's no comparison." Another, also from Zacatecas, says, "My children speak English; they speak to me in English and I answer them in Spanish because I don't want them not to be able to speak it themselves." In this sense, our interviewees do show a critical attitude toward the possibility of an acculturation process whose steps could include loss of the mother tongue.

Probably the interviewees' most common justification for preserving Spanish among themselves and their children refers not only to identity issues but also to opportunities to widen social and employment options. As an immigrant from Oaxaca puts it, "My daughters speak English among themselves but they talk to us in Spanish, and both of them speak it very well, and that's what I want. I tell them that it's much better for them to be able to communicate with more people and that's good for them in their work too." In fact, a good number of the interviewees stress the importance of bilingualism in the US context, in California, or specifically in Los Angeles. A Veracruzan immigrant mother describes her advice to her children: "I have always told them that they should speak Spanish with us. I tell them, 'Somebody who speaks two languages has opportunities to make more money here; you should learn to speak both languages.'"

The Mexican immigrants we interviewed point to a variety of strategies to guarantee preservation of the mother tongue. In many cases, the basic strategy revolves around making Spanish the official language of the home. Sometimes this norm is complemented by an outright prohibition of English within that realm. For instance, an immigrant from Veracruz says that "since they were little, the kids were not allowed to speak English at home. In the street, with their friends, at school, they could speak English, but at home they had to speak Spanish." The use of such strict criteria may be seen as an indicator of the importance surrounding the preservation of Spanish among the next generation. The interviewees placed a high value on bilingualism, in particular for their children, emphasizing the importance of their learning English alongside continuing their use of Spanish. Preservation of facility in the mother tongue is seen as fundamental not only for identity reasons but also as a form of human or cultural capital for themselves and their children—that is, as a way to broaden social and occupational options. A variety of strategies must be implemented to achieve this.

Among our interviewees, mastery of English, in spite of the many obstacles, is perceived as fundamental for integration. In some cases, this association is explicit, specifying the benefits that come with language acquisition. For example, a Oaxacan immigrant says:

> Yes, thank God I can [speak English]; I manage, pretty well I think, and that's how we make our way, little by little, because we have to integrate, because there's no way we can make the Americans join our way of living, or make them be like us—on the contrary, one has to adapt.

Linguistic knowledge is also seen by some as a means to access social circles beyond the Mexican immigrant community. For example, a migrant from Zacatecas, after stressing the importance of learning English, adds, "I have friends from India, and English is how we communicate. My son-in-law is American, so I have to speak nothing but English when we go to my daughter's house, which is also his house, where English is all I speak."

TRANSNATIONALISM AND SOCIAL INTEGRATION

A theme that permeates the comments and experiences of all our interviewees is the extent of ties to their places of origin in Mexico. Those transnational ties appear in various forms, including travel back to these communities, remittances, and frequent communication. However, as we have stated, although these ties continue to exist, they no longer take the form of earlier years, when transnationalism meant a regular and intense flow of people across borders. As we explained in our second chapter, such travel has been rendered more difficult by significant changes in both countries. On the US side, there has been increased border control and tighter enforcement of immigration law in the interior, alongside a weaker job market. On the Mexican side, increasing concerns about safety in the places of origin and during the journey make possible plans of emigration to El Norte more difficult.

Still, a primary element that stands out in the life of Mexican immigrants in the Los Angeles region is their preservation of family networks in Mexico and the United States, and an important reason for the survival of these networks is the sending of remittances. The majority of our interviewees send money to their relatives in Mexico, either on a regular basis or sporadically, so as to bolster their relatives' incomes or cover specific needs such as health care, education, or celebrations. Some interviewees also said that they participate in sending collective remittances through migrants' associations to support projects for the common good in their localities of origin.

However, what is most revealing is how transnational ties are compatible with the process of social integration in Los Angeles. For our interviewees, greater integration is not only desirable but also necessary for them to be able to maintain the flow of remittances. Most of them referred to the existence of relatives needing this type of support.

Also, in spite of changing circumstances in Mexico and the United States, the majority of our interviewees have made trips to their places of origin. In many cases the reasons are primarily familial—because of illness or death or to attend a baptism, wedding, fifteenth birthday celebration, or simply for vacations. These trips generally include the immigrant's nuclear family. Sometimes, these visits are judged to be important not only to fulfill specific family commitments but also to maintain ties with the family in Mexico more generally.

In other cases, the immigrants travel to attend festivals that honor the patron saints of their hometowns, or sometimes to fulfill community obligations arising from these festivals. This is particularly true for the Oaxacan immigrants, in whose towns the importance of such traditions and customs is very high. Pablo, of the community of San Lorenzo, had to return to Oaxaca to carry out his function as festival *mayordomo*. "I went back in 1992, not of my own choosing but because I had a commitment there in the town where we come from . . . they appoint *mayordomos* to organize the festivals of the patron saints, and this year it was my turn." Finally, in other cases, the immigrant does not travel to Mexico, but rather the family in the hometown comes to Los Angeles to visit.

As noted, for years this circulation between the places of origin and destination was quite fluid and could be maintained by many immigrants who were able to regularize their immigration status and even by some who were not. However, the growing series of restrictions affecting the border crossing between Mexico and the United States, the economic crisis in the United States, and the climate of insecurity in Mexico began to exercise a marked influence on such traveling. An immigrant from the state of Veracruz, Carmen, remarks, "We've gone and come back, but now lately since it's gotten hard to go and come, now it's not so easy, well, aside from the money, because they've raised the prices for bringing people across the border, so that's why we haven't gone at all in the past eight years, and so we've lost important things . . . at those times, you'd like to be with your family."

It might be inferred that Mexican immigrants' ties with their hometowns, which suggest a transnational dynamic between the places of origin and Los Angeles, also signify limited integration into Los Angeles society. However, some of our interviewees report that their transnational lives also involve the building of strong social ties with Los Angeles. For instance, Jairo, of Zacatecas, observes, "One time I made something like $55,000 and with that I went to Jerez to spend a year and half, so that my children would learn our traditions and go to school there, but after that year and half we had to come back, and they really didn't want to be there because they missed *their* country [emphasis added], Dodgers games and things like that, or McDonald's, which they like, and all those minor things." Casimiro, another Zacatecan immigrant, comments, "I haven't been there for three years now; my parents come every year, and all of us brothers and sisters, we're all here in California now. But if you do go now, the town is very different—it's not like it was when you left. You go with the mentality you had when you left, but if you go, everything you see is very different; it's like you don't feel right there anymore."

Such observations show that although ties with their localities in Mexico persist to greater or lesser degrees, the existence of important social ties in Los Angeles can be determinant in future plans. In the excerpt quoted above, the obligatory return from Zacatecas to Los Angeles due to the children missing emblematic referents of "their country" illustrates how having children who are born in the United States opens a substantial path for the eventual development of ties between the immigrants and the society of Los Angeles.

Also, the second interviewee's comments show that life in the society and culture of the United States results in transformation, even if partial, of the cultural referents of the immigrants themselves. Therefore, the idea that the transnational life of Mexican immigrants who live in the Los Angeles region denotes a clear inclination toward their hometowns and a disinterest in the society of Los Angeles constitutes a simplistic vision that does not capture the assimilation, on various levels, of the social processes in which they have been immersed ever since their arrival in the United States.

In sum, our interviewees show, on the one hand, various levels of integration in particular spheres of society in Los Angeles, and, on the other hand, insertion in a transnational arena that implies the presence of a variety of ties to their places of both origin and destination, through maintenance of extensive family or locality-based networks on both sides of the border. Although the ties to localities in Mexico persist (through constant communication, sending of remittances, etc.), the obstacles to a frequent return are accompanied by the growing strength of greater social commitments in Los Angeles, whether in work or family realms.

ASSOCIATIONS AND SOCIAL INTEGRATION

One of the most visible aspects of the social dynamic of our interviewees is their extensive participation in a wide spectrum of associations of various sorts, which reveals how the groups of Mexican immigrants in our study have constructed a social fabric in the Los Angeles region. In principle this is to be expected, given that our selection of communities and informants was based on contacts initially established with immigrant organizations serving those groups. Still, both the extent and the diversity of associations that prevail in the social lives of our interviewees deserve close attention.[16]

To begin with, the great majority of the immigrants interviewed point out that they participate, with varying degrees of intensity, in associations based on place of origin. Here we are talking about groups referred to as clubs, associations, or committees of people from the same town or region. In general, this is a more formal way of organizing the informal social networks that immigrants create in their host societies. Among Mexican immigrants in the United States it is a widely practiced form of organization, with two main goals. On the one hand, it creates a community of immigrants who may be scattered within a destination area but who have a common hometown or region in Mexico. On the other hand, it embodies a desire to help the community of origin through philanthropic projects. In the majority of cases, such locality-based associations group themselves into federations based on the Mexican state of origin; these larger groupings provide a greater voice in dealing with other social and political actors.[17]

Given the scope of Mexican immigration to the Los Angeles region, it is not surprising that this region also presents the greatest concentration of this form of organization in the United States. All the communities represented in our study have at least one association of this type, regardless of the number of years their members have been residing in Los Angeles. For example, the group California por un Yanga Mejor (California for a Better Yanga) has existed since the early 1990s, eventually evolving into the Fundación Yanga; it has allowed for the preservation of ties between US immigrants from Yanga who live in such scattered cities of California as Fullerton, Placentia, Long Beach, San Francisco, and San Jose.

Similarly, immigrants from Macuiltianguis, Oaxaca, have migrated to the Los Angeles region since the 1970s, particularly to such areas as San Gabriel, Santa Monica, and Tustin. In the 1980s, the Organización para la Ayuda a Macuiltianguis (Organization to Support Macuiltianguis, Spanish initials OPAM) sought to develop an organizational form among the immigrants from that Oaxacan town because, as one interviewee pointed out, "there was a need to feel united," and, on that basis, to try to help out "those who are still arriving," offering moral and economic support in difficult moments. This particular group has experienced ups and downs and splits over the course of its organizational life, but as with other organizations of its type, a central aspect of its operation has been to preserve customs and traditions among the community of emigrants. Thus a large number of its activities are cultural in nature, such as the celebration of festivals.[18]

The case of the Zacatecan immigrants in the Los Angeles region stands out because their organizations are more cohesive and experienced and have a greater track record of philanthropic initiatives to aid their communities. A clear example is the Federación de Clubes Zacatecanos del Sur de California, the oldest and most widely recognized for its achievements; the federation includes dozens of associations of Zacatecan migrants who live in the region and, in turn, has served as the launching pad for a variety of initiatives and community leaders. For instance, a member of the federation's board of directors who belongs to one of the local communities included in our study observes, "I saw the possibility that here in the United States it could be possible to attack the poverty that abounds in Mexico . . . and if we can do that through the mutual aid of those who are there and those who are here, then we should."[19]

A second type of association in which immigrants commonly participate is related to issues of education. Generally, such participation has centered on the education of the immigrants' children, with the parents serving as members of boards or participating in fund-raising, in various kinds of cultural activities (for instance, performing folk dances in schools), or in gathering information about programs of educational support.

The degree of our interviewees' participation in the educational sphere varies. Though some do not report participating actively as organizers, they do show interest and participate by attending meetings or helping to carry out activities. For example, an immigrant from Jerez, Zacatecas, says that "when I get a call that there will be a meeting to talk about things to do with my kids' school, then I get involved, to find out what's going on." However, there are also those who report more active roles. Antonia, an immigrant from Orizaba, Veracruz, participates very actively in a variety of organizations related to cultural activities among Veracruz immigrants; she is also a formal representative of her daughter's school at school district meetings.

In some cases, the immigrant associations come to function as informal educational institutions or as promoters of education. The Federación Zacatecana again stands out in this regard. As one Zacatecan immigrant points out, the federation's building in Los Angeles includes a community plaza where adult education classes are offered, from literacy to high school equivalency, and the federation even awards small scholarships to support attendance in college courses. In this regard, the growing role of such associations in promoting education among members and their families is a clear indicator of the associations' visions and goals. It shows them to be gradually devoting more attention to their membership's social integration, not just the preservation of ties with the place of origin.

A third organizational form among Mexican immigrants in Los Angeles involves religious groups. Interviewees' participation in this sphere includes religious practice, missionary work, and community support. In many cases, such participation includes some kind of transnational element. One common example is support for patron-saint festivals in the places of origin through sending resources generated by the immigrants in Los Angeles. In other cases, the religious groups have supported visits by religious leaders coming from Mexico, or they have been involved in the importation of cultural elements (for instance, holding "Oaxacan masses" in Spanish accompanied by wind instruments, or carrying out community responsibilities such as those of the *mayordomos*). As will be seen in greater depth in the chapter on cultural integration, religious ties are fundamental to promoting a sense of community identity among Mexican immigrants in Los Angeles.

A fourth type of association centers more specifically on cultural activities. Recreational activities based on Mexican culture are a constant in the organizational life of the interviewees, whether as part of the wider range of activities sponsored by the immigrant associations or as a main focus. As is the case in other spheres, the cultural associations' recreational activities do have a clear referent in the towns and regions of origin, but the sponsorship and implementation of these activities also represent an opportunity for greater interaction in the social environment of Los Angeles, and thus can be a means toward greater social integration.

A fifth organizational form is that of sports associations. As with the cultural organizations, a wide range of sports-oriented groups draw participation from Mexican migrants and their children throughout the Los Angeles region. As a Veracruzan immigrant explains,

> One guy in Los Angeles started to get in touch with other people from Orizaba; he had a soccer team, and the word spread from person to person until I heard about it, and we started playing here, in playing fields in Los Angeles, in a league where everyone could form their own team. There are a lot of leagues here, and we've been playing for years. We started about six years ago, at first just people from Orizaba, then people from Guatemala and El Salvador.

In fact, some immigrant associations originated as soccer, baseball, or basketball clubs, and they kept up those activities as their organizational life broadened. The federations, too, support the functioning of one or more sports teams.[20]

Finally, a sixth type of association has to do with businesses, professions, and trades. A number of our interviewees cite the importance of participating in associations related to their professional fields or to business promotion, both in their hometowns and in Los Angeles. For example, a Zacatecan immigrant mentions his participation in a company that distills and distributes mezcal; this involves people from the same Zacatecan locality living on both sides of the border, which makes it a true transnational business. In other cases, associations based around states of origin support small businesses in the places of destination; one example is the Asociación Oaxaqueña de Negocios (Oaxacan Business Association).

Similarly, especially among immigrants with more education or training gained from either postsecondary education or their own work trajectory, there is participation in professional development groups. For instance, a Oaxacan immigrant notes his membership in an international association for haute cuisine. Another case is a Zacatecan from Jerez, trained as an engineer, who participates in an international organization dealing with automation. "All of us are engineers, and if I have a problem in designing some kind of motor, I talk to them, we interchange ideas, and the problem gets solved." In general, it is the interviewees with the highest levels of education who report belonging to this sort of professional group.

In sum, the immigrants interviewed in our study display an intense organizational life through participation in one or more associations of various sorts. Thus the several dimensions of the process of social integration considered in our study (immigration status, families and family networks, access to health-care services, and education and language proficiency) are all permeated by participation in intermediary groups, which are a key element in shaping communities. Some of these associations have objectives clearly linked to Los Angeles (for example, school-based or professional groups). However, the majority reveal a strong presence of transnational ties, given that the place of origin is central to their identities.

As far as we can judge from the information provided by our interviewees, participation in one or more associations leads eventually to interaction with environments and social groups beyond the fellow immigrants from the same hometown who generally form the initial social base of these groups. Also, even if apparently focused on places of origin, and regardless of their degree of formality, these organization often function as sources of information and skills that facilitate interaction in a broader arena.

These results are consistent with other researchers' findings about these kinds of associations. Somerville, Durana, and Terrazas[21] stress the importance of such associations among immigrant communities in different parts of the world; they report that the associations function as effective intermediaries in the process of social integration, serving as important centers of social networks for new immigrants or offering goods and services they sorely need, such as language classes, information, and advice. Other analysts have observed the gradual transformation of the agendas of such groups, which tend more and more to deal with issues related to their members' futures in the United States, and thus with clearing a path for the social integration of their memberships, members' families, and communities.[22]

FINAL CONSIDERATIONS

This chapter presents the main findings of the ethnographic component of our study about the social integration process of Mexican immigrants living in the Los Angeles region. In general, those of our interviewees residing in the United States for more years arrived in the Los Angeles region in more favorable circumstances than those who came later. Therefore, not only were they able to eventually obtain documented status, but they also have more clearly established themselves within the new society.

Most of the immigrants from Zacatecas, a good number from Oaxaca, and some from Veracruz not only have US citizenship or legal permanent residency but also greater English proficiency and have succeeded in developing a wider range of social relations outside the Mexican community of Los Angeles. By contrast, a large share of the immigrants originally from Veracruz and some of those from Oaxaca have been in the United States for shorter periods, having arrived in the Los Angeles region mostly in the 1980s and 1990s; as a result, they tend not to have legal immigration documents, have less English proficiency, and have had to face more restricted occupational contexts.

Nonetheless, in spite of the different circumstances facing Mexican immigrants arriving in the region at different times, in general terms we can see that those from all three Mexican states do participate, to one degree or another, in a variety of social spheres, whether in preexisting spaces (for example, participation in the affairs of their children's schools, in religious practice, or in sports) or in spaces largely constructed by immigrants themselves (for example, migrants' associations or clubs, or recreational activities expressing Mexican culture).

One part of the explanation of this phenomenon is that the context in question, the Los Angeles region, has for decades been a relatively advantageous point of arrival for Mexican migration because social networks of relatives and fellow migrants from the same region, state, or nation facilitate the arrival and activity of the newest immigrants. As we have put it throughout this book, this is indicative of the immigrants' integration "into" the society of Los Angeles. Although some critics have pointed to the prevalence of closed Mexican immigrant communities whose only integration is with other Mexicans, the fact is that the Zacatecan, Oaxacan, and Veracruzan immigrants have had to integrate into a region that is highly segmented in socioeconomic, racial, and ethnic terms.

Another part of the explanation is that—as we will show in chapter 7, on political integration, and in chapter 8, on public policies—in the context of the entire United States, the Los Angeles region is relatively less hostile toward its immigrant population. Although a number of our undocumented interviewees comment on the need to avoid contact with immigration authorities (especially those in families with mixed immigration status), overall we have not found the sort of generalized fear that would prevent mobility or reduce participation in work and social activities. In the interviews we have excerpted in the various sections of this chapter, the interviewees display a positive assessment of their settlement and eventual integration in their destination society, notwithstanding the existence of continued ties to their hometowns. Their perceptions reflect the social fabric they have succeeded in creating in the United States , and thus they demonstrate that the stereotype of the monolingual, isolated immigrant whose only connection is to his or her place of origin is entirely simplistic and erroneous, in spite of its prevalence in many public and political arenas.

Finally, as some analysts[23] have observed, one of the central problems in the process of social integration of migrants to the United States is a decline in the membership of the institutions that have historically been fundamental to this process, such as schools, churches, businesses, unions, and local electoral committees.

In spite of such decline, the information shared by our interviewees reveals varied degrees of participation in such institutions, suggesting that immigrant participation has contributed to reinvigorating them. Furthermore, other analysts, after examining the trajectory of the first wave of migration to the United States and its members' eventual integration, have stressed the importance of what the destination society does—or does not do—about the presence of such immigrant communities in its midst (the importance of what we in this book have called integration of the immigrants "by" the society), rather than focusing only on what the immigrants do to promote their own social integration. For instance, Mary Waters[24] concludes that US society must rethink its immigration policies and its institutions for promoting social integration, but it must also ask itself, "What can we do about the pervasive inequalities in American life that often mean that becoming a black American or a Mexican American leads to a less bright future than remaining an immigrant?"[25]

In Los Angeles the immigrants' creation of their own institutions, such as migrants' associations or platforms for cultural events, has widened the range of intermediary institutions that facilitate their process of social integration. This participation and initiative on the part of migrant communities is important to emphasize because, as other analysts have pointed out,[26] US public opinion in general and in such states as California in particular habitually views the subject of immigration and immigrants in a negative light. Thus there is a need to reframe this discussion in terms of the positive contribution that immigrant populations make to their host societies, as well as their multiple efforts to build their lives and those of their families and communities in the United States.

CHAPTER 6

Cultural Integration

Redefining Identities in a Diverse Metropolis

The first chapter of this book stressed the two poles that have defined the discussion of cultural integration: the assimilationist perspective, which envisions the incorporation of immigrants through the dissolution of difference, and the multiculturalist perspective, which sees immigrants inevitably entering into a heterogeneous and conflictual space where they negotiate their belonging according to their own cultural particularities.

This debate can also frame examinations of the immigrants' own strategies, because it affects our understanding of the logic underlying migrants' decision making (whether individual or collective) as they pursue integration. Viewing immigrants as the subjects of this action, while bearing in mind that the receiving society is not homogeneous, makes it analytically possible to distinguish between two types of integration strategies. On the one hand, there are strategies that follow the logic of assimilation—that is, the pursuit of integration through dissolution or concealment of cultural difference. On the other hand, there are strategies that emerge from a logic of difference—that is, the pursuit of incorporation through negotiating one's own space within a heterogeneous society, making use of cultural particularities as a resource.

In the following pages we will try to show that the choice of one or the other of these paths to integration is affected both by the specific historically constructed characteristics of the receiving society and by the specific individual or collective characteristics of the immigrants themselves. These, in turn, are related to the particularities of their communities of origin and to the nature and strength of the ties they maintain with them.

Integration strategies, along with their eventual successes and failures, reflect the tensions or synergies established by the bidirectional nature of the integration process—integration by the receiving society and integration into it. The structural and conjunctural resources and obstacles facing such individual or collective strategies also reflect that two-directional relationship. In other words, resources for integration and obstacles to integration both demonstrate existing tensions between the space that immigrants seek to occupy within their new society and the space that this society assigns to them.

Given all of the above, in order to contextualize our analysis of the cultural integration strategies employed by the immigrants we have interviewed, we will begin with a brief account of the historical importance of "Hispanic" culture in the region. As will be seen later on, this context is key to understanding what it means to integrate oneself in the Los Angeles Metropolitan Area from the cultural perspective. Following those comments, we will analyze the immigrants' integration strategies along four main analytic axes: (1) identity and self-definition; (2) residential integration and segregation; (3) artistic, religious, and civic/community practices; and (4) life projects.

LOS ANGELES—A HISPANIC CITY?

To understand the processes of cultural integration we must begin with the cultural specificities of metropolitan Los Angeles. In the cultural sphere, what first strikes the eye is the significant "Hispanic" or "Latino" presence. This presence is important in both numerical (see chapter 3) and historical (see chapter 2) terms, and it becomes especially evident in the cultural sphere, whether through the music playing on local radio stations, local cuisine on offer, or the sight and sound of the Spanish language in public space. Nonetheless, it is important to avoid a simplistic reading of "Hispanic"; it's important to search out the origin of this category and identify the heterogeneity of referents that it encompasses.

The Hispanic character of Los Angeles dates from the city's founding in the second half of the seventeenth century. Thus, the first meaning of this term refers to the city's past as part of a Spanish colony. Though this referent is symbolically important, it provides no concrete line of continuity between that colonial past and the contemporary Latino population, which is composed mostly of immigrants from Mexico and their descendants.

Similarly, the period during which Los Angeles was a Mexican city (1821–1847), despite its brevity, also has symbolic importance because it has allowed for the construction of a legitimizing argument according to which the origin of Mexican American population is not immigration by its founders but the relocation of the border. The 1848–1920 period forms the counterpart to that argument, symbolizing the processes of "expropriation," loss of regional hegemony, and forced assimilation.[1]

Toward the end of the nineteenth century and in the early decades of the twentieth, immigration from the midwestern United States and the periodic restriction of Mexican immigration transformed the ethnic profile of Los Angeles, proportionally reducing the Hispanic share of the population. This process, which Soja[2] has called the WASPization of Los Angeles, was more than a regional demographic transformation, because it established the basis for the emergence of a strongly segmented metropolis. This period culminates the Hispanic culture's shift from being a hegemonic and majority referent to being a minority and subaltern one—a dramatic transition documented by Chicano historians,[3] who point to that historical period as the one that created the Chicano or Mexican American population in the region.

The establishment of Hispanic culture as the characteristic of a minority and subaltern population is particularly visible in the history of eastern Los Angeles. Historian Ricardo Romo has shown how, during its formative period (1900–1930), the poor living conditions that eastern Los Angeles offered to its workers discouraged both European immigrants and native-born workers, leaving the field open for the formation of what "would be the nation's largest Mexican barrio and by 1930 rival in size major cities in the United States."[4]

For George Sánchez, another expression of the process of concealment or segregation of the population of Mexican origin can be seen in the creation of an official history in which Mexican Americans were a forgotten people.[5] Thus, in spite of the growth of the Mexican-origin population in the 1940s because of increased immigration flows, for several more decades the presence of MexicanAmericans and their membership in US society continued to be rendered invisible, until the rise of the Chicano movement in the early 1960s.

Within the current of struggles for civil rights, the Chicano movement expressed and demanded a recognition that Chicanos are part of

US society while maintaining a specific cultural identity. Its originality consisted in demanding recognition of belonging not through assimilation but through assertion of difference. This major shift reflected, on one hand, the importance of new thinking about difference and, on the other, the historical context of segregation.[6]

After the Chicano movement, the specificity of Mexican American culture became still more complex because of a new intensification of immigration from Mexico, the economic restructuring of the region, and the new urbanization of Los Angeles.[7] The process of re-Mexicanization took place alongside a new diversification of the Hispanic population, in which the descendants of the Chicano generation were joined by a more recent Mexican immigrant population that maintained strong linkages to its sending communities. In particular, as people from additional regions of Mexico became part of the immigration flow to the United States, the referents underlying Chicano culture were no longer limited to the west-central part of Mexico. Thus, symbols like tequila and mariachis began to coexist with Sinaloan bands, Mixtec cuisine, and Norteño musical groups. The new immigration contributed to diversifying the Hispanic image and cultural panorama of the region.

Today, the Hispanic or Latino presence in Los Angeles has gained ground in two ways: through the struggles of the Mexican American community to be considered as an integral part of US history and through the accelerated growth of the Mexican immigrant population. This growing Hispanic presence, however, has not reduced segregation or reestablished Hispanic culture as hegemonic in the region. Hispanics are still concentrated in stigmatized neighborhoods and in jobs with poor pay and working conditions, and the Hispanic population has the lowest educational levels and the most undocumented immigrants. In spite of numerical and historical importance, the "Hispanic" is neither homogeneous nor hegemonic. On the contrary, unlike what happened with earlier waves of migration from Europe, the population of Mexican origin is "ethnified" by being rendered "Hispanic." Authors like Telles and Ortiz demonstrate how the adverse effects of such segregation continue to express themselves even in the third or fourth generation.[8]

In the pages that follow, we will show how the importance of the "Hispanic" and concretely the "Mexican" can constitute both an obstacle and a resource for the implementation of diverse strategies of cultural integration by immigrants in metropolitan Los Angeles.

IDENTITY, INTEGRATION, AND RESIDENTIAL SEGREGATION

In chapter 1 we described the debates stemming from two different conceptions of identity. The first links identity to citizenship and presupposes that national identities are exclusive. The adoption of a national identity thus requires giving up any other sense of belonging, so that the process of cultural integration of immigrants must be unidirectional and require the rupture of any preexisting senses of affiliation with communities of origin. The second perspective, on the contrary, holds that identities are composed of multiple referents and are relational—that is, they are constructed through interaction, they change constantly, they are negotiated between the assertion and the imposition of attributes, and they have concrete implications in the daily life of the individuals who assert these identities or take on their associated stigmas. In this second perspective, cultural integration is not understood as the giving up of cultural practices identified with places of origin, but as the negotiation of incorporation through reproduction or abandonment of such practices in the new context. The process is, necessarily, two-way: the immigrants can assert, abandon, or conceal their particular cultural practices, while the receiving society can reject them, incorporate them, or transform them. This negotiation occurs through processes as diverse as the enacting of laws, the reappropriation of cultural practices through commercialization that may be either ethnic or exoticized, or the construction of new hybrid, or syncretic, practices.

The comments about forms of self-identification put forward by the Los Angeles immigrants interviewed in our study seem to represent the second of these approaches. The majority identify themselves according to their states of origin—as Zacatecans, Oaxacans, or Veracruzans—but also explicitly show how their terms of self-identification are contextual and relational. Thus, for instance, the Oaxacan interviewee Marco explains, "It depends on who you're talking to. With people from other countries, we call ourselves Mexicans. If I'm among people from Mexico, I identify myself as Oaxacan, and if I'm among Oaxacans, then I say I'm from Macuiltianguis."

This tendency continues even among those who have acquired US citizenship, such as Abelardo, who recounts, "I tell them I'm from Mexico, from Zacatecas. Even though I lost my Mexican nationality when I got to be a citizen, later I got it back! I went and applied at the Mexican consulate and I got it back." Interviewees refer with pride to the transmission of this identification to the second generation, as in the case of Victoria, who explains, "Even if I do become a US citizen, I'm going to keep saying I'm Mexican, just like the way my daughters [born in the United States], the little ones don't even know where Mexico is, but they always say that's where they're from." The contextual nature of identity allows for renegotiating stigmatizing borders by means of praising positive attributes of the culture of the place of origin. Mixtecs from Oaxaca, for instance, have experienced the stigmatizing of their indigenous character in Mexico, but once they find themselves within the new set of relations established among people from Mexico in the United States, they seek to vindicate their particular background. Roberto says, "They always think I'm from Michoacán and I tell them, 'No, I'm from down there where we're short and dark and big-headed and ugly. 'Oh, you're a damn Oaxacan!' and I say, 'That's right, we're short and dark and big-headed and that doesn't bother me a bit, because those are my roots. I'm happy and proud to have Indian blood.'"

So, what does it mean for Mexicans to redefine their identity referents through the process of incorporation to the United States? Paraphrasing George Sánchez,[9] we might argue that Mexican immigrants are not Hispanics, but they become Hispanics through integration. The path to integration that the receiving society offers these immigrants consists of converting them into Hispanics. Our interviewees have learned that the space the receiving society allows them to occupy is to be found within the limits of the category "Latino" or "Hispanic." In most cases they take this identity on: "If it's for some type of identification, according to what they call things, one is Hispanic, so . . . *there's no other choice,* I'm Hispanic" (Elías, Oaxaca; emphasis added). "Almost always they classify us as Latinos [but] when you fill out papers or anything here, 'Mexican' never appears; always it's 'Hispanic,' so, *our place is to be Hispanic*" (Lorena, Oaxaca; emphasis added). This attitude of fatalism or relative conformity to segmented incorporation is particularly evident in response to residential segregation, as we will shortly see.

Constructing and Erasing Cultural Borders

Several authors[10] have shown that residential segregation by ethnicity prevails in the Los Angeles Metropolitan Area. This can be seen in the distribution of the Hispanic population within the area (see maps 2, 3 and 4); some cities in the region show percentages greater than 90 percent, while in others the Hispanic population is practically nonexistent.

As years go by, the ethnic composition of neighborhoods changes. That process is revealed by the urban landscape, as in the case of the Oaxacan restaurant La Guelaguetza. The oriental architectural style of its building, located on Olympic Street in Koreatown, reflects the traditional Asian presence in this central neighborhood, which today has a significant Hispanic population. Similarly, South Central, traditionally African American, became a predominantly Latino barrio at the end of the twentieth century, joining other Hispanic areas like East Los Angeles, El Monte, Downey, and San Fernando.[11] Thus, given the size of the region's Hispanic population and the history of ethnic segregation, it should come as no surprise that almost all our interviewees live in cities with high proportions of Hispanic residents, and they identify the neighborhoods where they live as Latino or even predominantly Mexican.

As can be seen in maps 2, 3, and 4, Zacatecans, Oaxacans, and Veracruzans are highly concentrated in the most heavily Hispanic cities. Twenty-three of our ninety interviewees live in cities that are more than 90 percent Hispanic, but there are also some concentrations based on social networks related with their places of origin in Mexico.

For example, there is a nexus of Veracruzans in East Los Angeles and the contiguous cities of Fullerton and Placentia. Oaxacans live along the Interstate 10 corridor, especially in Santa Monica, Los Angeles, and San Bernardino. Zacatecans—slightly more dispersed—are most concentrated in Long Beach and San Fernando. Concentration according to place of origin is also reflected in the interviews, which sometimes reveal the presence of a number of families from the same Mexican locality now living in the same neighborhood of metropolitan Los Angeles. In the case of Jerez, Zacatecas, according to Abelardo, "There are a lot of people from Jerez here, like if you go to the supermarket you find people from Jerez working there and shopping there, or among the yard workers, or in the restaurants, the majority around here are from Jerez." The most striking example of concentration of people from the same town is that of six families originally from one town in Veracruz who now live in the same housing project in East Los Angeles.

Given these observations, one might well ask, do these concentrations of Zacatecans, Oaxacans, and Veracruzans reflect the search for intra-ethnic comfort, or, on the contrary, do they reflect structural determinants of residential segregation that were present before the immigrants' arrival? That question, however, would be deceptive, and its answer could only be ambiguous, because this process must be explained as the result of a combination of factors. While it is true that the interviewees refer to the comfort derived—especially when on first arrival—from living near relatives and others from their hometowns, they also provide evidence of the subtle or not-so-subtle mechanisms through which inter-ethnic tension, alongside segmentation by income levels owing to the greatly contrasting prices of housing in different areas, pushes immigrants toward traditionally more disadvantaged Latino neighborhoods. Or, to put it another way, if the immigrants seek out intra-ethnic comfort, this is to a large extent because of the impossibility of living comfortably in other neighborhoods.

Ethnic segregation, meanwhile, is accompanied by less favorable living conditions. More than two-thirds of our interviewees live in cities with household incomes below the California median of $60,883. In addition, most of our interviewees reside in cities with high percentages of the population living below the poverty line that are significantly greater than the state average of 13.7 percent. Those percentages are 27.4 in San Bernardino and 24.1 in East Los Angeles.[12]

The ethnographic approach allows us to observe that social networks have the greatest impact on the immigrants' spatial distribution. This explains why some undocumented immigrants who recently arrived in the region are concentrated in higher income cities. For example, we observed that those who live in Placentia—a city with relatively higher income levels and a lower percentage of Hispanic population—are Veracruzan immigrants, mostly undocumented. The ethnographic research allows us to identify one of the first Veracruzans to settle in that city as a university graduate who obtained legal permanent residence after marrying a US citizen. The rest of the Veracruzan interviewees living in Placentia went to that city because of direct or indirect ties to that first immigrant.

Also, residential segregation can be found within city boundaries. The significant presence of Oaxacans in Santa Monica, a city with a high average household income, seems to provide a counterexample to the trend of concentration of immigrant population in poorer cities. However, all the Oaxacans interviewed in Santa Monica, members of a single social network, lived in rent-controlled apartments in the most disadvantaged area of that city.

Nevertheless, our interviewees' attitudes do not reveal clear opposition to or condemnation of residential segregation. One even seems to put a positive spin on residential concentration by ethnic group. Victoria, who is originally from Veracruz and later lived briefly in Chicago with her husband, decided to return to Los Angeles. She explains the differences between the two urban contexts this way:

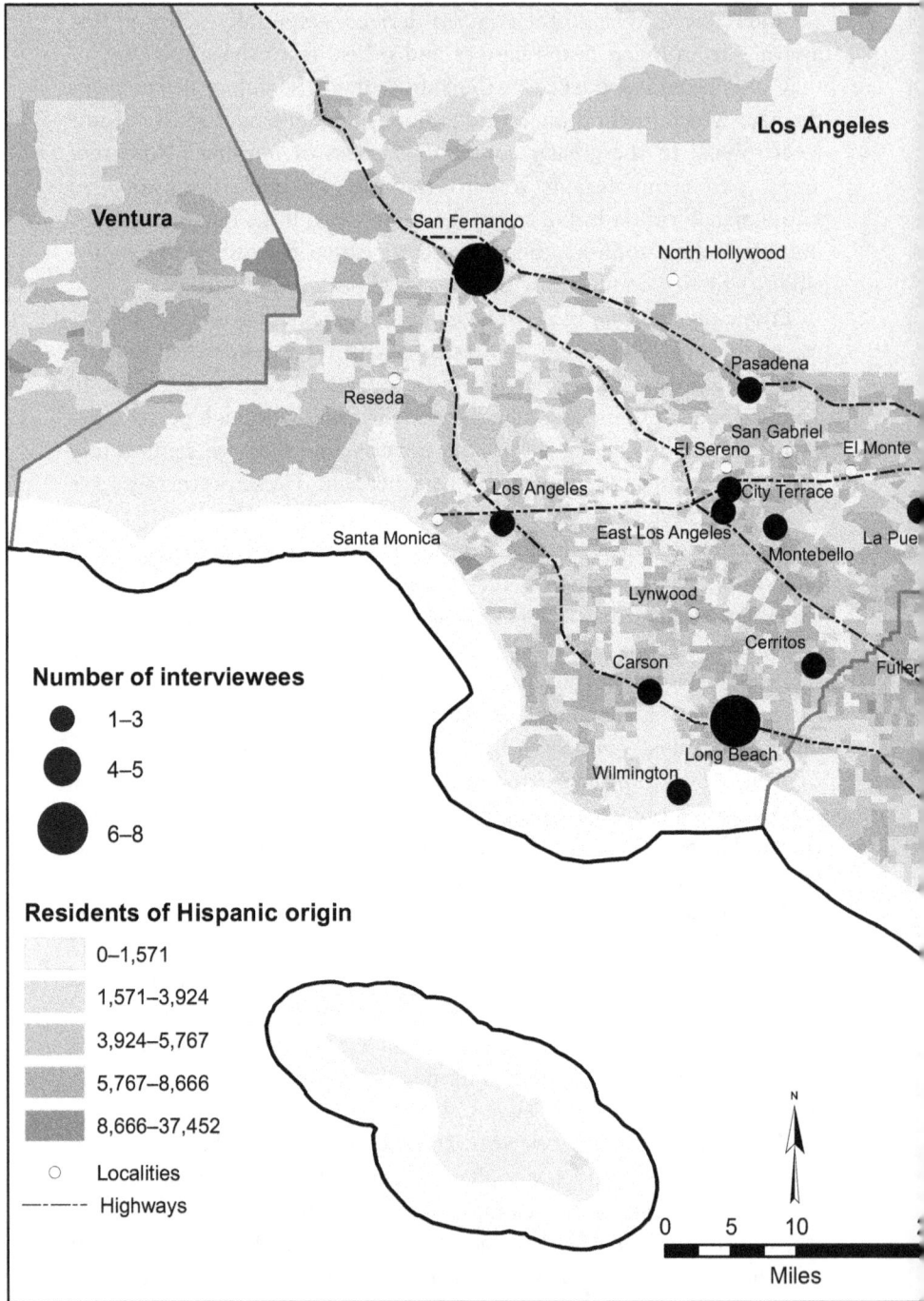

Number of interviewees

- 1–3
- 4–5
- 6–8

Residents of Hispanic origin

- 0–1,571
- 1,571–3,924
- 3,924–5,767
- 5,767–8,666
- 8,666–37,452
- ○ Localities
- ----- Highways

Los Angeles

Ventura

San Fernando

North Hollywood

Pasadena

Reseda

San Gabriel
El Sereno   El Monte
City Terrace
Los Angeles
Santa Monica   East Los Angeles   La Pue
Montebello

Lynwood

Cerritos

Carson   Fuller

Long Beach
Wilmington

0   5   10

Miles

N

MAP 2. Main cities of residence of interviewees from Zacatecas.

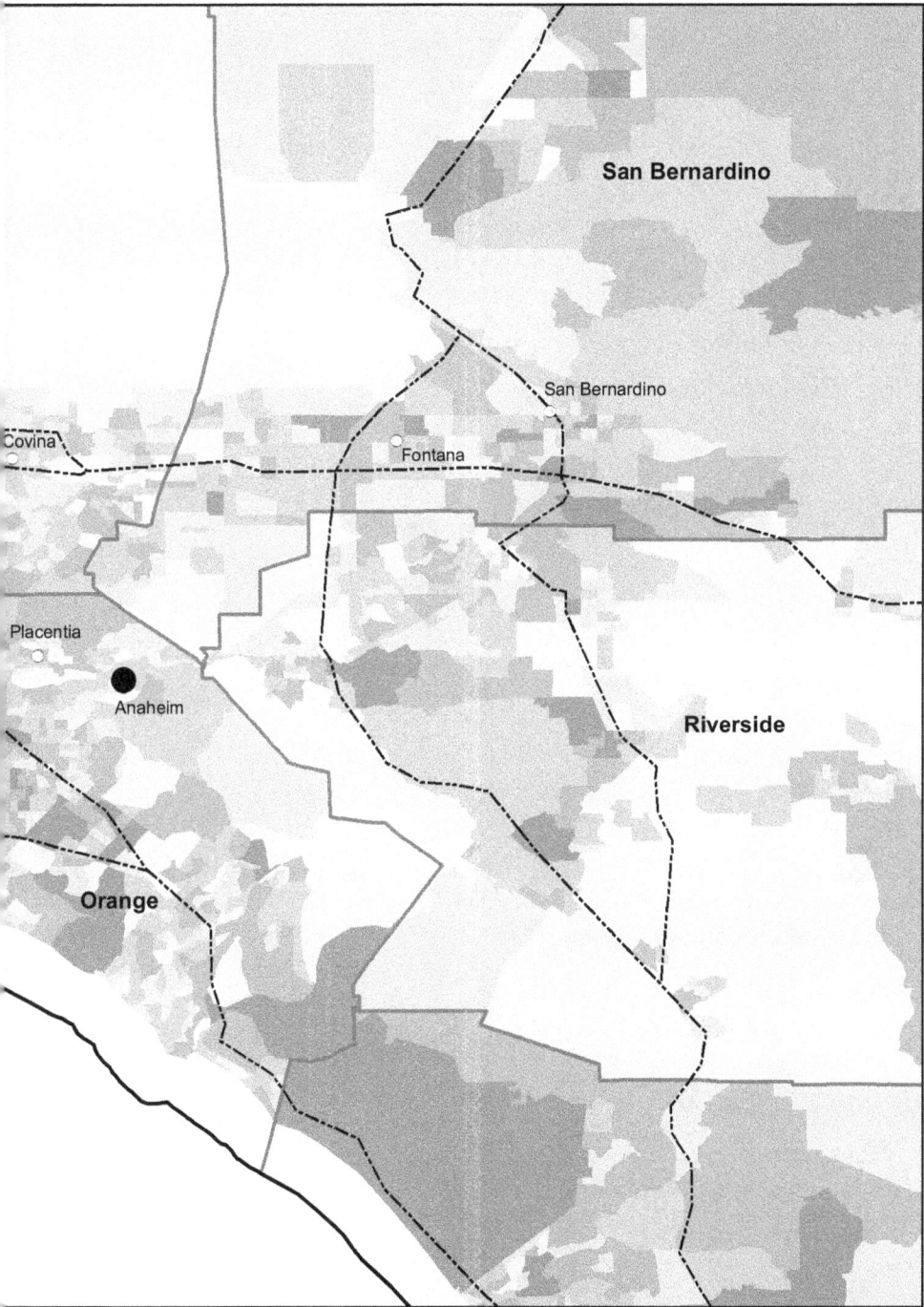

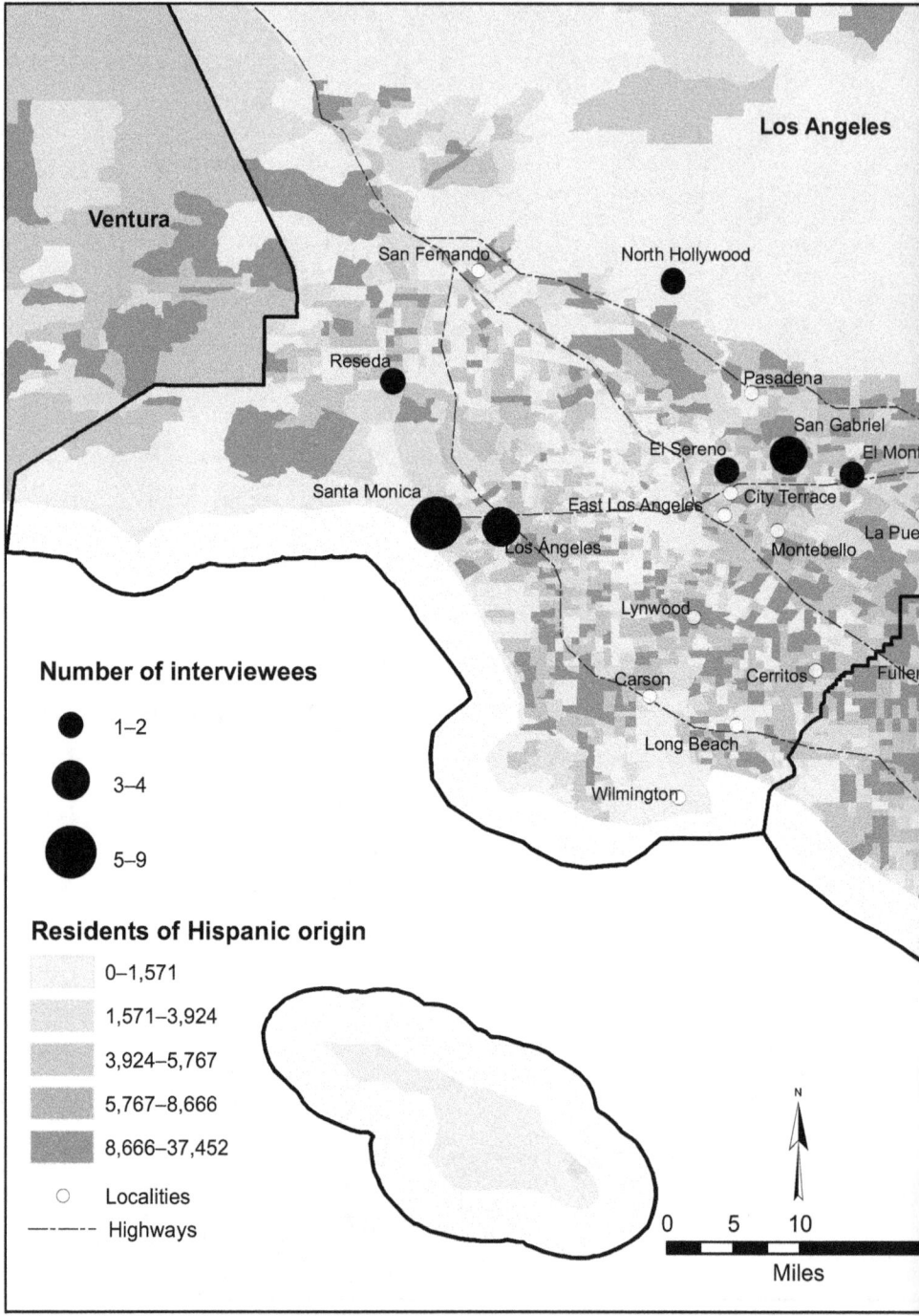

MAP 3. Main cities of residence of interviewees from Oaxaca.

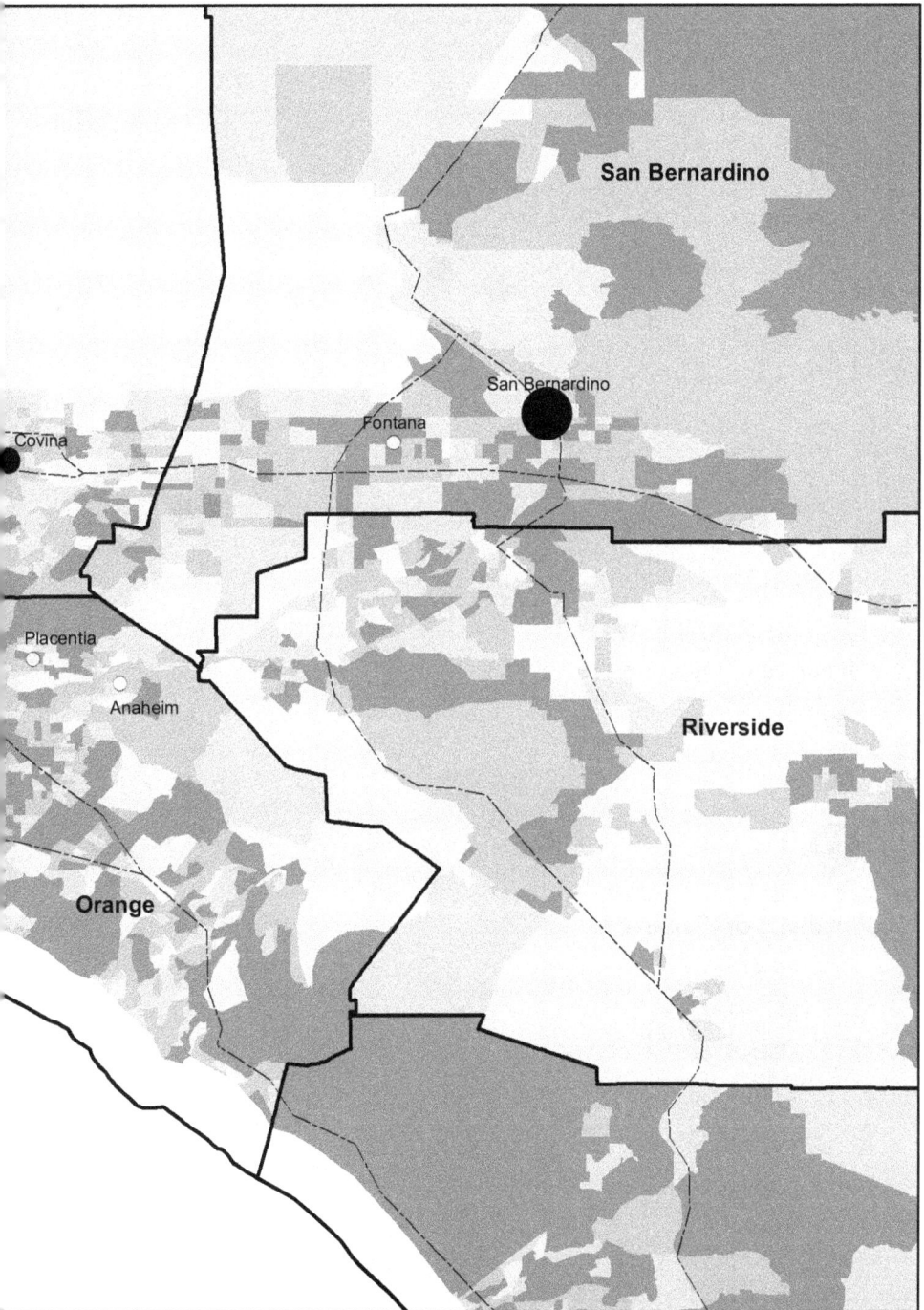

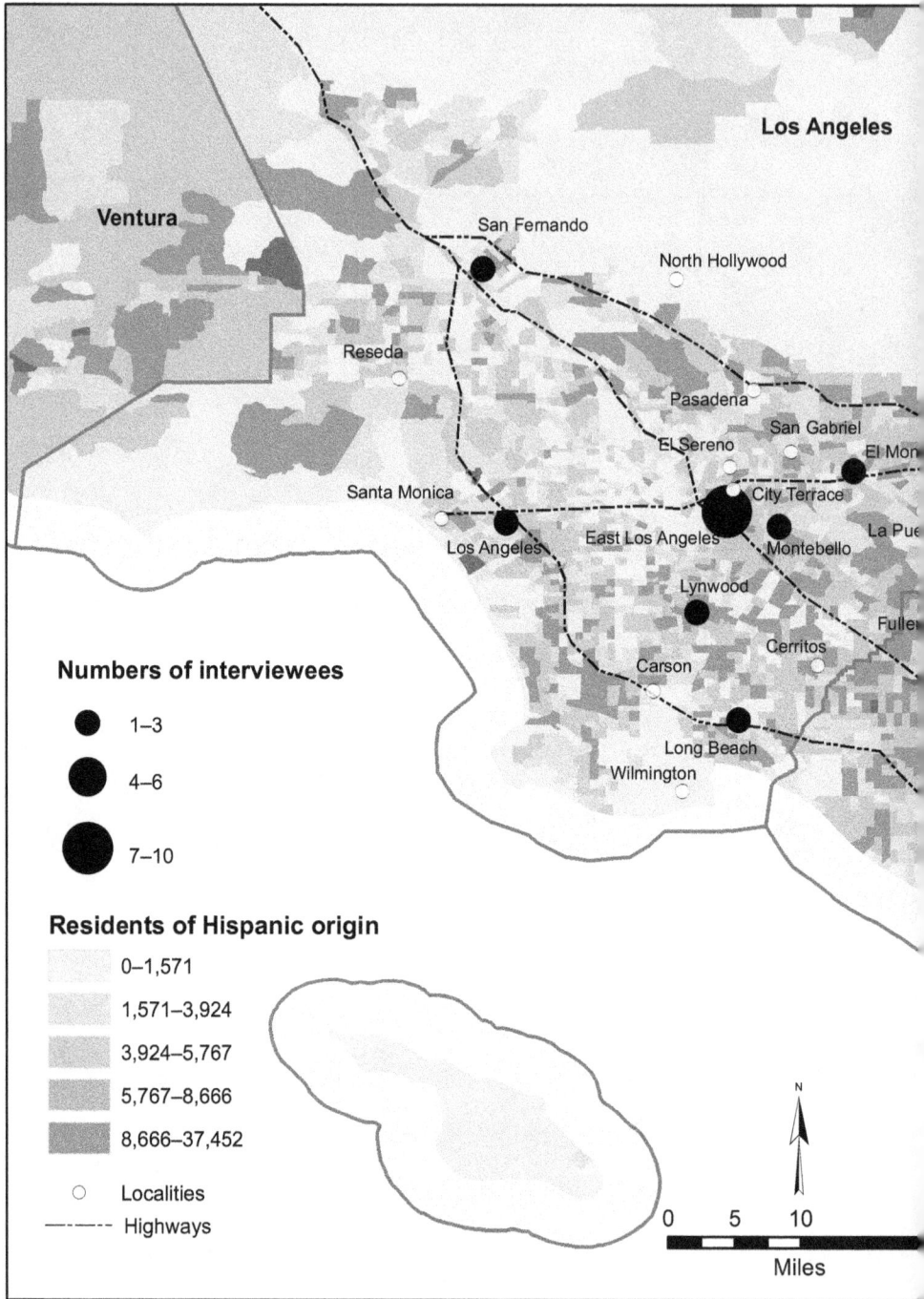

MAP 4. Main cities of residence of interviewees from Veracruz.

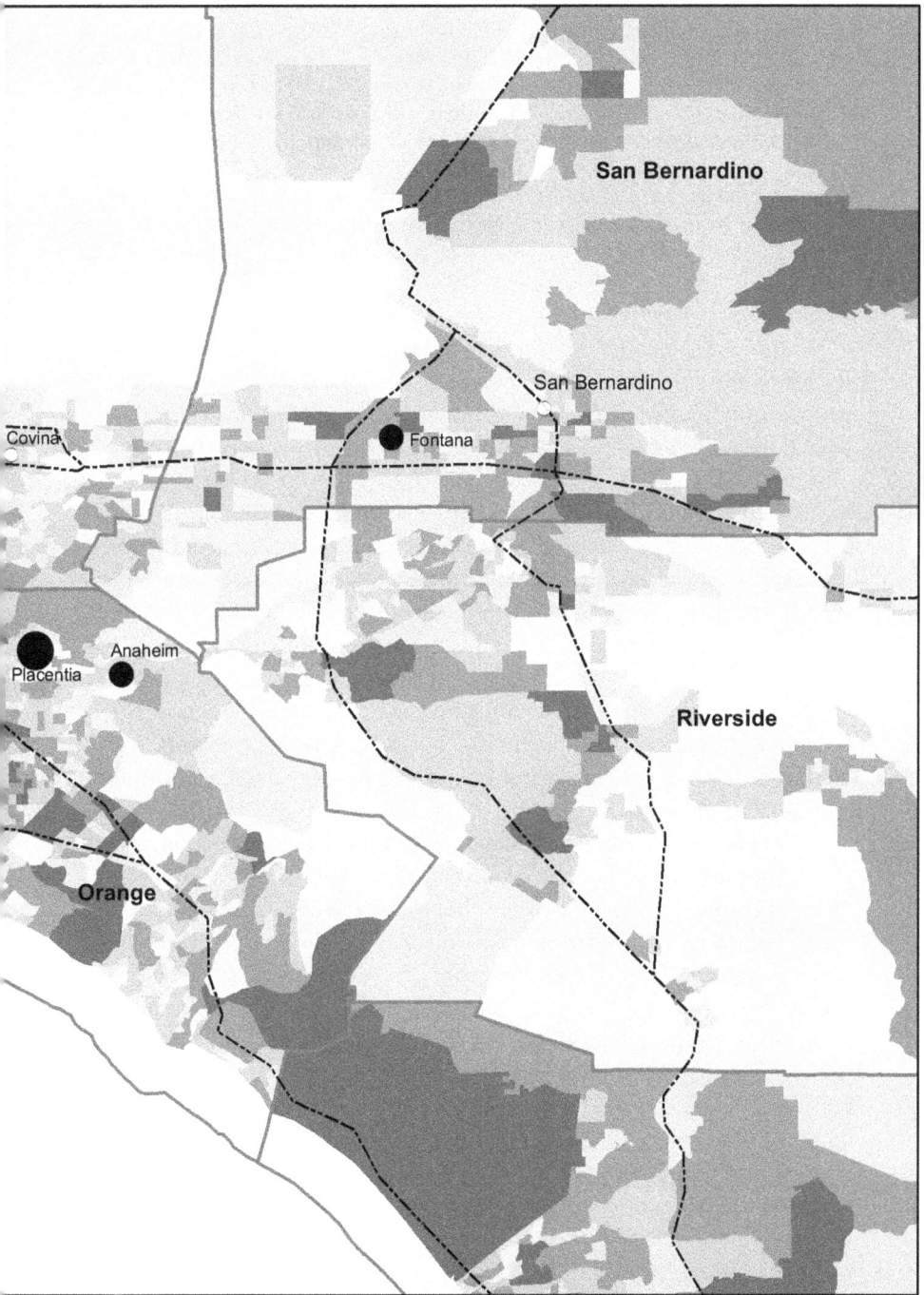

San Bernardino

San Bernardino

Covina

Fontana

Placentia Anaheim

Riverside

Orange

The thing is, Chicago wasn't like we were told it would be. Chicago is, I think, one of the poorest cities. Yes, there are a lot of Latinos, but the city is very ugly. The buildings where people live are all attached one to the other [rather than separate houses]. Here there are divisions; it's more orderly—like this area is all Mexican, another one is all Salvadoran, it's just Mexicans here and in East L.A. There in Huntington Park it's Latinos, I mean they're mixed together but all Latinos, in South Central, you know, that's all blacks, and then you come to where it's all Central Americans. But in Chicago it's not like that. In Chicago everybody's all mixed up; you've got blacks with Latinos, with Poles, all stirred together!

Despite the significant residential segregation, though, our interviewees also report sharing the spaces in which they reside and work with people from a great diversity of nationalities, whether these spaces are neighborhoods or workplaces. Although the majority of their neighbors are "Latinos" or even specifically Mexicans, almost all interviewees mentioned having good relations with neighbors or workmates from other nationalities or ethnic groups, such as Salvadorans, Koreans, Armenians, Filipinos, and Guatemalans, among others. In spite of some specific references to tensions stemming from occupational competition with African Americans and to conflicts with Korean employers, inter-ethnic conflict was not a recurrent theme. In sum, because of their life experience in metropolitan Los Angeles, and in spite of living in pre-dominantly Mexican neighborhoods, our interviewees have come into contact with an important degree of cultural diversity and have learned to coexist with others.

In general terms, the construction of ethnic barriers in residential space does not turn out to be a phenomenon that our interviewees see as an imposition. In spite of the scholarly literature maintaining that "reducing racial residential segregation may be the most critical step toward eradicating economic inequality,"[13] moving out of neighbor-hoods stigmatized as "Latino" was not explicitly mentioned as a prior-ity in the integration strategies of our interviewees. While leaving behind poorer cities is indeed an aspiration, relocation to non-Latino cities is not a frequent strategy even among those who have managed to regu-larize their immigration status and have accumulated more years of residence in the region. We therefore observe that residential segrega-tion by ethnicity is a characteristic of the society of Los Angeles that predates the arrival of our interviewees, which they themselves do not question; indeed they reproduce it because of social networks based on their Mexican communities of origin.

ARTISTIC, RELIGIOUS, AND CIVIC COMMUNITY PRACTICES AS IDENTITY REFERENTS

One of the most visible signs of the presence of groups of immigrants in destination societies is their reproduction in public space of "imported" cultural practices. The emblematic character of such displays frequently places them at the center of mass media debates. It is worth taking a deeper look at how these cultural practices are structured, reproduced, or reinvented by immigrant communities, and at the meanings attributed to them.

Toward that end, in the ethnographic work we carried out in metropolitan Los Angeles, we inquired about our interviewees' participation in artistic, religious, and civic community activities. In each case the interviewees were asked about both practices they carried out as individuals and those they engaged in as members of groups, whether inside or outside the Mexican community.

Artistic Practices

The important presence of Hispanic or Latino and especially Mexican culture in the area under study is reflected in an immense number of venues and offerings, both commercial and community based. Examples include the radio stations with the largest audiences, such as KLVE-FM, which in the late 1990s became the most-listened-to station in the metropolitan area,[14] or newspapers like *La Opinión,* with one of the largest regional circulations. Thus it should not be surprising that the majority of our interviewees say they listen to the radio, watch television, or read the paper in Spanish frequently. Also, they note the importance of access to local traditions and especially the traditional music of their regions.

When asked about free time, interviewees most frequently lamented its near absence. Still, in spite of long workdays, most of the interviewees find time on weekends for visiting relatives and friends and even for taking part in religious, cultural, or civic/community activities. In some cases, these activities demand a high degree of involvement, such as organizing folkloric dance groups, fulfilling responsibilities as *mayordomos* of religious festivalss, or creating musical groups. Although the range of artistic activities in which the interviewees say they participate in is very broad, one area that stands out among Veracruzans and Oaxacans is music and dance.

We will go on to present two cases in this sphere that are paradigmatic, each for a different reason. These are the Oaxacan group Guish-Bac and the Movimiento Jaranero de California, which specializes in the music of Veracruz. We should first, however, point out that these are only two cases out of many, selected to exemplify the participation of immigrants in such activities. Guish-Bac is an organization dedicated to promoting Oaxacan culture and traditional dance. It was founded in 2007 by a group that split off from COTLA, another Oaxacan group. Unlike COTLA, Guish-Bac defines itself specifically as a group for the arts.

Among the activities in which it has played an important role is the Los Angeles Guelaguetza[15] of 2008. This name refers to a music and dance festival held every summer in the city of Oaxaca, with participation from representatives of many areas within the state. Its antecedents can be traced back to the first half of the twentieth century,[16] but it was toward the end of that century that La Guelaguetza transcended its regional status to become Oaxaca's emblematic event on the national stage, seeking to promote the state's image as a place that celebrates both ethnic diversity and regional unity.

The roots of the emergence of La Guelaguetza as an international event go back to Oaxacan immigrants' settling in California, especially from the 1980s on, and to the festivals they held in the cities of San Marcos, Fresno, and Los Angeles,[17] among others. In the specific case of Guish-Bac, while there is no explicitly political component to its work, there is a clear link to religion. Thus, for instance, Nora from Oaxaca points out that the group attracted her attention through its participation in the festival of the patron saint of Tlacolula that is held every year in Los Angeles.

Guish-Bac's membership includes a significant Tlacolulan component. Alongside religious celebrations, the organization offers an opportunity for strengthening community ties. Its dance rehearsals constitute a meeting space where, besides practicing new dances, organizing performances, or choosing wardrobes, participants can talk about their daily lives, share news from their communities of origin, and share projects and plans for the future.[18] Due to the difficulties of transportation in Los Angeles, some of the participants who live in the same neighborhoods make their way to rehearsals together. This is particularly useful for Oaxacan women who have not learned to drive, which makes them dependent on other participants or on their husbands' availability to drive them. In this way, the trips to and from rehearsal also become occasions for talking with other members of the community.

Significantly, children born in the United States also take part in these activities, which thus create a space in which transmission of the region's artistic practices to the next generation can occur. Some traditional dances have even come to be seen as the province of the second generation. According to Israel from Tlacolula,

> I used to take part in *El torito serrano* dance in Oaxaca, and now it's gone through other generations. At first it was only the people who came from the town so they knew how to dance *El torito serrano* but later it's gotten to be their children born in the United States, and some more young ones born in Oaxaca, but really there's been an effort to keep it alive in the new generation.

In these rehearsals and performances, Spanish is spoken and traditional foods and drinks are consumed. To raise funds, Guish-Bac members hold fairs and food sales that simultaneously contribute to the revitalization of cultural practices and the reinforcement of community ties. In sum, Guish-Bac constitutes a clear example of an association that seeks, through the reproduction of cultural traditions, to preserve and stimulate intra-community solidarity. It is also important to note the strength of the organization's ties with people still in Tlacolula who send outfits for the performances and some raw materials for preparing traditional foods. But beyond this instrumental function, the ties with the place of origin are important for emotional, family, and religious reasons as well.

However, in spite of such transnational character, one of the explicit goals of Guish-Bac is to promote Oaxacan culture in California. Its activities, which are held in a variety of public spaces—plazas, squares, parks, and churchyards—are also intended to make Oaxacan cultural traditions known in the destination society. So, through daily assertion and vindication of specific cultural practices, identity borders are renegotiated within the public sphere of the receiving society.

In contrast to Guish-Bac, the Movimiento Jaranero de California does not reproduce the structure of a particular community, is not centered in immigration networks, and does not seek, as one of its main priorities, to bring together fellow immigrants who have settled in California. On the contrary, it is above all a transnational artistic movement— yet it does have direct implications for immigrants originally from Veracruz.

To understand the origins of the Movimiento Jaranero de California (renamed Encuentro de Jaraneros, Inc., in 2002), we must locate it within the resurgence of Verucruzan music that took place in Mexico in the last quarter of the twentieth century. This musical movement produced two main currents. The first, more linked to the logic of the market, led to large international sales of recorded music through labels commercializing "world music." The second, more concerned with recovering and preserving traditional Veracruzan music, focused on the defense of that musical heritage and its organizational forms.[19] Both currents experienced rapid growth and overflowed national borders. Thus the arrival of the *son jarocho* in California and the founding of the first associations dedicated to its performance took place by way of musical networks (of the traditional, commercial, and "high-culture" varieties) and predated the formation of Veracruzan immigration networks.

Still, in spite of this movement's having arisen independently of Veracruzan immigration networks, there are at least two intersections worth pointing out. First, since Veracruzan immigrants maintain a taste for their traditional music, its performance and the associated festivals—the *fandangos*—allow the Veracruz community to converge and interact. Veracruzans who migrated to Los Angeles in search of work have also joined the Movimiento Jaranero, which has come to constitute a space of interaction with non-Veracruzan *jaraneros* and with lovers of *jarocha* music from outside the immigrant communities. Examples include the annual *"noches veracruzanas"* at Hollywood's Ford Theatre,[20] where prestigious scholars, college students, and the families of Veracruzan workers, among others, all rub elbows for a night. The existence of the Movimiento Jaranero has served as a platform—sometimes conflictual—for the emergence of many musical groups in which a marked heterogeneity prevails. Veracruzan musicians recently moved to Los Angeles come to the *fandangos* along with Mexican Americans, University of California professors, Mexican folkloric dancers from other parts of Mexico, US and Mexican music producers, and so on. Naturally, their interaction is not always harmonious, but that does not alter the important fact that an intense and diverse interaction is going on.

Second, the existence of a musical movement that celebrates the Veracruzan ethos reveals that the negotiation of identity borders may proceed along of axes outside the immigrant communities themselves. In addition to the participation by the University of California in the diffusion of *jaranero* music, for example, the Mexican Cultural Center of Santa Ana, California, offers weekly *son jarocho* classes to the general public. Naturally, these expressions may have a relatively limited impact in the broader society—lovers of *son jarocho* are a relatively small subculture—but the potential that the music thus acquires as a resource for

Veracruzan immigrants in their process of identity formation and assertion should not be underestimated.

Finally, there is the fact that, independent of the Movimiento Jaranero, this music constitutes a fundamental referent of identity within the Veracruzan immigrant community, although musical tastes and abilities also transcend this particular genre. Several of our Veracruzan interviewees report being members of professional or semi-professional musical groups in many different genres, but all express a liking for Veracruzan music.[21]

Religious Practices: Observant Catholics, Nominal Catholics, and Converts

Several authors have pointed out the important role played by religion in immigrant communities' processes of becoming settled in receiving societies,[22] in the establishment of transnational ties,[23] or even in changing their attitudes toward religious diversity.[24]

The ethnographic research we carried out in metropolitan Los Angeles confirms these findings, but it also shows some interesting differences: religious practice occupies an important place in the processes of cultural integration, but not always in the same way. While for the Zacatecans adherence to Catholicism is generally (though not always) a personal identity referent, for the Oaxacans the most important resource for the reconstruction of community is the celebration of the festivals of their patron saints. The Veracruzans, on the other hand, report the most attachment to non-Catholic religious communities.

These three forms of religion/identity/integration are directly linked to some of the prevailing characteristics of religious practice in the states of origin. While Mexico has been predominantly Catholic since colonial times, it has also undergone an important process of religious diversification since the last quarter of the twentieth century, making room for the growth of other denominations, especially evangelical and Bible churches.[25]

The degree of religious diversification has varied widely by region, being most prominent in Mexico's southeastern and border regions, while the west-central region (including Zacatecas) continues to be the stronghold of Mexican Catholicism.[26] Both Oaxaca and Veracruz display a heterogeneous distribution of religious diversification, with some areas that have seen accelerated religious change over the past three decades, and others where the percentage of Catholics remains above

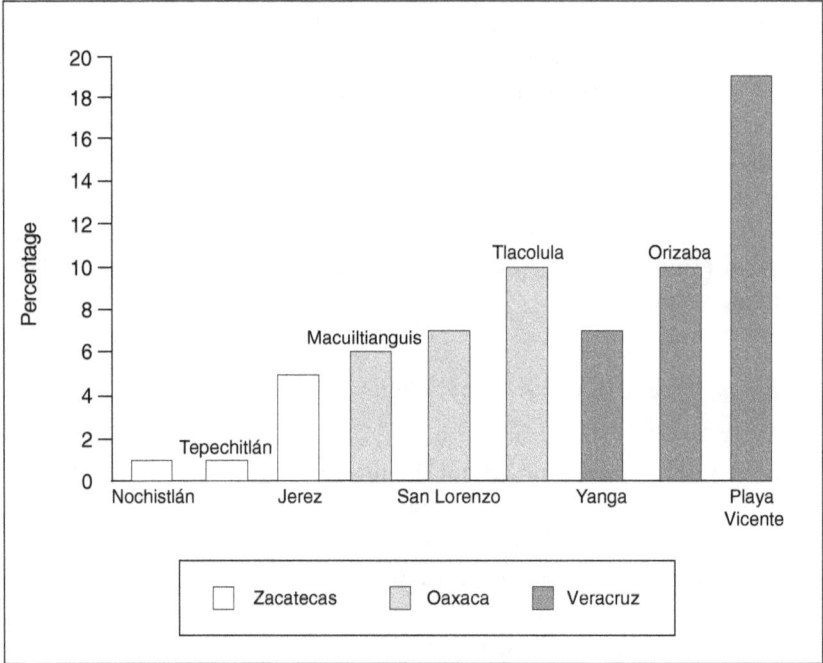

FIGURE 7. Percent distribution of the non-Catholic population in interviewees' municipalities and states of origin in Mexico, 2000. Mexico's Census of Population and Housing, 2000.

the national average. Mexico's 2000 Census of Population and Housing reports a 95.1 percent adherence to Catholicism in Zacatecas, 84.8 percent in Oaxaca, and 82.9 percent in Veracruz.

As can be seen in figure 7, the municipalities from which our interviewees have come reflect the religious adscription tendencies of the states where they are located. This figure shows that between 1 and 5 percent of the population is non-Catholic in the three Zacatecan municipalities considered in our study, while the Oaxacan and Veracruzan municipalities were between 6 and 10 percent and between 7 and 19 percent, respectively. Likewise, from our ninety interviewees, all but one of the Zacatecans identify themselves as Catholics, while five Oaxacans report they are not Catholic. Among the Veracruzans, on the other hand, we found eight to be non-Catholics. The allegiances of the non-Catholics are primarily to Protestant and evangelical denominations, as well as two cases of conversion to the Church of the Latter Day Saints, better known as Mormons.

Most of the interviewees report having neighbors or workmates belonging to other religious denominations. Thus, even those who retain their allegiance to Catholicism have more exposure to religious diversity than they did in their communities of origin. The non-Catholic religions most present in the domains of our interviewees are "Christian" churches,[27] Jehovah's Witnesses, and Mormons, but they also mention neighbors or workmates who are Seventh Day Adventists, Presbyterians, Muslims, and Buddhists. Living in metropolitan Los Angeles has brought a need to learn to live with religious diversity.

Also, beyond the range of religious affiliations in the communities of origin reflected in figure 7, we found in the ethnographic study some important differences in the forms and frequency of Catholic observance. The Zacatecans have greater participation in daily religious practice, the Oaxacans mostly identify as Catholic but have much less of this practice, and the Veracruzans are still more distanced from it. Thus, for instance, the majority of Zacatecan interviewees report attending mass quite regularly. A recurrent response is that they go to mass at least once a week, and there are frequent cases of greater participation, such as Ricardo from Zacatecas, who points out, "We never miss a Sunday, and we also go during the week whenever we can," or Jacinta, also from Zacatecas, who reports, "I go to church regularly. I'm a lay Eucharistic minister. I help out—I go to church in my free time. I like to go because in the church I can relax, and every Tuesday I go for the prayer."

We also found constant reference to participation in prayer groups, catechism, and church choirs. Some interviewees, like Ladislao from Zacatecas, underscore the importance of daily prayer: "I try to show respect for God our Father, and for the Virgin of Guadalupe, who is very important to every Mexican. I don't go to mass, I mean I only go on Sundays and also if I'm going to play music, but I do pray every day, I pray two or sometimes three rosaries; when I'm driving the car I'm also praying."

All of these forms of participation can be described as individual. That is, though prayer groups, choirs, and masses are religious practices that create community, each participant attends on his or her own responsibility, not as member of a village or region or a system of offices with responsibilities. A more illustrative case of this individual practice can be seen in the testimony of Abelardo: "I've got a statue of the Virgin of Guadalupe there in the bathroom, and I've got the Santo Niño de Atocha, and Jesus, and right there I light their candles—I've got a little altar right there." Another example frequently mentioned by the Zacatecans is to pray daily so as to thank God or to ask for his help and protection.

Besides regular religious practice carried out on an individual basis, most of the Zacatecan interviewees report taking part in the December 12 celebrations of the Virgin of Guadalupe. For some, this means making a monetary contribution and attending the celebration, while for others it includes active participation in organizing the event. Unlike the previously cited examples, this is a case of a collective religious practice that re-creates a preexisting community and—above all—a national identity (rather than a local or regional one) that involves coordination with Catholics from many different parts of Mexico.

In contrast to the primarily individualized religious practice of the Zacatecans, the Oaxacans' practice is firmly anchored in the community. Although there are exceptions, daily practice and especially attendance at mass seem to be less intense. For example, Esteban points out, "We're Catholics, but we only go to church once in a while"; or Sergio, who notes, "We go to mass two or three times a year." Rather, Oaxacan Catholicism seems to be expressed more intensely in collective practices, reproducing the organizational forms of the indigenous communities of origin by way of transnationalization of the system of responsibilities, extending the traditional roles of Oaxaca to California. The special times and places when the local community congregates include the Oaxacan mass in the church of St. Cecilia, the worship of the Señor de Tlacolula in the church of St. Sebastian, and the celebrations of the Virgins of La Soledad and El Rosario. These constitute important pillars in the edifice of transnational community ties.

During our fieldwork we had the opportunity to attend the celebration of the Virgin del Rosario, in which nearly a hundred Oaxacan faithful took part. The system of responsibilities replicates traditional Oaxacan organization. The celebration begins with a breakfast in the house of la mayordoma (the female mayordomo), followed by la calenda, in which the worshippers parade, generally in traditional dress; then comes la marmota, a giant sphere constructed out of wire and cloth that dances to the rhythm of traditional music. Then the faithful march in a procession, carrying the statue of the virgin, arriving at the church for a mass, followed by the festival, with traditional food and regional dances. This celebration is carried out simultaneously in Oaxaca, Los Angeles, Las Vegas, and other locations.

About the Oaxacan mass in the church of St. Cecilia, Guillermina explains, "Two years ago they brought the image of our patron saint, the Señor de Tlacolula, which is where I am from, and just a year ago they started holding the Oaxacan mass with a musical group and wind instruments on the fourth Sunday of every month." Likewise, one of the main organizers of the celebration of the Virgen de la Soledad explains, "We like to be able to take part in things in the area of faith, of religion, especially as a way to keep our people united, all of the Oaxacans." Given the large numbers of participants who gather on these special occasions, we can see that it is collective events—more than individual religious practice—that mobilize the Oaxacan Catholics, by means of widespread transnational networks.

In terms of cultural integration, this form of religious practice is oriented toward the reproduction of cultural difference. Yet it is also true that the organizational complexity of these celebrations requires participants to have a good understanding of the administrative forms governing public spaces in California, so as to secure permits for the processions, to formally register the organizations, and so on; it also requires developing strong ties with the local Catholic Church.

The construction of these spaces specific to Oaxacan religiosity has come about through tension and negotiation. One striking expression is the transformation of the church of St. Cecilia into a gathering place for the Oaxacan community. Located in South Los Angeles and founded in 1927, this church had mostly white immigrant parishioners until the 1960s, when it became primarily African American. Starting in the 1990s, the Latino population—especially Oaxacans—became the majority, after which Spanish began to occupy a central place in the liturgy, and the Oaxacan celebrations and images became fixtures. This transformation is interpreted by Father Luigi Zanotto, the head of this church, as a positive element in the integration process: "This church now is the definition of a parish—which is the communion of communities."[28] Or, as a Oaxacan parishioner named Hector Mata is quoted, St. Cecilia's "gave us a great opportunity to . . . open ourselves to the broader world."[29]

In the case of the non-Catholic Veracruzans, we find the opposite integration strategy. The clearest example is that of Carmen, who remarks that the Presbyterian church she attends is a space that allows her to socialize with the white population and better understand their way of thinking. She values the potential that this socialization might have for her children and the importance of moving out of a stigmatized Latino niche.

Another Veracruzan interviewee, Rita, remarks that she finally decided to "put away her saints" and join the Mormon community because of the support offered by the missionaries who visit her every week in her East Los Angeles apartment. The Mormon community allows her to acquire practical tools for integrating into US society and achieve a degree of social mobility. Besides taking classes in reading and writing, Rita got support that encouraged her to protest against the domestic violence she was suffering, to start learning English, and to broaden her social network through female "friends in the church." This widening of networks also implies widening the range of customers for the traditional Veracruzan food that she sells to make her living. As she explains, "I went on for a long time having faith in my saints, but I see they didn't give me anything. It's only been a month since I turned to the celestial father [Mormon conversion] and now I can see the dollars coming in. I'm living better. I'm not crying. I've got a lot of friends in the church."

In sum, religious practices seem to be an important referent for Zacatecans, Oaxacans, and Veracruzans, but for different reasons. In each case, the characteristics of the religious domain in their states of origin are reflected in the form in which each individual interprets and adapts to the religious field of Los Angeles. But beyond the specifics of religious practice in their sending communities, the religious sphere shows us the variety of strategies constructed by individuals and communities who may seek integration through the reproduction of cultural particularities or through adoption of new religious referents.

Notably, each of these strategies has allowed the immigrants to take active part in the religious realm of California and to establish new ties with the destination society, whether through participation in daily observance, organization of special celebrations, or membership in new denominations.

Civic and Community Practices

As described in the chapter on social integration, Zacatecans, Oaxacans, and Veracruzans all participate significantly in clubs or associations of fellow immigrants, whether these are demarcated by locality, region, or state. Such associations are at the center of a great number of activities that we will call civic practices, which are parallel to the artistic and religious activities already discussed. Beyond their importance to the process of social integration and in the building of transnational ties, they are also part of the recomposition of identity referents, and in a broader sense, of cultural integration.

While the most visible contribution of these activities to immigrants' lives may be the reproduction of intra-community social networks, they have also helped create spaces of interaction in which the immigrants participate as California residents. That is, alongside the nostalgic evocation of the sending communities, these are spaces of socialization where the members of these associations must exercise their organizational capacities within the institutional framework of California, and where their identities of origin are complemented by a sense of belonging to the city where they live now. In this sense, on the basis of their experience in the receiving society, they differentiate themselves from those who remain in the land of their birth. Quite visible examples of this process are the parades held on Mexican patriotic holidays such as September 16 or May 5. Making these celebrations a success requires a wide network of relationships involving members of the community of origin by way of their clubs, the Mexican consulates, and local and state authorities from whom the necessary permissions to occupy public space must be secured.

Within the framework of organizing and carrying out such parades, groups from many different Mexican regions and groups of other nationalities converge, making this an important social arena for the exchange of experiences relative to the immigrants' negotiation of their own space within US society.

This interchange has important implications. For instance, we can observe how the Veracruzans have achieved a significant level of organization in spite of their recent arrival. The speed with which the Veracruzans have been able to create a variety of clubs and a federation[30] is linked, doubtless, to their previous organizational experience, but also to their rapid learning about how US society functions, derived in part from their interaction with other immigrants' associations. Domingo Martínez, president of the Fundación Yanga, recalls that "thanks to these contacts, information was shared about current consular programs, mechanisms to arrange participation in civic parades with the local authorities." At the time of that interview, the Fundación Yanga and the Casa Guanajuato were sharing office space and exploring the possibility of undertaking joint educational projects.

Thus, the realm of civic activities generates intense interaction of both intra- and inter-community sorts, while demanding the use of California public space for promotion of the immigrants' specific cultural practices. That is, these activities are congruent with the integration strategy that departs from classic assimilationism to seek incorporation into the receiving society not through dissolution of difference but through negotiating the inclusion of immigrant particularities within the broader society.

The range of such civic practices is not limited to parades. Among the three groups under study, those who best exemplify the importance and diversity of such activities in cultural integration are the Zacatecans. Those who have settled in the United States have successfully built a complex organizational framework including clubs, federations of clubs, and a confederation. Through this structure, alongside activities that revitalize identity ties to localities of origin and participation in the above-mentioned parades, Zacatecan immigrants carry out activities as diverse as the Miss Zacatecas contest, the organization of concerts in California with performances by the Zacatecas Symphony Orchestra, and the granting of scholarships to young Zacatecan students. All told, these activities allow the participants to strengthen their ties with the society of California, build or strengthen their life projects in that place, and simultaneously assert their particular cultural heritage.

LIFE PROJECTS

The third and last indicator we examine here is the construction of life projects. Probably this is the indicator that best reflects the degree of incorporation into the receiving society. On the one hand, life projects synthesize the complex of cultural models that determine the expectations, longings, and desires of Mexican immigrants. To what extent are these longings constructed through the internalization of cultural patterns of the host society or, on the contrary, are they constructed according to the cultural logic of the sending communities? On the other hand, plans for the future also correspond to senses of belonging. To what extent do individuals feel that the Los Angeles region is the place where they want to—and are able to—build their lives and the lives of their children? Or, on the contrary, to what extent do they see their stay in metropolitan Los Angeles as a stage in life, but not where they desire to—or are able to—construct their futures?

Our findings in this area are quite revealing. Most of our interviewees consider their future to be in Los Angeles and are not thinking of returning to Mexico on a permanent basis. This indicates a very significant shift in the immigration pattern from Mexico to the United States, in which the return to Mexico was an important aspiration among Mexican immigrants after a lifetime work in the United States. In our study, approximately one-third notes they would like to go back but do not have any concrete plan to do so, nor any tentative date. This is particularly the case for those who think their work life will unfold in the United States but imagine returning after retirement.

Of the ninety interviewees, seven see their stay in Los Angeles as more or less a means to the purpose of returning home, as a necessary phase in building a life project in Mexico. One such case is Miguel, from Veracruz, who is saving money to set up a restaurant in his hometown, where he plans to go in the near future. However, with the exception of a few cases like this, where a return is projected for the near future, the others, even if they have well-defined plans, expect their realization to take a number of years more.

The motives cited for remaining permanently in the United States range from access to medical services to their US-born children's difficulty in adapting to the place of origin, educational opportunities in the United States for their children, the availability and comfort of services in California, or simply that "you get used to it; now we're from here" (Artemio, Oaxaca), "now my life has gotten to be here and going back would be like starting over again" (Caterina, Veracruz)," or, "you get used to it, your family grows, and it's hard to say, 'I'm leaving'" (Cecilio, Zacatecas). Another important reason for staying permanently in Los Angeles is the economic crisis in Mexico. As Zaira from Veracruz comments, "I don't feel capable of returning to my country now; how would I find a job? If I couldn't find one when I was younger, even less so now with the crisis—there's no work there at all."

Similarly, the perception of a generalized increase in violence in Mexico is given as a reason for canceling the idea of a permanent return, and even for postponing plans for a temporary visit. According to Leandro, "Zacatecas is such a pretty and peaceful city, but because of the infamous Zetas cartel it has started to come apart." Maritere from Veracruz notes, "Personally, I'd like to go back to Mexico because that's my tradition—the folklore, the food, the desserts—but the truth is, I wouldn't go back now, because there's so much violence in Mexico, a lot of kidnappings; it's frightening to me."

Thus the violence leads to modified plans. Valente from Veracruz points out, "I had some plans to go back but now that I've just been there, I went two weeks ago, you don't want to anymore! There's so much violence." Similarly German from Zacatecas comments, "I'm not going back to Jerez anymore, not now anyway, because we used to hear about the narco wars, but we always thought that was in Sinaloa and Ciudad Juárez, but now the *narcos* are right there in Jerez with their machine guns and all."

Another recurrent element is expectations for the lives of the next generation. First, there is a widespread belief that children will have a better future in the United States. Second, those interviewees who have young children or teenagers frequently state that the children would not accept the idea of going back. Therefore, the idea of returning is canceled or postponed more or less indefinitely, put off until some more remote future after the children have become independent.

Finally, another revealing finding is the proportion of those who have constructed life projects in the United States even among undocumented interviewees, even though the interviews were conducted during a time of intensified deportation from the interior of the United States. Carmen and Jaime, undocumented parents of US-born children, say they are tired of living under the threat of expulsion. For Carmen, the idea of being detained during school hours and not being able to pick up her children is a recurrent nightmare, but she nevertheless repeats her desire to stay in California. Victoria, an immigrant from Veracruz, comments, "Unless they actually throw me out, but otherwise, if I have the chance to stay here and bring up my daughters here, that's what I'll do."

This contrast between a significant internalization of the norms and values of US society and the impossibility of political integration (stemming from the absence of ways to regularize immigration status) are a source of constant frustration and anxiety. Without a doubt, this represents the principal obstacle to full cultural integration.

FINAL CONSIDERATIONS

Cultural integration to Metropolitan Los Angeles is marked by the important presence of Hispanic or Latino culture, both demographic and historical. This presence is made up of at least three elements: the Spanish colonial past, Mexican American culture as represented primarily by the Chicano movement, and recent increased immigration from Latin America, predominantly from Mexico, and with a growing regional diversity.

The growing visibility of this Mexican presence, however, has not brought about its repositioning as a hegemonic culture or as an important component of the dominant one. "The Hispanic" today is a visible but segregated component within a diverse cultural universe. As a result, although the size of the Hispanic presence in the region facilitates the process of adaptation for newly arrived immigrants, in the long run it also has negative implications for this process because it reduces oppor-

tunities for interaction with the non-Hispanic population, thus reproducing the pattern of segmented integration.

In spite of exhausting workdays, the immigrants take an active part
in artistic, religious, and civic associations, centered mostly though not
exclusively around the cultural referents of the places of origin, thus
helping to reinforce transnational linkages. Empirical observation confirms that most artistic, cultural, and religious activities adapt to the
ethnic segregation of the Los Angeles region and reproduce it through
the pursuit of recognition of the immigrants' own cultural referents—
dance, music, religious worship—within a diverse cultural field. This
constitutes a differentialist integration strategy that makes use of specific cultural referents in negotiating inclusion in a heterogeneous society. In turn, this suggests that the maintenance of transnational ties with
sending communities is not an obstacle but rather a resource, employed
in the process of negotiating space in a segmented cultural sphere.

The interviewees left no doubt that they participate actively in the
cultural life of the city, making use of its spaces to do so—whether
parks in which to hold picnics and gatherings, sports fields to organize
various kinds of competitions, auditoriums and other spaces for rehearsals of traditional dances, Catholic churches for worship and festivals,
streets and avenues for religious processions and civic parades, and plazas for outdoor concerts and dance classes, as well as venues for the
organization of *jaripeos, coleaderos,* and other rodeo events. To achieve
all this, they avail themselves of intermediary groups (clubs, artistic
groupings, civic associations) that reproduce the structure of cultural
segmentation characteristic of the region.

Thus, cultural integration is marked by the bidirectionality of the
processes of incorporation, in which the immigrants develop strategies
that fit within the social structure they find upon arrival. In this sense,
in order to integrate Mexican immigrants, the Los Angeles society
transforms them into Hispanics, defining a designated geographic and
symbolic space. For their part, the Mexican immigrants internalize the
principles, norms, and values of the receiving society, including the
incorporation of ethnic and cultural fragmentation. As a result, Mexican immigrants become Hispanics, and from within that category they
seek to re-negotiate their identity and cultural borders through the
assertion of specific practices.

In this way, and in spite of some significant exceptions, their integration is deep but occurs fundamentally within the sphere of "Hispanic"
culture. An expression of the solidity of their integration process can be

found in the construction of life projects, in which the immigrants clearly demonstrate that metropolitan Los Angeles is the place they call home, where they plan to continue their lives and construct a future for their children. The return to Mexico is not considered as a viable option in light of the rampant violence and deep economic crisis.

Finally, the exceptional examples of a few trajectories that tend toward exiting from a segregated ethnic condition—joining "white" churches, relocating out of Hispanic neighborhoods—also makes them examples of the difficulty of pursuing paths that the receiving society does not open for immigrants. In other words, the integration strategies of Mexican immigrants seeking full integration into the receiving society come into tension with the barriers that limit integration, erected by a society that remains culturally fragmented.

CHAPTER 7

Political Integration

From Life in the Margins to the Pursuit of Recognition

Political integration in destination societies is a facet of immigrant integration that has gained greater visibility in recent years. This attention stems from large-scale processes that unfolded in the second half of the twentieth century. Widespread population mobility has brought new challenges that confront the national states from which migrants come, through which they pass, and in which they arrive, including the definition of their political status. At the center of these processes and redefinitions is the concept of citizenship. This concept in turn implies the establishment of criteria for membership in a national community, along with the corresponding access to rights or lack of such access. The increased movements and presence of immigrants have led to reexamination of old relationships among national states, populations, and territories, requiring states to question their relations and responses to population mobility.

In societies such as the United States that receive the largest numbers of immigrants, the issue of political integration arises in the context of immigration processes that differ from those of earlier periods. In contrast to the integration of European immigrants at the beginning of the twentieth century, the great waves from Asia and Latin America in the later part of that century brought the presence of a vast population with differentiated levels of integration within US society, but without access to citizenship and thus without the power to influence the political community of their new environment. As some analysts have pointed out,[1] the restrictions with respect to this access are largely the result of US immigration policies, which center on border enforcement rather than integration. As synthesized by Nathan Glazer,[2] these restrictions and omissions in public policy have led to a situation in which "the settlement, adaptation, and progress, or lack of it, of immigrants is largely, in the US context, up to them, the immigrants themselves."

In general terms, what we mean by political integration is obtaining access to spaces and processes of influence and decision making within the political community of the nation in which immigrants have arrived. In practical terms, what we must do is to examine the achievements of immigrants in terms of citizenship. Full citizenship includes acquisition of legal citizenship, or naturalization, which depends largely on the regulations established by receiving nations. It also includes, though, what has been called substantive citizenship,[3] which implies participation in the political life of destination societies ranging from keeping informed about political events to seeking to exercise rights and participate at various levels. Thus, this second dimension refers to the strategies employed by immigrants themselves to achieve such participation, which we have considered crucial to examine among our interviewees.

In the case of Mexican immigrants in the United States, as was pointed out in chapter 1, levels of naturalization remained low for much of the twentieth century but showed an important increase toward its end. As documented by the historical research of Manuel Gamio,[4] the first decades of that century saw very low levels of naturalization. This resulted from the marked racialization of Mexicans as a social group on the part of the dominant society of the day, and the stigma attached to Mexico at that time. Yet by the end of the 1990s, Mexicans accounted for 20 percent of the naturalized immigrant population. This change resulted from a combination of factors. First, Mexican immigrants were the main beneficiaries of the amnesty included in the 1986 Immigration Reform and Control Act (IRCA), which was the first step toward naturalization over the decade that followed. The later enactment of the Illegal Immigration Reform and Immigrant Responsibility Act (IIRIRA) in 1996, with its heightened criminalization of undocumented immigrants in the United States and its limiting of access to social services even for legal permanent residents, served to consolidate the rising rate of naturalization among Mexicans. Second, in the 1990s the Mexican government adopted a more proactive role with respect to Mexican communities in the United States by offering irrevocable dual nationality, thus making it easier for immigrants from Mexico to naturalize without ceasing to be Mexican citizens (so-called dual citizenship). Third, in the face of the anti-immigrant climate in states such as California, with Proposition 187 in 1994, a growing mobilization on the part of the Mexican immigrant population itself translated into greater electoral participation and therefore decisive influence in the electoral geography of several states.[5]

However, in spite of all this, the rate of naturalization of Mexicans remains low as compared to that of other immigrant groups. As we documented in chapter 3, American Community Survey figures show that in the Los Angeles region, slightly more than 70 percent of Mexican immigrants lack US citizenship, in contrast to approximately 36 percent of immigrants coming from Europe and Asia.

Clearly, these figures on formal citizenship among the immigrant population in the United States illustrate not only vulnerability but also limited access to various benefits. This situation is further complicated by the limitations of integration policies in the United States. As Fix, Laglagaron, et al. and Fix, McHugh, et al.[6] observe, the low levels of citizenship among Latino immigrants can be attributed in part to such requisites as a minimum five-year waiting period after obtaining legal permanent residence before being able to apply for citizenship (three years in the case of spouses of US citizens); the high monetary costs of the application process; and the requirement of high English proficiency in a population whose incomes, years of schooling, and English competence are limited.

Nonetheless, the restrictions on formal citizenship do not mean that Mexican immigrants remain on the margins of US political life. Our goal in this chapter is to show the varying perceptions and practices of the ninety Mexican immigrant interviewees in regard to their citizenship status and their political participation in the Los Angeles region. We will discuss four key dimensions that reveal the perceptions and practices among our interviewees as related to the process of political integration: the naturalization process, the political perception of Mexico and the United States, participation in political actions in the United States, and electoral participation. We will also examine the role of two additional processes that may influence the political integration of Mexican immigrants in the Los Angeles region: transnational ties and participation in intermediary groups.

ACCESS TO CITIZENSHIP AS AN INTEGRATION STRATEGY

As we pointed out in our chapter on social integration, legal immigration status is a central factor in the process of immigrants' integration.

Still, as we have stressed previously, a central problem confronted by Mexican immigrants in the Los Angeles region is that a considerable proportion of them is undocumented in comparison to other immigrant groups. This greatly affects their access to many rights, including the considerable difficulty of obtaining legal immigration status. In the case of our interviewees, just under a third (twenty-eight cases out of ninety) has such status. Most of these individuals come from the state of Veracruz, meaning that they arrived in recent years and in more difficult conditions than their predecessors from other states. To these twenty-eight undocumented interviewees can be added the twenty who have legal permanent residence, making a total of forty-eight interviewees who do not have US citizenship as compared to forty-two who do.

As we observed in chapter 5, most of the undocumented interviewees arrived in the Los Angeles region more than ten years ago, have children, have established strong ties with their communities, and show marked expectations of settling permanently in the region. This is directly related to the process of political integration in that practically all of our interviewees are informed about developments in the political life of the United States and specifically California and Los Angeles, and in that they express some type of position in response, whether in terms of political opinions or through their participation in specific actions. For example, a recurrent theme in the opinions of the interviewees was the initiative to promote a new amnesty for the undocumented immigrant population in the United States, and in particular (given that the interviews were conducted in 2008) the expectation that such a reform could occur with Barack Obama's election as president.

The eventual acquisition of legal permanent residence and citizenship in the United States is perceived among the interviewees in a variety of ways—with indifference, resignation, pragmatism, or conviction—depending on what arrangements they have already been able to make to maintain their situation in the country. For example, Abundio, from Veracruz, came to California without documents in 1987 and, like many of his compatriots, has been working in low-skill jobs that have not required him to worry very much about his immigration status: "At least in my case, I'm OK, I'm fine. I've spent more than half my life here. I came at sixteen and now I'm thirty-seven. Now I'm used to things; I mean, I don't have papers but I make out OK." For another immigrant from the same state, access to documented status has not been a priority because he has always been able to work using false documents, largely because of the type of jobs he's been able to get in that situation: "We've always worked with fake papers, that's the reality—that's how things go."

However, in other cases, lack of access to permanent residence or US citizenship is seen as a serious impediment to fully integrating in the United States. For instance, a couple from Oaxaca whose life project includes buying a house to consolidate their settling in the United States have run into the impossibility of getting mortgage credit because of their undocumented status. Even for those who have begun the application to obtain legal permanent residence, the slow pace of that process is a serious obstacle. Gerardo, from Oaxaca, expects the legal process of becoming a legal permanent resident to take a number of years, during which he will not be able to leave the United States: "Because if I do that, then I'll lose what I'm trying to get, but a time comes when you just get mad, so much time not seeing my mother, my brother, because of waiting for the papers. I'm tired of that, and I'm thinking of everything I need to do back in my town."

Yet other interviewees stress the advantages of success in getting full US citizenship. An interviewee from Zacatecas reports that naturalization provided him with access to more and better credit: "If you're just an immigrant, they won't give you much credit; you're way down on their list, but for a citizen it's different—they do give you preference." To achieve this result, the strength of family networks is sometimes decisive, and it can speed up the application process involved in getting legal residence and eventual naturalization. For example, an immigrant from Oaxaca explains how he acquired his status this way:

> I got my legal permanent residence through my wife. She was illegal too when she first got here, but her father was a legal resident, here in California, and he saw there was a program that let you apply for your children, and it worked. In 1992 her father put in the application, and they accepted her, and in '95 she got her work permit, which she used for about three years, and then in 2001 she got residency and waited the five years you have to wait to become a citizen. Once she did that, she applied for me . . . and six months later I got the interview and thank God now I'm a legal resident.

In other cases, some of our interviewees reported that their main motive in becoming naturalized is to exercise their political rights in the United States. Ramiro, from Zacatecas, comments, "Yes, I got to be a citizen in '96 or '97, before all this revolution [the mass demonstrations of 2006 demanding immigration reform in the United States]; I got to be a citizen because I wanted to vote." In other cases, it is more a matter of accepting that fully exercising one's citizenship is a part of being firmly settled in the country.

Equally, access to US citizenship opens the possibility of getting the new status of dual nationality and so achieving a fuller sense of belonging in both countries. As a Zacatecan immigrant puts it, "We got the chance to have dual citizenship, so now we're free to be there in Mexico without feeling that we don't belong there; they gave us this and we also got it for our children, so I think we can be on either side now without any problem."

In sum, our interviewees present different stances with respect to naturalization, depending on their immigration status and their perceptions of that status—stances that run the gamut from indifference and resignation for the undocumented to more pragmatic visions for those who have achieved a change. Similarly, there are those who show more conviction about exercising their new US citizenship, whether as a sign of their incorporation into the United States or as a way of making use of political rights through the ballot box.

POLITICAL PERCEPTIONS OF THE UNITED STATES

As we saw in the first chapter, an important step in any assessment of immigrant integration is to examine perceptions of politics and political processes, because this reveals the sense of membership in the political community of the new society. In general, the Mexican immigrants we interviewed have, at least, basic knowledge about political developments in both the United States and Mexico. In the case of the United States, this can be perhaps explained by the fact that our interviews, carried out in the second half of 2008, coincided with the presidential campaign culminating in the November victory of Barack Obama. As a result, there was abundant information in circulation about US politics. Some interviewees stress the differences between the Democratic and Republican parties, particularly in relation to the immigrant population. Some feel that neither the Democratic nor the Republican politicians are a good option, but the majority do have a preferred political party. The interviews show notable sympathy for the Democrats, whom some interviewees consider more "tolerant" of immigrants, while others additionally express rejection of Republicans for being "racist." Mauricio comments:

> Republicans are always attacking us; they're the ones proposing laws that go against us, the immigrants, and they're the ones who always make war when they come into power, who plunge the country into crisis . . . Because of all this, I would never vote for the Republicans, even if they put forward a Latino candidate.

Besides the Republican position with respect to the immigrant population, the US war against Iraq is cited as an additional reason for rejecting the policies of the Republican Party when it was in power. As one interviewee puts it, "I think the Americans don't want to continue the doctrine of [then-president George W.] Bush. Look at what he's spending on the war—millions and millions of dollars a month—while the economy here is suffering." Indeed, an additional constant in the interviews is criticism of former president Bush's performance, and several respondents mention that it is time for a change in party and government so that things can improve. Petra, a Veracruzan immigrant, comments:

> The Republicans' time is up, the people want change and the war is the result of the economic situation, really the result of voting for Republicans for eight years, and it's incredible that a single man [Bush] could put the country in the spot it's in now, that a man with such a selfish way of thinking should have put such a great country in this situation. There needs to be a change, and although maybe a lot of people think Obama is not the best, still he's going to bring a change. I don't know what change he's going to bring, but at least we'll change parties; that will be interesting.

The above opinions exhibit a generalized knowledge of US politics among the majority of our interviewees, as well as their electoral preferences based especially on three issues: the treatment of the immigrant population, the country's economic situation, and the war in Iraq. Although such widespread knowledge can be explained in part by the abundance of information circulating during the presidential campaign, the retrospective visions expressed by a good many of the interviewees extend back several years, showing that they not only are aware of political developments in the United States, and in California and Los Angeles specifically, but also have a history of taking of positions on these political matters, rather than one of rejection or indifference toward political life.

PARTICIPATION IN POLITICAL ACTION

Between March and May of 2006, demonstrators in many US cities marched to demand immigration policy reform. As some analysts have reported,[7] the largest of these marches took place on May 1. In Los Angeles, many thousands of immigrants from Mexico and other countries took part in that mobilization, making the march in that city the largest in the country. In their research on the twenty largest marches, these analysts[8] estimate the size of the Los Angeles action at between 650,000 and 700,000 participants. Although the purpose of the marches was to demand a reform that would benefit the millions of undocumented immigrants living in the United States, the demonstrations were truly multinational and multiethnic. Participants included immigrants from many nations who already had legal permanent residence, as well as US citizens of many origins (especially but not only Latin American), who joined the action in solidarity with their compatriots, relatives, and friends.

The participation of immigrants in these marches, as revealed in the testimonies of our interviewees, can be classified into three categories according to the groups with whom they attended the demonstration: those who went with their families, those who went as members of community organizations, and those who went as associates of broader organizations. As an example of the first category, we can cite the experience of Mari Luz, from Veracruz:

> We went to the first one, in March—my husband, my children, my brother-in-law, and his wife. My brother-in-law is a citizen but he went too and we heard on the radio that there were so many people they had to get there on foot because the buses were all full, and the march filled three different streets, and I had such a great feeling! My son said, "We're going down in history now!"

Baltazar, another Veracruzan immigrant participating with his family, says: "A bunch of us went and I remember how I made some T-shirts with messages in Zapotec, and people took pictures of us; there were about five or six of us who marched. We all had on these white T-shirts, and people took photos, they interviewed us. We still have photos of my daughters marching." These two cases are similar to those of many of Mexican immigrants who have been living in Los Angeles ten or more years, whose children were born there but who are still undocumented. Despite their status, they found in these mobilizations an ideal means through which to take a public position.

In the next category are cases like that of Efrén, from Oaxaca, who describes his participation as a member of the Organización para la Ayuda a Macuiltianguis (OPAM): "We went to the marches with OPAM, both the early ones and also on May Day." As described above, OPAM is an organization made up of immigrants from the community of Macuiltianguis, Oaxaca, with a primary goal of cultural preservation.

Those in the third category, that of allying with other pro-immigrant organizations to participate in the marches, are Zacatecan interviewees. This can be explained to some degree by their longer history of immigration and organization, which has allowed them to establish linkages with a variety of organizations that fight for immigrant rights. Martina points to the alliance between the Federación de Clubes Zacatecanos del Sur de California and other organizations taking part in the marches:

> The march needed to be something big, something overwhelming, so we wouldn't be afraid to go out there. Here in Los Angeles we started to organize along with different federations, churches, unions, community organizations. For our base of operations we used the Placita Olvera [Olvera Street, the restored downtown historical center of Mexican Los Angeles]; that's where we organized from, and more than eighty-five organizations of immigrants from different parts of Latin America took part.

In this wave of demonstrations, immigrants with legal permanent residency or US citizenship joined the thousands of activists and the undocumented who were marching for immigration reform. Among our interviewees, the need to stand in solidarity with compatriots to fight for their rights motivated legal immigrants like Astrid, from Veracruz:

> Yes, we went, and my daughter—the one who has her doctorate—she made T-shirts, she made them for all of us because everyone likes to be part of things, and we got lots of photos taken of us because of her T-shirt, where she put a logo that said, "Immigrant's daughter educating future leaders," and this really caught the attention of the media because she was already teaching classes at the university. We all participated, even my son-in-law from El Salvador.

In fact, we found cases of documented immigrants who stayed out of work in order to support the actions, as is reported by Roberto, from Oaxaca: "I didn't go to the march, but I didn't go to work either because we had said that everyone needs to support each other. We used to be illegal ourselves, and in our own family we've got people who don't have papers and who want to have them, so that they're not out there struggling to get a driver's license, or insurance." Like Roberto, others also point out that although they did not go to the Los Angeles march, they did support it by staying out of work that day, even if that meant they would receive several days of temporary layoff for having missed a day at their jobs.

The fact that a large proportion of our interviewees played some part in these mobilizations clearly shows one form of their participation in Los Angeles political life. This is significant because for a number of the interviewees it was the first time they had decided to take part in any demonstration of this sort, and they justified their actions in terms of their desire to be part of the mass demand for US immigration reform—

a demand that has resonance among immigrants with varying immigration statuses—and to make their position evident through open and public participation. Thus, even though that wave of demonstrations constituted an unusual rather than a typical event in the US political arena, in terms of integration we can conclude that the strategies employed by our interviewees, regardless of their immigration status, reveal not only opinions and knowledge within the political dimension, but also the will to participate in actions as one more way to express their sense of being individuals with "substantive citizenship," of being included in the political community.

ELECTORAL PARTICIPATION

Electoral participation is another of the activities through which immigrants intervene in Los Angeles political life, denoting evident integration into the social and political life of the region, although of course the right to vote can be exercised only by those who have US citizenship. Among our interviewees who do have citizenship, a significant share participated in elections before 2008, while for others 2008 represented their first voting experience.

Throughout the interviews, these Mexican immigrants express interest in participating in the election of officials in the Los Angeles region. For instance, Marcia, from Zacatecas, reports having been a legal permanent resident for many years before deciding to acquire US citizenship, which for her meant access to elections: "Finally, when I got to the end of the process of becoming a citizen, they gave me a paper about elections, and I've been voting ever since." Some responses show internalization of the sense of voting as a mechanism for citizens to elect officials who will fulfill their expectations. Mauricio, from Oaxaca, remarks that for him the acquisition of US citizenship implies the civic duty to vote: "Yes, definitely I vote, even in the local council elections I always participate, I take time out, I go and vote, and I feel I've fulfilled a duty that I have, you know?" A similar commentary is offered by another interviewee from Veracruz: "I believe in elections, I'm a firm believer in voting, and that's how I've taught my family and they all vote. Even the youngest, when he turned eighteen, I said, 'Now it's your turn, you go, and register, and vote, do it for me.'" This last opinion is particularly suggestive since the interviewee himself is undocumented; he demonstrates clear civic convictions even though he does not have access to formal mechanisms of political integration such as the right to vote.

The elections of 2008 constituted a historic event in US political life, since for the first time a citizen of African American origin, representing the Democratic Party, won the presidency. Given the political climate in the city of Los Angeles during and after the election, we learned a good deal about the opinions of the Mexican immigrants we consulted. Some were interviewed before the elections and others after, but all except one openly expressed their inclination toward Obama. Esteban, from Oaxaca and by that time a US citizen, recounts how his sympathies have always tended toward the Democrats, for whose candidates he has voted since acquiring citizenship in the mid-1990s: "I'm a Democrat," he says. "I'd like to see Obama be president of the United States, and I'm going to vote for him." Undocumented interviewees also express preference for the Democratic Party and its candidate. As Victoria, a Veracruzan immigrant, puts it: "If I had to choose one party or the other, I'd say the Democrats, because the Republican Party is more conservative and as immigrants we have more problems with them." The interview results show that the preference for Obama stems not only from his being a Democrat, but also from his African American origins. Israel, from Oaxaca, expresses this perspective:

> He's a Democrat and we have confidence in the Democrats. Clinton did good work in his two terms. With Clinton the economy was good, he directed our attention toward domestic politics, whereas if we were to vote for the Republicans we'd be following along the road taken by Bush, which brought us practically to bankruptcy. Look at the economic problems right now; if he hadn't taken us to war in Iraq, most likely the economy would be different. Obama's father is an immigrant so he understands, and being of the black race, too, it's a real advantage to have someone who understands us better. But, of course, it doesn't just depend on him, but anyway we'll support him because we need a change.

Once again, these responses reflect the issues repeatedly brought up by interviewees (the war in Iraq, the recent economic recession in the United States, the increasing anti-immigrant policies) and associated expectations of positive change with the election of Barack Obama. They reveal a variety of forms of political integration, ranging from mastery of information about political life in the US society to clear political preferences to direct participation in political mobilization—all this regardless of citizenship status.

TRANSNATIONALISM AND POLITICAL INTEGRATION

Another recurrent topic in the interviews is Mexico, about which these immigrants express both knowledge and opinions. Although many of the interviewees have been in the United States a long time, are clearly settled there, and have future life projects that involve staying there (as described in the chapters on social and cultural integration), this does not necessarily mean they are detached from Mexican political life. While the majority report that they do not participate in Mexican elections, they also say they are informed about political developments in Mexico. They report several channels that provide a constant flow of information that allows them to stay abreast of Mexican political realities: mass media, telephone conversations with people in their places of origin, and growing internet use.

The interviewees' perception of Mexican politics is generally negative, associated with corruption, violence, poverty, and incapacity to govern—regardless of political party. A very significant indicator is that none of the ninety interviews contains a single positive opinion about Mexican politics. A Oaxacan interviewee puts it this way:

> The PRI [Partido Revolucionario Institucional, or Institutional Revolutionary Party] governed us seventy-some years; it was always a corrupt party, and inside the PRI they were even having assassinations, one against another, and this led to a different, more conservative party taking office, which was just a continuation, just power changing hands, and we can't expect anything from the PAN [Partido Acción Nacional, or National Action Party]. The PRD [Partido de la Revolución Democrática, or Democratic Revolution Party] has had a lot of internal struggles lately; it's going through a breakdown, but it's another party that does the same thing in some places, falls into corruption. It has some good people, but not all of them are good.

This opinion reflects a series of negative perceptions constantly expressed by the immigrants from all three states, illustrating the deep lack of confidence in Mexican politics that, in general terms, prevails among them.

Corruption, particularly, appears over and over in the interviews as a constant in Mexican political life at all levels of government. An interviewee from Oaxaca describes it this way:

> I think we really need very drastic changes in Mexico. I think we're continuing with the same pattern of corruption we have; the Mexican mentality needs to change, to say "enough!" about these abuses that are so common. Above all, believe me, when you go to request any document, in the tiniest office, you still need to give them a tip so they can buy their sodas or whatever, and we have to change this idea, because pretty much the mentality is

that the first time you go, they won't give you the document—you have to bring them something and then they'll be very happy to take care of you. So I think we ourselves are feeding this corruption; it's gotten inside our minds.

One last but extremely important issue in Mexican politics that surfaces in the interviews is the growing level of violence in Mexico. This refers in particular to murder, extortion, and kidnapping—increasing in recent years—for which the government is seen as responsible. A Zacatecan immigrant says:

There's a very touchy situation in Zacatecas, which is that nobody feels safe; they get kidnapped and what worries me is that everybody is going around armed now. The peasants are arming themselves for defense against those guys, because the government isn't defending them. So, why would I want to go there? Instead of me going there, I'm thinking of bringing my family here; I'm going to do that.

Practically all the interviewees demonstrate awareness of both the violence prevailing in Mexico as a whole and the ways this violence has penetrated their specific sending communities. The preceding statement is consistent with the formulation of life projects to be carried out in the United States, as discussed in our chapter on cultural integration, and the elaboration of strategies to achieve these goals. That tendency in turn accompanies a disapproval of government and politics in Mexico and an explicit fear of returning to live or even visit there. Ramón, from Oaxaca, says there was a time when his life project included possibly returning to Mexico at some point, but now he has changed his mind: "Things in Mexico are so ugly now, so it's hard for me to, I mean—to go live in Mexico? I don't think so."

The growing climate of violence in Mexico and the ingrained and traditional corruption are prevailing characterizations of Mexican politics among the interviewees. Thus their perception of the political dimension of Mexico is not only negative but also involves serious distrust. While some interviewees display a degree of preference for one or another of the three major parties (the PRI, the PAN, and the PRD), they believe that the Mexican political system needs to be restructured before they would consider participating in it.

Nonetheless, the issue of political participation is not exempt from the transnational relationships created by immigrants themselves, which opens the possibility of their having a political presence on one side or the other of the border, or both. There are well-known cases of Zacatecan immigrants, for instance, participating in politics in their states of origin in Mexico, which, once again, is perhaps attributable to their longer immigration history. An emblematic case is that of Andrés Bermúdez, better known as the Tomato King, a Zacatecan immigrant from the town of Jerez who ran for mayor in that town's local elections after a long and successful period as an immigrant in the United States. His example has been followed by other immigrants as they aspire to political office in their hometowns. This kind of participation has been examined in detail by some analysts, as well as the impact it could have in transforming the Mexican political arena.[9] Such links between immigrants to the United States and local governments in Mexico have been forged largely around immigrant associations' sending of resources or collective remittances to their communities of origin for use in projects of social benefit. These projects allow immigrants and local authorities to exchange ideas and work together, and at the same time they built or consolidate relationships between immigrants and local politicians. Although the immigrant associations declare themselves apolitical in formal terms, the growing weight of the resources they send for local development has won them important access to politicians in their states in Mexico.

Thus, the gradual consolidation of ties between immigrant associations and local or state governments in Mexico, and the associated economic power of the immigrants, has allowed them to deepen their influence on the politics of their communities of origin. Even in the cases of Oaxaca and Veracruz, US immigrants are organized into associations or clubs, send collective remittances, and participate in programs of cooperation with the Mexican government, such as Three for One (Tres por Uno), so they too are able to establish ties with authorities at different levels of government.

Among our interviewees, some do not see any problem with transnational or translocal political participation, in the sense of living in the United States while aspiring to political office in Mexican states of origin. Others, however, are skeptical and critical, because they see such inclinations as better directed toward political integration in the destination country. Rosendo, a Zacatecan immigrant, puts it this way:

> I don't live there, and I can't make decisions for those who do, but I'm against having emigrants who become legislators or local board members because, I mean, what could I know about the needs of those who are living there, maybe they need just the same as me, but we came to make our life here in the United States and we have to respect this place. There are comrades in the Federación Zacatecana who are there—there's one who wants to become a legislator in Mexico. Others who want to be municipal presidents

in Mexico, while they don't even know who their representative in the US might be. What I tell them is, let's educate ourselves here first.

This opinion reflects what we pointed out earlier: the fact that there has been an increasing inclination among Mexican immigrants to participate in the political sphere and that in most cases this takes the form of gradual reorientation toward the politics of Los Angeles rather than Mexico.

What we want to emphasize now through these cases, however, is the existence of differentiated strategies for political participation. Although we have often pointed to immigration history as the main factor explaining the reorientation toward US politics, the specific US context has also been important. The national debate on the immigration issue and the enormous wave of demonstrations throughout the United States in March to May of 2006 (with Los Angeles being the scene of the largest one) has been the main catalyst motivating such participation. In fact, practically all of our interviewees were aware of the Los Angeles marches at the time, and a third of them (thirty-one cases) took direct part. So a convergence of elements has generated life projects that mostly produce actions in the United States.

In the case of Oaxacan immigrants, one element related to political participation in their communities in Mexico is the traditional system of local posts or responsibilities. In many Oaxacan communities, citizen obligations include fulfilling both civic and religious responsibilities in order to maintain rights (especially, access to communal means of production, along with rights to political participation) and thus maintain status as a citizen. Some of the Oaxacan immigrants in Los Angeles report that this system formerly was more rigid, to the point where even for those living outside the community, the local authorities pressured them to return to fulfill obligations even if that meant giving up their jobs in the United States and moving back, generally with the whole family. However, over time there have been some changes, so that now the immigrants who are summoned to fulfill an obligation have other options to avoid losing their community rights.[10]

In the case of the Veracruzan federation and associations in Los Angeles, there is no clear presence in the political arena of the state of Veracruz or its local communities, probably because these groups are still relatively new. According to our interviewees, there is some recognition of the immigrant associations on the part of the Veracruzan state government, partly for past philanthropic work in their hometowns or elsewhere in Mexico. For example, the Fundación Yanga has donated toys to children in Tijuana, Baja California, but especially because some of the associations have participated in Tres por Uno, the government program designed for emigrants, which has allowed them to establish ties to local and state authorities.

In sum, although transnational participation in political affairs ranges from communication to more direct participation, the information we have gathered shows that our interviewees are more active electorally in the United States than they were in Mexico. Only nineteen of the ninety interviewees say they voted in Mexico before emigrating, either because they left before reaching voting age or for lack of interest. Others express interest in participating in Mexican elections, but argue that they cannot do it because they do not have voting credentials and, if they have tried to obtain them, they have not been able to supply or meet all the requirements. Some express complete rejection of voting in Mexico because of the reigning corruption in the politics of their communities of origin. This seems to reflect an antipolitical position in response to perceived Mexican realities, rather than an apolitical one.

In 2006, as a result of the previous changes in the Mexican Constitution, emigrants were offered the right to vote from abroad in Mexican presidential elections.[11] Despite expectations that emigrants would display significant interest, in fact very few voted. Only five of our interviewees did so, and they voted in the border region. Esteban, from Oaxaca, states his position categorically: "I like to vote, I went to Tijuana to vote; I voted for López Obrador of the Partido de la Revolución Democrática. Here in Los Angeles I had my sister and my sister-in-law, and I said, 'I want to go vote in Tijuana,'—that's where I got my voting card—and we went and voted."

However, not all interviewees who voted express the same enthusiasm. Unlike Esteban, who is convinced of the importance of voting in Mexico, a Oaxacan immigrant couple who voted from Los Angeles expressed doubts about the procedure: "We voted from the United States, by mail, because they set up stands where they handed out the applications, but we still didn't trust the process very much." Among those who did not participate, reactions range from complaints about not getting the necessary information on time to characterizations of the offer as one more form of corruption. David, from Veracruz, notes, "I wanted to do it [vote in the Mexican presidential election], but they kind of played a trick on me because really they didn't inform the community very well, so we didn't know what we had to do here to vote." More emphatically, Clara, who is a US citizen and votes in the United

States, explains, "I didn't vote, not me, because they just do what they want, regardless of anything else, they do what they want to do. Do I have a desire to vote in Mexico? Since I started to see what dirty corruption there is, I don't vote anymore." Clara's opinion reflects that of a number of our interviewees, who say they have lost confidence in Mexican politics and, although they exercise their right to vote in the United States, they do not do so in Mexico.

These opinions once again reflect the existence of differentiated strategies of political participation, but within a prevalence of life projects oriented toward becoming more firmly established in the United States. Another stated reason for not voting from abroad is that Mexican politicians are to blame for the migration to the United States in the first place. Edgardo, from Veracruz, expresses this view:

> I didn't care about voting. I don't know whether I've got the wrong idea, but the reason we're here on this side of the border is the fault of Mexican politics; it's because of those politicians that we're over here, and yet they keep pressing us to vote in Mexico, which seems illogical to me, right? So it really doesn't interest me.

All of this evidence suggests that in spite of the existence of forms of transnational political participation that run the gamut from staying informed to taking positions in both the places of origin and those of arrival, such participation by Mexican immigrants is more prevalent in the United States than in Mexico. Some analysts have argued that the very low participation rate by US immigrants in the Mexican presidential elections of 2006 can be explained by misinformation and the complexity of the voting process (see the account by Rivera-Salgado[12]). The interviewees' comments also reflect different strategies of political participation. Still, their responses clearly show marked interest in involving themselves in political life in the United States. This involvement in turn means that whether through becoming more knowledgeable, through taking political positions, through voting, or through joining demonstrations in public space, the Los Angeles immigrants in our study have shown an inclination to incorporate themselves into political life, which, as we have pointed out above, is not restricted to those possessing formal citizenship.

ASSOCIATIVE FORMS AND POLITICAL INTEGRATION

In addition to any other participation or electoral preferences, practically all the interviewees judge it important to affect US politics by demanding respect for their rights as immigrants. In this area, the role played by the immigrants' own organizational forms as vehicles to facilitate and promote such participation stands out. These associations have traditionally been oriented toward promoting the welfare of Mexican sending communities or preserving their cultures in the United States, which makes them apolitical in fact and in law. That is the case of those registered with the Internal Revenue Service as 501[c][3] nonprofit organizations, which are distinct from political groups. Yet changes in the context of the United States seem to push them in the direction of becoming platforms for political participation at some level.[13]

The Zacatecan immigrant clubs have gradually taken on greater roles in the civic and political life of Los Angeles, including actively adding their voices to the demand for immigration reform in the United States. This has led them to participate not only in the marches held toward that end but also in public forums where they express their disagreement with the US government's policies toward immigrants. The account by Martina from Zacatecas is illustrative:

> The good thing about the Federación [of Zacatecan clubs in Los Angeles] is that it has led to our knowing the different leaders on a world level, and it all began with the idea of going to Washington and having a press conference where we told President Bush, "This is not what we want, this is not what the migrants want," and we mobilized quite quickly at the national level.

Martina's account shows once again how much Mexican immigrant associations have learned about exercising pressure and influence within the US political system, and it suggests the work of socialization and teaching that the Federación Zacatecana de Los Ángeles has taken on with respect to other groups of immigrants. Mexican immigrant groups' playing a more proactive political role in Los Angeles or the United States is consistent with what some analysts[14] have concluded about the changing behavior of these organizations: after being centered mostly around events in their Mexican hometowns, these groups are reorienting their agendas and actions toward the United States.

FINAL CONSIDERATIONS

The ninety Mexican immigrants we interviewed have indeed participated in the political life of Los Angeles, although at varying levels. Those who are US citizens—that is, are part of a political community—have access to electing the officials who govern them. However, as we have seen, legal permanent residents and the undocumented are present in political mobilizations and are in touch with what is going on in political life in both the United States and Mexico. In spite of many being long established in the United States, they have not completely detached from Mexican politics. There have been some cases of transnational political participation on the part of immigrants who decide to participate in electoral contests in their places of origin, which demonstrates the use of differentiated strategies for political participation. However, our interviewees offer a very negative vision of Mexican politics, which they consistently associate with corruption, violence, and poverty.

Nonetheless, in terms of political integration, the point to underline is the gradual shift of the interviewees' political participation toward the United States. In explaining this trend, although we must consider settlement in the United States and the concomitant changes in immigration status as important, the growing negative political climate in the United States with respect to the immigration debate is also a fundamental factor.

This chapter has centered on documenting and examining the diverse strategies that the immigrants we interviewed employ to participate, at different levels, in the political system of the United States, and with it their achievements in political integration (or, as we have put it earlier, immigrants' integration "into" the society). But another important element that must be examined in order to understand this political integration is action at the governmental level to promote it (that is, immigrants' integration "by" the society). In practical terms, this means examining not only the relation of immigrants to politics, but also the government policies that exist to further this process.

As we stated in the first chapter, United States policies to further immigrants' integration are quite limited, as has been discussed by several analysts.[15] Such policies would include promoting integration in overall terms, but would above all involve awarding effective citizenship. Similarly, some analysts who have evaluated the process of immigrants' integration in the Los Angeles region[16] stress the importance of a context and an institutional framework in societies of arrival that would promote such integration. We will take up this issue in chapter 8, which discusses public polices that influence the integration process of immigrant communities in the Los Angeles region.

PART THREE

Government Intervention and the Immigrant Population

Public Policies and Mexican Immigrant Integration in the City and County of Los Angeles

To complement the discussion of a number of issues raised in the ethnographic section of this book, this chapter will describe the public policies affecting the integration of Mexican immigrants in the Los Angeles region. This review of public policies will highlight the importance—for achievement of greater or lesser integration—of initiatives by political actors in the region. As we have argued, analysis of immigrant integration involves understanding immigrants' perceptions and actions in relation to the economic, social, political, and cultural life of the receiving society, but also requires examining the actions of various levels of government to promote or restrict such integration. In the specific case of the Los Angeles region, the main entities we will examine, which are fundamental to such initiatives, are the Los Angeles city council and Los Angeles county government.

Unlike in previous chapters, the perspective of this chapter is time-specific to 2008, when the ethnographic research was carried out. It is based on extensive documentation and analysis of proposed or enacted legislation as well as academic and journalistic reports about the impacts of those laws on the immigrant population. The reports available on the internet were consulted between September and December of 2009.

One premise orienting our analysis is that the US debate over immigration is not limited to the federal government. Immigration, on the contrary, is a topic of growing importance in state legislatures, county governments, and city councils.[1] According to a recent report from the

TABLE 17 LAWS AFFECTING THE IMMIGRANT POPULATION PASSED BY US STATE LEGISLATURES, 2008 AND 2009

Main subject matter	Number of laws passed, 2008	Number of laws passed, 2009
Education	12	27
Employment	19	21
Health	11	28
Human trafficking	5	16
Driver's licenses, identification documents, and other licenses	32	46
Law enforcement	12	16
Legal services	2	—
Multiple-issue measures	39	49
Public benefits	9	15
Elections	1	4
Total laws	142	222
Resolutions	64	131
Total laws and resolutions	206	353
Vetoes	3	20
Total enacted	203	333

SOURCE: National Conference of State Legislatures, "State Laws Related to Immigration and Immigrants."

National Conference of State Legislatures,[2] as of November of 2009 these legislatures had adopted, in that single year, 222 laws and 131 resolutions in forty-eight states related to immigrants in general and undocumented immigrants in particular, for a total of 353 laws and resolutions. In the same year, a total of 1,500 proposed laws were considered in the legislatures of the fifty US states. Classified by content areas, the legislatures passed forty-six laws related to identification cards and driver's licenses, twenty-eight to do with access to the healthcare system, and twenty-seven dealing with education, as is shown in table 17.

Clearly, this does not mean that the federal government has disappeared from the immigration arena. There are currently important public policy initiatives being discussed at the national level that will have an impact on the lives of immigrants, including the debate on immigration reform and the health-care system. Nationally, at the level of state legislatures, the anti-immigrant movement has not gained much ground because it is only the more conservative legislatures, such as that of Arizona, that have passed punitive laws. In the states where most undocumented immigrants are concentrated (California, New York, Illinois, Texas, and Florida), no important anti-immigrant laws were passed.[3]

Given that Los Angeles has more Mexican immigrants than any other city in the United States, and given that the city has generated a considerable number of Latino political leaders (most of them of Mexican origin) who can now be found in key positions within the local power structure, a more positive climate for advancing public policies that effectively contribute to the full integration of immigrants is to be expected.

In general terms, public policies are laws and regulations enacted by the government within a given community, behind which lies a complex process of interactions among many actors with different degrees of power. As Schneider and Ingram[4] point out, "Policies are revealed through texts, practices, symbols, and discourses that define and deliver values including goods and services as well as regulations, income, status, and other positively or negatively valued attributes." This implies that to understand the process of creating public policies related to the Mexican immigrant population in Los Angeles, we must locate that phenomenon in the context of the debate about immigration policy in the United States. This, in turn, implies an examination of how the images of the immigrants themselves have been socially constructed as a part of this debate.

In that regard, Schneider and Ingram assume that policy makers make strategic decisions to socially construct or develop a particular public image of the population that will receive the benefits or experience the limitations that policies establish. They argue:

> The social construction of target populations refers to the cultural characterizations or popular images of the persons or groups whose behavior and well-being are affected by public policy . . . [This] theory contends that the social construction of target populations has a powerful influence on public officials and shapes both the policy agenda and the actual design of policy.[5]

Thus, the social construction of the target population by the politicians in office has a notable influence on the way the public in general perceives particular policies. This helps us to understand why, in recent years, the debate on immigration in the United States (and thus the debate on the possibilities of integrating immigrants, at least in the case of Mexicans) has taken place in such a polarized way, because the image of the immigrant population in the public arena has clearly been a negative one. As we shall see below, the policy makers are the principal agents in the construction of the public image of the immigrant population, toward the end of influencing the public perception of any social problem that justifies government action.

The polarization around the topic of immigrants in the United States results from several factors, among which are serious reservations that have been raised about whether undocumented immigrants should be present and what their characteristics are—especially in the case of Mexican immigrants. Attacks on the presence and character of that population have been carried out in many public forums and have succeeded in creating widespread rejection. As a result, rational discussion of the immigrant population in general, and that of undocumented immigrants in particular, has become very difficult.

Although this quality of the public debate on immigration in the United States stems from diverse factors, mass media representations have been an important contributor to the negative perception. Clear examples are the television commentators who have adopted a decidedly anti-immigrant position in recent years (the most evident cases being Lou Dobbs and Glenn Beck of CNN[6] and Bill O'Reilly of Fox News), whose presence in the mass media has given them great influence over US public opinion. A report by Media Matters Action Network[7] found that their programs disseminated feelings of hatred and resentment against undocumented immigrants. Of these commentators, Dobbs[8] was clearly most obsessed with this topic; the study found that, during 2007, 70 percent of his programs contained such feelings. The program The O'Reilly Factor was next, with 56 percent of its content dedicated to this subject, while Glenn Beck devoted 28 percent, though with some of the most incendiary statements.

Another illustration of the increasingly negative public perception of immigrants is the sizable growth of extremist groups in the United States. According to the Southern Poverty Law Center, the number of Patriot Movement affiliates grew from 602 in 2000 to 926 in 2008.[9] Such "second wave" racist groups, as the study calls them, are distinguished by their paramilitary nature and their aggressive public tactics, such as the Minutemen American Defense's patrols on the Mexican border and their public meetings. Another example of this new patriotic-paramilitary tendency is the Oath Keepers, whose members swear to obey the Constitution of the United States, not the political authorities. The members of this organization are primarily ex-soldiers or ex-police. The election of the first black president in US history and the massive immigration from Latin America have served as justifications for the exacerbated racist positions of these organizations' activists. Though they constitute a minority in social terms, they do influence public perceptions and policies on the immigration issue.

Finally, there has been an increase in the persecution of undocumented immigrants by US authorities. Homeland Security raids on workplaces continued after the election of Barack Obama in 2008, and that department likewise sought to expand programs of cooperation between federal agencies and local police departments aimed at identifying, arresting, and deporting noncitizens who become involved in the judicial system. Other government policies include the strategy of intensified patrolling of the Mexican border and expanding the border wall, in spite of the evidence that this strategy is not working and carries a high human cost.[10]

It is not surprising that the spread of all these elements has created a dangerous atmosphere for immigrants in the United States, especially for Mexicans. This political context of the social construction of immigrants, especially the undocumented, frames the debate about immigration policies in the Los Angeles region. We will go on to survey the public policies recently implemented in the city and county of Los Angeles with respect to the immigrant population.

GOVERNMENT STRUCTURE IN THE LOS ANGELES AREA

Los Angeles County is the largest county in the United States in terms of both population and budget. On January 1, 2009, the county population totaled 10,393,185 inhabitants—more than those that reside in the majority of the states of the union. Within Los Angeles County lie eighty-eight cities, including the city of Los Angeles itself, each with its own local government. In one way or another, all these cities sign contracts with the county to provide municipal services.[11]

For fiscal year 2009–2010, the county budget was $23.6 billion. In terms of funding sources, 22 percent comes from the state of California, 22 percent from the federal government, 20 percent from local property taxes, and 36 percent from other sources. In terms of expenditures, the largest share, 27 percent, goes to pay for public safety services, while 26 percent is directed to public health services and 25 percent to social services.

The voters of the county elect the five members of the L.A. County Board of Supervisors, which is to say that each supervisor represents slightly more than two million people. The board operates in legislative, executive, and quasi-judicial capacities. Regulations affecting the population of the entire county must be ratified by the governments of the various cities within its jurisdiction. As an executive body, the board determines the policies of all county departments and instructs them as to how to implement and interpret both state and federal laws. As a judicial body, it is the maximum authority for the whole process of urban and regional planning, and it carries out public hearings about many related issues.

Los Angeles County is in charge of providing many services that affect the lives of all its residents. Among the services it is required to provide are public safety, property valuation, tax collection, public health services, public social services, and support of the indigent. Other specialized services are flood control, water conservation, parks and recreation, and cultural activities. This is, in principle, the government structure encountered by residents of the region and the one that develops and carries out public policies affecting immigrants' integration. In the following pages, we will examine the policies of immigration and public safety, public health and welfare, jobs and immigration, education, and identification cards in the city and the county of Los Angeles, and the possible implications for immigrants in the integration process.

IMMIGRATION AND PUBLIC SAFETY POLICIES

One of the main public policy areas directly impacting immigrants in Los Angeles County is the justice system. Once immigrants enter into it, especially the penal system, the effects of county policies related to immigration increases exponentially. The county liaises with the Department of Homeland Security and specifically with its Immigration and Customs Enforcement division, better known as ICE, by means of three programs of strategic cooperation. The first is the Secure Communities Program. Under this program, ICE tries to identify unauthorized immigrants once they are in jails and prisons, and then deports them to their countries of origin. The second functions in the Mira Loma Detention Center, a county penal facility devoted specifically to detention of undocumented immigrants awaiting either deportation or a hearing before an immigration judge. The third operates by way of a Memorandum of Understanding with ICE to implement a program referred to as 287(g), which involves the questioning and detention of undocumented immigrants in the county jails. Section 287(g), of the Illegal Immigration Reform and Immigrant Responsibility Act (IIRIRA) of 1996, made it possible for ICE to establish accords with state, county, and city police agencies, in which officers are trained to enforce federal immigration law.

Currently, in Los Angeles County the detention, interrogation, and deportation of undocumented immigrants is governed by the 287(g) program.[12] This program is essentially an agreement between local police departments and ICE under which the police may carry out certain tasks that previously were exclusive to federal immigration agents. According to an ICE report, 287(g) agreements currently govern cooperation between ICE and sixty-seven US police departments. In the period 2006–2008, seventy-four thousand undocumented immigrants were deported through this program.[13]

In February 2005, Los Angeles County became the first entity in the state of California to sign a Memorandum of Understanding with ICE to implement the 287(g) program. By 2008, there were similar agreements in place between ICE and the neighboring counties of Riverside, Orange, and San Bernardino, though the agreements vary in terms of what specific prerogatives the county accepts. For the Los Angeles County Sheriff's Department, 287(g) means that some of its officers must be trained to question immigrants detained in county jails as to their immigration status, evaluate the evidence that justifies eventual deportation, administer oaths, take legal depositions, and prepare the paperwork that will bring the detainees before immigration officials.

Critics of the 287(g) program argue that as public policy, it suffers from two serious defects. First, several well-known organizations, such as the Coalition for Humane Immigrant Rights of Los Angeles (CHIRLA), charge that the officers working in the program routinely send undocumented immigrants to ICE for violations of the law. Thus the immigrant population in general, and especially the undocumented, live with the constant fear of being deported for any minor infraction they might commit, which in turn creates an atmosphere in which this population is very unlikely to collaborate with the sheriff's department in the work of reporting crimes or of promoting a social environment that would favor integration. Second, pro-immigrant organizations criticize the program because it does not guarantee immigrants any legal representation. Once detained, undocumented immigrants do not have any secure access to that right, and the great majority does not have sufficient means to hire an attorney to represent them before the immigration authorities. This is especially problematic for those who may have legitimate grounds for political asylum or other legal bases for remaining in the United States.[14]

However, a significant number of cities within Los Angeles County have not signed 287(g) agreements with ICE. The city of Los Angeles, in fact, has internal regulations that prohibit its police department from enforcing immigration laws in an excessive manner. Special Order 40 prohibits the Los Angeles Police Department (LAPD) from carrying out actions for the purpose of investigating an individual's immigration status.[15] This policy was adopted in 1979 to send a clear signal to the immigrant population of the city that the police did not represent the federal immigration service (then known as the INS) and that police officers would not question or arrest anyone on the mere suspicion of being an undocumented immigrant.

Still, this order does not bar the police department from collaborating with immigration authorities. The LAPD can send undocumented immigrants before ICE and carry out joint operations with that agency. Indeed, when Los Angeles police process immigrants in municipal detention centers, they ask the detained person's country of birth, and that information can be used by other authorities, such as the sheriff's department, which under program 287(g) carries out more intensive interrogations about immigration law violations.

Nonetheless, according to a statement issued by CHIRLA, Special Order 40 has clear positive effects. CHIRLA argues that the resident immigrant population in the city of Los Angeles has less fear of cooperation with the local police and has more effective communication with them because the immigrants are less anxious about being arrested and deported if they enter into any kind of contact with the police. This is the philosophy behind the so-called community policing strategy implemented by the LAPD. Another positive effect is to encourage immigrants who have been victims of a crime to report this to the police. Thus, Order 40 does, in principle, promote a more favorable context for possible integration of the immigrants along various dimensions by facilitating communication between immigrants and the police department and assuring some attention to their rights.

For example, according to Gail Pendleton of the American Bar Association Commission on Domestic Violence, immigrant victims of domestic violence who live in the city of Los Angeles, in particular, benefit from Special Order 40 because when police enforce immigration laws, undocumented female immigrants who have been victims of domestic violence—even in cases where they have been severely hurt—refuse to seek police help for fear that either they or the person who has committed the abuse will be deported.[16]

In sum, according to CHIRLA, Special Order 40 has three positive impacts. First, the immigrant community sees a clear separation between the responsibilities of the local police and the actions of immigration agents. Second, the order respects and strengthens the equal protection clause of the Fourteenth Amendment, which establishes that state and local government must apply the laws in an equal and just way for every inhabitant. And third, it contributes to reducing the discriminatory police practice of racial profiling, in this case detaining someone simply for looking like their image of an undocumented immigrant.[17]

PUBLIC HEALTH AND WELFARE POLICIES

The budget crisis that first hit in the state of California during the 1990s has had a direct effect on the social services Los Angeles County can provide to its immigrant population. For example, in March of 2009 then-governor Arnold Schwarzenegger eliminated the budget item for the Cash Assistance Program for Immigrants (CAPI), which provided economic aid to more than ten thousand legal immigrant seniors who were ineligible for Social Security or other financial assistance programs because federal regulations had severely cut back on immigrants' access to these programs, even for legal residents.[18] Blind immigrants or those over the age of sixty-five had been potentially eligible for CAPI, whose benefits were comparable to the average of $700 to $900 a month that other seniors receive from the Supplemental Security Income and State Supplementary Payment programs, better known as SSI/SSP.[19] The requirements for eligibility for that program and others managed by Los Angeles County—such as access to public health services and economic aid—are very strict; officials demand identification, valid Social Security numbers, verification of legal immigration status, and verification of age.

By contrast, a social welfare program with positive impact on immigrants is the Program against Hate Crimes, administered by the Human Relations Commission. Under California law, hate crime charges can be pressed when there is evidence of prejudice as a substantial factor in the commission of a crime based on the victim's real or perceived identity in terms of race, ethnicity, religion, national origin, disability, gender, or sexual orientation.[20] Through this program, Los Angeles County funds organizations that document and report hate crimes, and those that educate victims in their communities who have suffered from this kind of crimes. The program has been of special importance for the Mexican immigrant community in the county because several immigrant rights defense groups participate in the network of organizations that monitor and report such crimes.[21]

According to data on hate crimes in Los Angeles County, in 2008 there were 729 documented cases, a slight drop from the 763 in 2007. Of these totals, in 2008 eighty-three hate crimes were committed against Mexican residents, while in 2007 that figure was seventy-one.[22] The motivations for the great majority of cases documented during 2008 were race, ethnicity, and nation of origin of the victims (452), compared to 535 in 2007.[23]

JOBS AND IMMIGRATION POLICIES

E-Verify Program

As part of the growing cooperation between federal and local authorities with respect to the enforcement of immigration law, Los Angeles County has explored joining the E-Verify system, which is administered by the Department of Homeland Security. E-Verify is an internet-based system that allows employers to confirm whether or not an individual's immigration status allows him or her to work legally in the United States by inputting the information reported on the I-9 Employment Eligibility Verification form that all employees must sign and employers must archive. For most employers, the use of E-Verify is optional, and it is used only to determine the eligibility of new hires.[24]

In June 2008, then-president Bush signed an executive order instructing all companies with federal government contracts to use E-Verify. Until this expansion, the program had been used only by federal agencies for their own hires. According to official data from the Department of Homeland Security, more than 175,000 employers participated in the program nationwide, making more than 8.5 million verifications in fiscal 2009.[25] Immigrants' rights organizations have strongly criticized E-Verify, arguing that the databases used (from the Social Security Administration and the Citizenship and Immigration Services) have wide margins of error. Workers whose verification comes out negative must undertake a tortuous process to correct any erroneous information that renders them ineligible to work legally in the United States.[26]

In an effort to expand this program, the Department of Homeland Security has tried to persuade state and local governments to participate and to issue orders requiring more employers to do so. For example, the state of Arizona has made the use of E-Verify obligatory (the only such

state-level requirement in the country). Although in California participation is completely voluntary, in August 2009 the Board of Supervisors of Los Angeles County voted to explore the possibility of requiring
companies with county contracts to participate. Later the city of Lancaster, in the northern part of the county, passed an ordinance requiring
all businesses operating within the city limits to use E-Verify to check on
the immigration status and work eligibility of all new hires.[27]

Lancaster's then-mayor R. Rex Parris, explaining about the motives
for adopting this municipal ordinance, commented that "we're trying
to guarantee that the available jobs in our city go to citizens who are
dedicated workers and respect the law." In the context of the recent
economic crisis, unemployment in that city had reached a rate of 17
percent. Remarks like Parris's offer evidence of the negative social construction of undocumented immigrants, presenting them as undesira-
bles who do not deserve the right to a job while US citizens and legal
immigrants are suffering high levels of joblessness. The manner in which
this anti-immigrant discourse functions in the United States has been
widely studied. It seeks to blame the undocumented immigrant population for the great majority of social and economic ills, especially in
states with a high proportion of immigrants, such as California.[28] Not
only are immigrants in general and undocumented Mexican immigrants
in particular accused of causing high unemployment in cities like Lancaster, but they are also blamed for the California state budget crisis, as
then-governor Schwarzenegger did in a statement on the CNN television network.[29]

The social construction of a potential target population for public
policy benefits is related to the prevalence of a positive or negative
image in public opinion and political discourse, with political authorities being those who finally decide the nature of the policy. While immigration law belongs to the federal domain, debates about implementation occur at the local level, which is also where immigrants become
integrated or not. Municipal and county authorities debate what policies should be implemented based on the assumed negative or positive
impact of immigrants on the local economy and society.

Immigrants and Informal Employment in Los Angeles

For many years, Mexican immigrants in Los Angeles have had recourse
to street vending. Among their major activities are food sales. Street

vendors are part of a larger informal but regulated labor market that also includes day laborers, gardeners, car washers, taco makers, housekeepers, and cooks and nannies. The concentration of undocumented Mexican immigrants in this sector stems from multiple reasons, including lack of immigration documents for formal work, low educational levels, work skills that are not transferable to the Los Angeles labor market, low levels of English proficiency, and an over-concentration of immigrant social networks in the informal sector.

There is widespread evidence of the growth of this informal sector in the city and county of Los Angeles. As we pointed out in chapter 4, and as is supported by a report issued by the Los Angeles Economic Roundtable, many poor residents of the city and county, including US citizens, join the informal sector out of desperation after being unable to find formal work.[30] The report finds that the group with greatest difficulty getting work in the formal sector is recently arrived migrants. In 2004 there were an estimated 679,000 informal workers in L.A. County on any given day, representing 15 percent of the county's total labor force of nearly 4.5 million. In the city of Los Angeles, informal sector workers represent 16 percent (289,700) of a labor force of 1.8 million workers.[31]

The majority of workers in this informal sector are undocumented Mexican immigrants. Out of nearly a million undocumented workers in Los Angeles County, nearly 60 percent were born in Mexico.[32] The main sectors that hire them are construction, restaurant and food services, car washing, gardening and landscaping, self-storage warehousing, garment making, and families employing domestic workers. These sectors not only represent the least desirable jobs in terms of pay and working conditions, but also the most dangerous. According to a federal report,[33] Mexican immigrant workers suffer 70 percent of all work-related deaths among Latino workers in the United States. Of those deaths, 34 percent occur in the construction industry. Between 1992 and 2006, the report states, 11,303 Latinos died at work, of whom 95 percent were male.

Both the city and county of Los Angeles have tried to regulate street vendors more strictly, especially food vendors, a sector that in this region is dominated almost completely by Mexican immigrants. At the municipal level, since early 2007, the LAPD has boosted its patrols and its enforcement of ordinances against street vendors in the central areas of the city, which previously had received very little attention. That initiative forms part of a broader strategy to reduce crime around these marginal areas as part of the process of urban revitalization taking place there. One result is that vendors of hotdogs, tacos, fruit, ice cream, and corn who have concentrated for more than a decade in adjoining zones with considerable foot traffic such as the Fashion District and MacArthur Park have become the object of fines, arrests, and even confiscation of their carts and merchandise. As one vendor told a *Los Angeles Times* reporter, "When downtown was ugly, they didn't say anything. Now that it's pretty, they want to get rid of the hotdog vendors."[34]

From the perspective of the police and the local authorities who launched the Safer City Initiative in late 2006, the goal was to maintain order and create a law-abiding environment that was apparently lacking in the past. The initiative added fifty police to patrol in the area. For the immigrants who continue to sell food, these measures impose new requirements such as a business license and a certificate from the city public health department. Thus, immigrants working as vendors are collateral victims of the Safer City Initiative and its attempt to control the population of poor people who concentrate in a marginal area.[35]

At the county level, another new ordinance focuses specifically on regulating taco trucks. The Board of Supervisors in April 2008 approved an ordinance that made it a misdemeanor to park a taco truck in an unincorporated area for more than an hour. Unincorporated areas are those outside city boundaries, in which county rather than city authorities are responsible for basic safety and health services. This ordinance provoked a variety of reactions. In May 2008, a vendors' support group was formed and launched a website (www.saveourtacotrucks.org) to publicize the vendors' problems. This organizing effort, which was started by the lunch vendors of Anaheim when they won the court case *Barajas v. City of Anaheim* in 1993, led to the formation in mid-2008 of a group of taco truck workers and owners called the Asociación de Loncheros Familias Unidas de California (www.loncheros.com). These two groups waged a legal battle against the county regulation and later against another similar one that had already existed at the municipal level but began to be more tightly enforced toward the end of 2008. In August of 2008, a county superior court judge overruled the county ordinance as being unconstitutionally vague.[36] The Asociación de Loncheros also won a similar suit against the city of Los Angeles when another superior court judge overruled a 2006 city council order barring taco trucks from parking for more than an hour in a commercial area or for more than half an hour in a residential zone.[37]

Day Laborers, or "Esquineros"

A national study of day laborers[38] estimates that there are about two hundred thousand such workers in the United States, with a high concentration in the city of Los Angeles, where some twenty-five thousand immigrant workers resort to this type of work. It is worth noting that none of our ninety interviewees are day laborers. The same study estimates that 56 percent of all Los Angeles day laborers are Mexican immigrants, most of them undocumented, and that more than half complain that they do not receive minimum wage and/or are not offered any water or food while carrying out their work.[39] These workers gather in certain points of the city seeking jobs for the day. The gathering points are established informally or formally in front of large construction material chain stores (such as Home Depot and Orchard Supply) and have been the target of a variety of city government regulations.

On August 14, 2008, the Los Angeles City Council approved a municipal regulation requiring construction and home improvement material retailers who want to open new stores or expand existing ones to meet certain requirements to guarantee safety and order among the day laborers gathering there.[40] This regulation was framed with Home Depot in mind because the chain operated eleven stores in Los Angeles and planned to open a dozen more in the region over the coming years. The regulation requires such establishments to provide an area with shade, potable water, bathrooms, and garbage cans for the use of the day laborers. Passage of the measure was a clear victory for organizations defending immigrants; such a regulation had been under discussion for three years and had provoked strong opposition not only from Home Depot executives but also from anti-immigrant groups like the Minutemen, who argued that it was an illegal regulation because it promoted and facilitated undocumented immigrants' entry into Los Angeles.[41]

Car Wash Workers

Some of the most grueling and lowest-paid jobs in the informal sector are those in car washes. These are deemed part of the informal sector because of the general irregularity of this industry and its high level of exploitation. According to the Community Labor Environment Action Network (CLEAN), in 2007 there were between seven and ten thousand workers in this sector in the Los Angeles region, almost 92 percent of them immigrants, of whom almost a third were undocumented.[42] In fact, several of our interviewees work in this sector. On the basis of a 2000 survey conducted by the US census, Nazario and Smith[43] estimate that more than 90 percent of car wash workers in Los Angeles County are not US citizens and a third are undocumented. If Mexicans form the largest immigrant group in Los Angeles County (almost 43 percent in 2007) and represent 57 percent of all undocumented immigrants in the Los Angeles region,[44] we can assume that the great majority of car wash workers are from Mexico.

Car washing businesses reported $251 million in revenues in Los Angeles County in 2002, which means that each such establishment reported an average gross income of $1 million. For the entire state of California that total was $872 million, which means that nearly a third of all revenue came from Los Angeles County.[45] Among the most common documented labor law violations in this industry are work schedules that sometimes exceed ten hours a day, six days a week, without including any overtime pay; pay rates below minimum wage, including establishments that pay in tips only, sometimes totaling as little as $30 or $40 a day, likewise below the state minimum; and damage to workers' health through constant exposure to water and chemical products without adequate protective equipment, with workers reporting kidney and respiratory problems due to prolonged contact with those chemicals.[46]

Labor laws are generally not seen as connected to the immigration laws that permit or impede immigrants' incorporation into US society. In the case of regulation of commercial auto washing, however, enforcement of labor law represents the enforcement of immigration policy in an indirect way, for the notable impact it can have on the life and welfare of immigrant workers. The same is true for other sectors with a high concentration of immigrant workers, such as street vending, domestic work, gardening, building cleaning, and hotel work.

An example of how labor policy directly impacts the welfare of immigrants is the Car Wash Worker Law that was originally enacted by the California legislature in 2003. This law requires all commercial car washes to register annually with the California State Labor Commission. The registration process is supposed to improve these establishments' compliance with local and state labor regulations. Though passed in 2003, the law did not go into effect until 2005, when the Industrial Relations Department published internal regulations for its implementation.[47] Due in large measure to pressure from a grassroots workers' group organized by the Steelworkers Union, that law was modified by the passage of Assembly Bill 236, known as the Car Wash

Worker Law, signed by then-governor Arnold Schwarzenegger in October 2009. This modification extended the law through 2014 and continued the registration requirement for all car washes, but it added a provision that allows the state to deny registration to establishments that have violated the law in the past. Another innovation obligates owners to post wage insurance bonds and to contribute to a car wash workers' restitution fund.[48]

Despite the existence of this law, there is evidence that many car washes in Los Angeles are still not fully complying with all its requirements. For example, a *Los Angeles Times* article of March 2008 reports that inspections by the California Labor Department found violations of one or more legal requirements by 60 percent of the car washes inspected, while the remaining 40 percent were unregistered—and the department itself had only a dozen inspectors supervising car washes for the entire state of California.[49] Still, implementation of the Car Wash Worker law has generated $10.6 million in fines for labor law violations, including $5.9 million from unregistered car washes.[50]

Farm and Domestic Workers

Some labor laws and regulations, in their application to specific sectors of the labor market, have a notable impact on the Mexican immigrant population not only in the Los Angeles region but throughout California. Such is the case for the laws that regulate domestic work (housecleaning, care of children and the elderly in the home, etc.) and agricultural work. As many of our interviewees have pointed out, these are the types of jobs that have served as their entry points into the metropolitan Los Angeles economy.

A key element to bear in mind is that workers in both of these sectors were excluded from the most important turning point in the history of US labor law, the New Deal reforms spearheaded by Franklin Roosevelt in the late 1930s. One of the most important pieces of legislation was the Fair Labor Standards Act (FLSA) of 1938, which established a minimum wage that applied throughout the nation. It also contained specific rules about overtime pay for certain jobs. Due to pressure from conservative Democratic representatives and senators from the southern United States, however, Roosevelt decided to exclude domestic workers and farmworkers—who at the time were mostly African American—from coverage by this law. The effect on these workers was devastating; they did not benefit from the growing waves of unionization, wage increases, and improved working conditions that occurred in industries such as steel, automobiles, and mining as a result of the New Deal.

It was not until 1966, after farmworker leader César Chávez began his struggle in support of agricultural workers, that some of them won protection under the FLSA. The 1975 California Agricultural Relations Act granted agricultural workers not only better regulation of working conditions but finally, for the first time, the right to organize. However, this has not been the case for domestic workers, including many of our female interviewees. So far, federal labor laws like the National Labor Relations Act, the FLSA, and the Occupational Safety and Health Act do not provide protection for domestic workers. Although it is true that in practice immigrant women who work in domestic service in one or more family homes have some legal recourse under the FSLA, this is not the case for those who work as nannies in informal arrangements, those who care for the elderly (and are considered "companions"), or those who live in their employers' houses.[51]

Thus domestic workers remain in a very vulnerable situation. Still, thanks to increasing organized strength, they have sought to bring about changes in the labor laws. One victory was the passage by the California state assembly and senate, in 2006, of the California Domestic Workers' Bill of Rights; however, the bill was vetoed by then-governor Arnold Schwarzenegger. This initiative, which was reintroduced in the legislature in 2010, would provide some basic rights to domestic workers such as overtime pay, annual cost-of-living wage increases, one day of vacation per week, and pay for sick days, holidays, and vacations. It would also require advance notice of layoff or firing and a right to corresponding compensation.[52]

Regulations against Wage Theft

The city of Los Angeles has stood out in recent years for its growing commitment to use new municipal ordinances to try to improve the working conditions of immigrants in low-income occupations. To combat the prevalent practice of employer wage theft—that is, leaving workers unpaid or only partially paid for a day's work—Los Angeles has committed to passing a municipal ordinance against such theft.[53]

A study of labor conditions in the low-wage sectors of the three most important cities in the United States (New York, Chicago, and Los Angeles) found that 26 percent of these workers are paid less than minimum wage and 76 percent do not get overtime pay. The same study shows that 70 percent of those who work "off the clock" outside their regular shifts do not receive any compensation, and 12 percent of workers who receive tips report that their employer retains part of that money.[54]

However, in spite of the enormous evidence about labor law violations affecting immigrant workers in Los Angeles and local politicians' growing interest in legislation to attack this problem, public opinion in general does not appear to support these types of local laws.[55]

EDUCATION POLICY AND THE IMMIGRANT POPULATION

There are two major areas of education policy that affect the immigrant population in the Los Angeles region—policies that affect immigrants' children's access to Los Angeles public schools and those related to the use of English as the official language and to learning and teaching English as a second language. The basic right of access to the educational system for immigrants and the way this education is imparted are very controversial political topics. In California these issues are discussed and contested in election campaigns, the mass media, and even the courts.

A federal government policy directed explicitly to integration of immigrant communities in the United States is the promotion of English as a Second Language. Such programs are generically known as ESL (English as a Second Language) or ESOL (English for Speakers of Other Languages), and are under the US Department of Education's Office of Vocational and Adult Education (OVAE). In the states where it operates, OVAE offers the necessary resources to develop educational systems, including training, technical assistance, and materials. As evidence of the need for this policy, supporters cite federal agency reports[56] detailing the increase in demand for language-learning services.

In practice, it is the states that have taken more initiative in promoting the teaching of English, with or without federal funding, with the goal of promoting the integration of immigrants through language learning. In California, the federal program funds classes in about four hundred community colleges throughout the state, thirty of them in the city of Los Angeles, offering various educational options for adults, in addition to English, either free or at very low cost.[57]

However, in California the debate on access to education for immigrants entered a new phase in 1994, when the electorate approved Proposition 187 (known on the ballot as Save Our State) by a margin of 59%

of the votes. The explicit goal of the ballot measure was to eliminate undocumented immigrants' access to health and education services supported by public funds. It also required school officials (such as teachers and principal), the staff of public health clinics (doctors and nurses), and other public servants (such as local police) to verify the immigration status of children and their parents before providing any public services.[58]

Although this measure was overruled by both federal and state courts, the court battle dragged on for five years and ended only with the election of a new, Democratic governor, Gray Davis, and the Democratic Party taking control of the state assembly. This, along with the state and federal courts having decided that regulation of immigration should be the responsibility of the federal government alone, allowed the parties to settle the long suit. But two events signaled the emergence of a new series of regulations and laws that, although less ambitious than Proposition 187, negatively affected immigrants in California.

At the federal level, the Clinton administration promoted two federal initiatives that made immigrants more vulnerable. In 1996, Clinton signed the Personal Responsibility and Work Opportunity Reconciliation Act, which restricts certain immigrants' eligibility for federal, state, and local benefits and services. In the same year Clinton signed the Illegal Immigration Reform and Immigration Responsibility Act (IIRIRA), which categorically bars undocumented immigrants from receiving financial benefits underwritten by federal funds.[59]

At the state level, Proposition 187 proved to be the forerunner of other similar initiatives in California and elsewhere. Anti-immigrant groups flourished amid a new atmosphere that favored wiping out the concessions obtained by immigrants and minorities during the previous two decades. In 1996, California's Proposition 209 sought the elimination of affirmative action (the complex of laws seeking equality of opportunity for minorities in employment and education). Two years later, in 1998, Proposition 227 sought to suppress bilingual education in the California public schools.

With the support of 61 percent of voters, Proposition 227 eliminated the model of bilingual education (with some exceptions) that had prevailed as the de facto curriculum for the sons and daughters of immigrants, replacing it with the structured English-immersion model.[60]

The bilingual education model that had prevailed in California before the approval of Proposition 227 contained a degree of flexibility. The ideal was for students to first learn to read and write in their native language, and then in English. They could continue to study mathematics and natural sciences in their mother tongues until they had achieved sufficient fluency in English.[61] When this model was eliminated, the newly imposed model classified the children of immigrants as "Limited English Proficiency," a category that required them to make a transition to regular all-English classes in a period of one year. In the campaign for Proposition 227, supporters did not base their message on any scientific or technical body of knowledge about the best pedagogical model for learning English, but rather insisted on promoting a conventional model of immigrant assimilation and eradicating any form of multiculturalism. The voters clearly expressed their preference, with 61 percent in favor and 39 percent against.

According to a report by Brock et al., assessing the first five years of Proposition 227's implementation, although all students of all languages who were in the process of learning English showed an increase in scores on national academic exams (SAT-9 and CST), a gap still persisted between the scores of the students learning English and those who were native-born. This difference appeared at all grade levels and in all subjects. This study also found no demonstrated superiority of the total English-immersion method as compared to the bilingual model.[62]

The evidence that this public policy is not succeeding in its mission is not very encouraging, since it affects a large number of immigrant families. Besides casting doubt on the efficacy of the English teaching program currently implemented by the Los Angeles School District, this kind of data also reveals important changes in the avenues for social integration for immigrants and their families.

IMMIGRANT STUDENTS AND HIGHER EDUCATION

The Dream Act (AB 540) is one of California's most progressive laws, allowing for more effective integration of immigrants into society. This law facilitates undocumented students' access to higher education. It passed the state assembly and senate in September 2001 and became official in October of that year when it was signed into law by Governor Gray Davis. In January 2002, the law went into effect for community colleges and the state university system. Shortly thereafter, the authorities of the University of California decided to adopt this law's requirements as well.[63] Undocumented students are allowed to register for higher education and, if they the meet certain requirements, they are exempted from paying the rates charged to out-of-state residents, reducing their tuition from $22,000 annually to $8700.

In understanding such policies, it is important to note the influence of increasing activism of the part of undocumented students in recent years. The students have formed a nationwide organizational coalition called the Dream Network that has been able to stop the deportation of several students[64] and has proposed that the Dream Act should become a federal law that could award legal permanent residency.

IDENTIFICATION CARDS FOR IMMIGRANTS

Another issue that particularly impacts Mexican immigrants in the Los Angeles region is access to identity cards. Both the LAPD at the municipal level and the sheriff's department at the county level have internal policies authorizing law enforcement officers to consider the *matrícula consular*, described in chapter 2, as a valid form of identification. In Los Angeles County, Policy 3.050 (adopted in June of 2002) specifically mentions the Mexican *matrícula consular*. It

> establishes a County policy to accept foreign consulate identification cards as valid photo identification for County services/programs," under which, "the policy of the county is to accept identification cards with photographs of the foreigner as valid identification for county programs and services. When members of the public are required to provide identification, County departments are authorized to accept as valid identification a photo identification card issued by the Consulate of Mexico known as the Matricula Consular Identification Card.[65]

In the city of Los Angeles, an identical ordinance (Ordinance Number 17853) was passed by the city council in March 2004.[66]

At the state level, since his election to the California assembly as a representative from Los Angeles in 1998, Gil Cedillo has fought for the state to issue driver's licenses to undocumented immigrants. In September 2003, then-governor Gray Davis signed into law SB 60 (Senate Bill 60), which allowed undocumented immigrants to receive official driver's licenses. However, the next month Davis was recalled from his post and replaced by Arnold Schwarzenegger. In early December, the new governor approved a retraction of the law on licenses, fulfilling a campaign promise to reverse SB 60 within his first hundred days in office.[67]

Despite its short life, this law offers a good example of a public policy seeking to aid the integration of immigrants into the society in general so they could obtain certain basic rights as California residents. As a number of our interviewees point out, in an area with the sprawling geography of

Los Angeles, acquiring a driver's license (and the opportunity to buy auto insurance) is fundamental to being able to move about in the area and get access to expanded job options and social ties, which are means of integration for immigrants, their families, and their communities.

FINAL CONSIDERATIONS

In this chapter we have presented the results of our review of the public policies that directly or indirectly impact the lives of Mexican immigrants in the Los Angeles region. Our objective has been to document the policies that make up the framework in which Mexican immigrants and their families live and work. This review of both policy initiatives and the laws themselves delineates the context in which immigrants implement the variety of integration strategies we have described in previous chapters. We also argue that the shaping of these policies is tied to the way their possible beneficiaries are represented and perceived in the public domain.

Although the chapter stresses some of the most controversial and negative of the immigration policies at the federal, state, and local levels, it is important to point out that California and especially the city and county of Los Angeles present a more favorable stance toward immigrants than many other regions of the United States. As we have shown, not all the local and state policies and ordinances are negative; several initiatives serve the goal of integration for immigrants. It is also worth stressing that almost invariably, when positive policies for immigrants are created, there is some tie to efforts by organized civil society. That is, the positive aspects of policy initiatives—such as those combating wage theft or those defending the rights of domestic workers and day laborers—are intimately tied to the capacity of immigrant workers to organize and demand respect for their rights, and to the backing provided by the civil organizations that support these initiatives.

Conclusion

In this book we have analyzed the integration process of Mexican immigrants in the Los Angeles metropolitan area. One of every three immigrants in the United States was born in Mexico, and Mexicans constitute the largest group of legal and undocumented immigrants. From the Mexican perspective, around ten percent of people born in Mexico now resides in the United States. The major destination of this migration is the Los Angeles region. Within that large metropolis, one out of every seven residents was born somewhere in Mexico.

Although immigrant integration has been a popular subject in US academic circles, this particular study has been carried out by Mexican researchers based in Tijuana—a border city emblematic of migration, with the highest index of border crossings in the world. However, that does not mean this is the first such book authored by Mexican scholars. In the late 1920s, the Mexican anthropologist Manuel Gamio[1] and his assistants conducted more than seventy interviews with Mexican immigrants in the United States on such subjects as assimilation and economic adaptation. For this research, following Gamio, we conducted ninety interviews with Mexican immigrants, which we have complemented with other research strategies.

We designed a methodological and analytic approach that would allow us to capture the distinct components, dimensions, and levels implicit in the process of integration. Therefore, unlike the majority of existing studies, which tend to observe the process of immigrants' integration from clearly disciplinary perspectives, we adopted a multidisciplinary, multileveled approach. Our methodology employs a combination of quantitative and qualitative techniques, in three directions. First, making use of descriptive statistics, we have analyzed the economic and social integration of Mexican immigrants residing in metropolitan Los Angeles based on data from the American Community Survey of 2007. Second, from an ethnographic perspective, we have analyzed the integration process in its economic, social, cultural, and political dimensions, which we have also considered in relation to transnationalism and participation in intermediary groups. This part of our examination of the integration experience is based on our ninety interviewees from Zacatecas, Oaxaca, and Veracruz. We conducted lengthy recorded interviews so that these immigrants themselves could recount the personal histories of their own lives in the United States, their strategies, and the prejudices and obstacles they have encountered in their efforts to be part of that society. Finally, in the third part of this book we have examined the public policies that recent administrations in the county and city of Los Angeles have implemented to facilitate or restrict the integration of Mexican immigrants.

The first finding of our study confirms what has been documented by other authors: since the 1990s, Mexican immigrants have shifted from the circular migration pattern dominant in earlier periods to a process of settlement in the United States. This change from migrants to immigrants has been accompanied by deep processes we have observed in our study. In the first place, the majority of our interviewees live in Los Angeles with their families, which were either formed in the metropolis or brought from Mexico. This economic pressure has led to a perspective that prioritizes investing in their children's education, buying a house, or starting a business in Los Angeles, while reducing family and collective remittances sent to Mexico.

The fundamental finding of our research is that there is no single path toward immigrant integration, but rather a multiplicity of strategies that lead to distinct results. In contrast to the argument put forward by Huntington,[2] we have not found any consensus formulation about how to define the goal of integration, but rather a diversity of individual and collective projects that occupy various points on a broad spectrum that stretches from classic assimilationism to radical multiculturalism. Thus, we cannot measure economic, social, cultural, and political integration as if we were dealing with a race being run along a clearly delineated track (with bigger or smaller obstacles) toward a single goal.

In this sense, our findings coincide partially with what has been expressed by advocates of the theory of segmented assimilation, which, as we have noted, questions the direct relation between assimilation and upward mobility by emphasizing diverse paths in the assimilation of immigrants. Our analysis of direct interviews with first-generation Mexican immigrants about their progress in integration in the economic, social, cultural, and political dimensions has given rise to a richer and more complex view of this process. We have observed that our interviewees seem to have more varied choices than that of reinventing themselves as white, middle-class Americans, that of becoming members of an underclass, or even that of combining successful economic integration with the maintenance of the values of their community, as described by Portes and Zhou[3] in their analysis primarily of the adaptation of members of the second generation.

Another important finding of our study has been to identify noteworthy differences in the objectives and in the obstacles encountered—and consequently in the achievements attained—in the distinct realms of economic, social, cultural, and political integration. For example, the operation of broad and solid social networks allows for strong social and cultural integration in the form of various trajectories that lead to the life project of becoming settled and established in Los Angeles. Economic integration, on the other hand, has a more ambiguous quality because for the majority of our interviewees significant insertion in the labor market has not led to clear economic upward mobility. Similarly, in the majority of cases the efforts of our interviewees to integrate themselves politically have run into the barrier of restrictive immigration laws that offer very limited access to legal permanent residence and citizenship for those who are undocumented. Such differentiated rates of progress in integration along different paths in different spheres mean, concretely, that Mexican immigrants have made their homes in Los Angeles and want to remain there, but they have scant opportunity to become citizens with full membership in that society.

The statistical and ethnographic analyses of the *economic* integration of Mexican immigrants in metropolitan Los Angeles, which are presented in our third and fourth chapters, reveal that these immigrants have followed diverse routes to try to achieve upward economic mobility, with varying results. Mexican immigrants in general, and those from Zacatecas, Oaxaca, and Veracruz in particular, show very high labor market participation rates, but many are concentrated in labor niches that offer low salaries and deplorable working conditions. This condition is not limited to unskilled immigrants; a high proportion of those with college degrees are working in nonprofessional occupations. The majority of Mexican immigrants find unsatisfactory jobs in the formal and informal sectors and, faced with such a lack of opportunity, some opt for creating informal businesses, especially in the area of food sales, an activity generally tolerated by local authorities in the Los Angeles region.

Nonetheless, some of our interviewees have achieved more successful integration into the economy even though they began in conditions similar to those who have not achieved such upward mobility. These more upwardly mobile immigrants have had to confront and overcome the structural barriers described in the literature of the segmented assimilation theory, such as national origin, low socioeconomic status (especially in terms of education and ability to speak English), a context of adverse reception for those who are undocumented, and meager financial resources.[4]

These immigrants have developed successful economic trajectories of work and entrepreneurship that have allowed some of them to become homeowners in Los Angeles and to reach a comfortable retirement. Among our interviewees, the Zacatecans have, in general, achieved relatively more upward economic mobility. The main factors explaining their more successful economic integration are their legal immigration status and long residence in the United States, which have allowed them to minimize the impact of their few years of schooling and limited English proficiency. In this sense, the Immigration Reform and Control Act (IRCA) of 1986, which led to the legalization of more than two million undocumented Mexicans, has been key to the upward economic mobility of longer-time immigrants such as the Zacatecans and to a lesser degree the Oaxacans. The bulk of the Veracruzans, on the other hand, because of their more recent arrival in Los Angeles, have been excluded from such regularization of their immigration status and, therefore, from opportunities to reach better economic outcomes.

Buying a house requires a burdensome investment over a long period of time. Yet this commitment has been taken on by a significant share of Mexican immigrants in metropolitan Los Angeles, at a rate fairly close to that of immigrants from Europe and Asia. This demonstrates a clear decision on the part of Mexican immigrants to settle definitively in the Los Angeles region, as well as to assure an inheritance for their children and a symbol, at least, of membership in the US middle class. In such life projects of individuals and families, any properties they own in Mexico serve as additional investments or as vacation homes.

In this regard, we argue that in spite of undocumented immigrants' heroic exploration of various strategies and pathways to achieve economic integration, that process always remains unfinished. Only those immigrants who are legal permanent residents or who have become naturalized citizens can take full advantage of access to the dense social immigrant networks in the region, shaped over several decades, that facilitate contacts with employers, opportunities for entrepreneurship, and the opportunity to achieve full economic integration.

Moving on to the process of *social* integration of Mexican immigrants in the Los Angeles region, a first element to note is one that also appears in our analysis of economic integration: in general terms, our interviewees who have been living in the United States for longer periods of time have enjoyed more favorable circumstances, allowing them to attain not only documented immigration status but also solid insertion into the social fabric.

A good share of the immigrants from Zacatecas, some from Oaxaca, and a few from Veracruz now not only have US citizenship or legal permanent residence but also have greater English proficiency and have developed a bigger network of social relations in the United States. Meanwhile, a good many of the immigrants originally from Veracruz and some from Oaxaca have been in the country for fewer years, are undocumented, have more limited English proficiency, and confront more limited labor market opportunities. Also, many families from Oaxaca and Veracruz have mixed immigration status.

Nonetheless, we have seen that immigrants from all three states participate to one degree or another in intermediary groups—whether these are preexisting spaces such as schools and churches or self-created spaces like immigrant associations, artistic and recreational activities, or sports clubs. In the process of insertion into Los Angeles society, the presence and use of social networks has been a key factor in assuring some participation, if in differentiated ways.

The Los Angeles region has been the preferred destination of Mexican immigrants for many decades, and the resulting social networks of families and townspeople ease the arrival and settlement of new immigrants. Although some immigrants use these same networks to facilitate circulating back and forth between Mexico and the United States, the tendency has shifted toward more permanent settlement in Los Angeles. Thus we can observe an intense deployment of actions and strategies to promote integration. In some cases these actions and strategies include consolidation of ties among immigrants from the same regions of Mexico, while in others they involve the creation of networks with other actors and connections with social spaces outside the Latino community, especially for immigrants with mastery of English. A clear example of this growing diversity of ties is the presence of intermarriage among our interviewees, analogous to the similar tendency among post-IRCA Mexican immigrants, and indicative of becoming settled and integrated.

In terms of access to services, our interviewees report a variety of situations reflecting different forms of social integration. In the case of health services, we found some immigrants with secure access to these services by virtue of their being documented and in stable jobs. However, the majority of our interviewees have to employ other strategies to receive a minimum level of health-care services, which reflects the overall deficiencies in public health coverage in Los Angeles.

In terms of access to educational services, the profile of our interviewees—like that of the rest of the Mexican immigrant population in the Los Angeles region—is significantly limited in comparison to those of other immigrants or native-born residents. However, all the interviewees have undertaken some type of study in the United States, thanks to their convictions about the importance of schooling and especially their attempts to learn the English language. Still, the interest in education tends to gradually wane among the majority as a result of their work and family responsibilities in Los Angeles.

One of the central problems in the process of social integration of immigrants in the United States is the membership decline in the institutions that have historically proven fundamental, such as schools, churches, companies, unions, and local electoral committees. In spite of this decline, however, the information supplied by our interviewees reveals varied participation in such institutions, which in turn suggests a certain revival.

Immigrants' creation of their own institutions, such as immigrant associations or the vast array of cultural activities (which, let it be said, reveal the importance and breadth of transnational ties to the places of origin), allows for a broadening of the range of mediating institutions that facilitate social integration. Our interviewees point out that in spite of maintaining constant communication and exchange with their communities in Mexico, the process of establishing themselves in Los Angeles and getting on with their lives there has gradually prevailed. Such participation and initiative on the part of the immigrant communities is important to emphasize because, as described in chapter 5, US public opinion in general and that of states like California views immigrants and particularly Mexican immigrants with habitually negative connotations. It is important to reframe that debate in terms of the positive contributions of these immigrants.

However, in the context of the whole United States, the Los Angeles region is generally less hostile toward the immigrant population. Although some of our undocumented interviewees speak of their worries about deportation by immigration authorities, we do not detect a generalized fear that would drastically restrict their mobility or reduce the scope of their social and employment activities. Therefore, we think that the public policies of the Los Angeles city and county governments have provided more accommodation and support for the immigrant presence than those of other regions. De facto, we would say, they fall closer to the multiculturalist perspective than to the classic assimilation model. All in all, our interviewees offer a positive assessment of their settlement and eventual integration in Los Angeles society. Thus their perceptions testify to an important part of the social fabric they have constructed in the region, and so demonstrate that the stereotype of the isolated monolingual immigrant who is linked only to his or her place of origin in Mexico is simplistic and mistaken.

As explained in chapter 1, we think that the study of *cultural* integration should begin with an examination of the specific characteristics of the society that immigrants encounter upon arrival. Thus, far from imagining that immigrants must incorporate themselves into a receiving society that is culturally stable and homogeneous, it is necessary to recognize the framework of historically constructed relationships within which each new immigrant must negotiate his or her sense of belonging.

In the specific case of the culturally diverse Los Angeles metropolitan area, what stands out is the important demographic and historical presence of "Hispanic" or "Latino" culture, nourished originally by Mexican American culture, which was in turn "re-mexicanized" by the immense waves of immigration from Mexico in the twentieth century. The great visibility of this Hispanic influence, however, does not mean that it constitutes the mainstream or hegemonic culture. On the contrary, the construction of the category "Hispanic" reflects tensions among groups that are differentiated within US society, a visibly fragmented society that, historically, has both constructed and questioned internal ethnic and cultural borders. This is the culturally diverse and socially segmented context that the immigrants from Zacatecas, Oaxaca, and Veracruz encountered when they arrived. As a result, the challenge facing them has been that of integrating themselves in the broadest possible way into a fragmented society.

The Hispanic or Latino character of Los Angeles constitutes, simultaneously, both a resource and an obstacle in this process. On the one hand, the presence of familiar cultural codes—beginning with the widespread use of the Spanish language—can facilitate the process of adaptation in its earliest moments. On the other hand, it is equally true that from the moment they cross the border, Mexicans are converted into "Hispanics," a categorization that channels them toward spaces previously defined by the logic of social segregation, especially in the spheres of employment and housing.

The objectives and strategies deployed in pursuit of cultural integration are also diverse, reflecting in some cases a search for shelter within the ethnic community and in others an attempt to dissolve cultural difference. We have found this diversity in the wide participation of Zacatecans, Oaxacans, and Veracruzans in artistic, civic, and religious activities—in which the immigrants move fluidly within a spectrum that reaches from the assertion and preservation of cultural difference, as in the case of Veracruzan music or Oaxacan religious celebrations, to the pursuit of integration through the dissolution or concealment of difference, as in the case of religious conversion to denominations seen as "American."

Here again, we can see the ambiguous character (resource/obstacle) of the Hispanic presence in Los Angeles. The great numbers of Hispanic cultural groups, whether artistic, religious, or civic, offer a broad field of participation for new immigrants. In contrast, the pathways to spaces of interaction with non-Hispanics are clearly more limited. These barriers, though, seem to become more porous over time and as the immigrants acquire English proficiency. When the Zacatecans arrived in the region, they could not count on the wide network of Hispanic or specifically Mexican associations that exists today, but they also did not need to confront the obstacle of today's anti-immigration political and social context. At the other extreme, the Veracruzans, who arrived most recently, found a solid community of people of Mexican origin, which has eased their access to goods and services linked to their cultural traditions, but they have also faced a more restrictive legal context and a growing threat of deportation by the Department of Homeland Security. In the face of all these contradictions, we have found one indicator that most likely best permits an understanding of both the effort invested by the immigrants in their social incorporation and the achievements that result. This indicator is the construction of life projects. Our interviewees, both documented and undocumented, show a clear orientation toward remaining permanently in the United States, the country where they are building their lives and those of their children. Clearly, the violence sweeping Mexico, as well as the economic crisis, has reinforced this orientation toward permanent settlement in the United States.

Our examination of *political* integration in chapter 7 leads us to conclude that there are varying levels of political participation among the Mexican immigrants interviewed and distinct forms of political integration. In principle, opportunities for broad involvement in the political domain are limited by the restricted access to citizenship facing a significant part of the region's Mexican immigrant population because of their undocumented status. As reported in chapter 3, slightly more than 70 percent of Mexican immigrants in the Los Angeles area are not citizens, as compared to 37 percent of European and Asian immigrants. Only the minority of Mexican immigrants who are naturalized citizens have access to political rights, including that of electing public officials. However, in spite of this limitation on political participation, both documented and undocumented immigrants participate actively in other forms of political expression such as demonstrations and mobilizations. Thus, those immigrants show that they are informed about political processes both in the United States and in Mexico.

Although a large share of the interviewees have now established their homes in the United States, this has not led them to detach completely from Mexican politics. In fact, we have found some forms of transnational political participation by immigrants who decide to take part in elections in their places of origin, reflecting the deployment of differentiated strategies with regard to political participation. However, we have also found that the interviewees have a generalized negative perspective on Mexican political life, which they consistently associate with corruption and with the violence sweeping Mexico in the first decade of the twenty-first century. That perception thus is added to the other factors that explain why the interviewees' life projects are so clearly oriented toward remaining in the United States.

A related point we stress in this chapter is the interviewees' growing political reorientation toward the United States. Practically all of our interviewees have access to information about political developments both in the Los Angeles region and in the United States as a whole, which has led to their forming an array of opinions in this respect and to participating in specific actions. The interviewees offer a variety of perceptions about obtaining legal permanent residence or citizenship, depending on the arrangements they have made to deal with their situations. In that process, the anti-immigrant political climate in the United States is a fundamental factor that explains a growing interest in naturalization and with it access to formal citizenship. We also note, however, that for many of our interviewees the interest in naturalization is purely pragmatic, responding to the well-known fact that becoming a naturalized US citizen aids in obtaining faster legal permanent residency for spouses, minor children, and parents.

As we stated above, our analytic strategy involves examining the integration process in its economic, social, cultural, and political dimensions, which are intersected by immigrants' practices in relation to transnationalism and participation in intermediary groups. In what follows we discuss the subjects of transnationalism and of public policies in the city and county of Los Angeles.

In the introduction to this book, we described the academic community's growing interest in understanding what effect maintaining linkages with communities of origin in Mexico may have on immigrants' processes of integration. This interest focused at first on the importance of new developments in communications media and transportation that allowed for maintenance of an important degree of circularity in international migration, facilitating the construction of transnational communities. Then, in a second period, the focus shifted to the possibility of maintaining such transnational ties in spite of the decline in migratory circularity, thanks to the development of new communications technologies that allow information to circulate in real time, which in turn makes possible a significant degree of interaction between those who have migrated and those who remain in Mexico.

The issues raised by new media and new communication dynamics are vast, and it has not been our intention in this work to take on all of them. On the contrary, our focus is limited to one important aspect of this discussion, which is to ask how the transnational ties established by Zacatecans, Oaxacans, and Veracruzans residing in the Los Angeles metropolitan area facilitate or obstruct the process of integration in its economic, social, cultural, and political dimensions.

Answering this question requires, first, identifying the nature and importance of such ties, so as to then consider their impacts on integration processes. In the specific context of our study, given the longevity and magnitude of the Mexican community in Los Angeles and its geographic proximity to Mexico, it should not be surprising that we have identified a great variety of transnational ties. Nor is it surprising that, with the heightened border enforcement since 1993, both the circular pattern of migration and the practice of occasional visits to Mexico have gradually diminished or been suppressed, particularly among the undocumented.

It has been more surprising, however, to find that documented immigrants have displayed the same trend due to the growing violence and insecurity in Mexico, as perceived by our interviewees, who cite it as a strong motivation for reducing travel to their places of origin—a tendency displayed by the Zacatecans, Oaxacans, and Veracruzans. We think this is striking because it shows once again a significant waning of the traditional circularity pattern of Mexican migration to the United States, and the reorientation of that migration toward integration in the receiving country. That reorientation is accompanied by a decline in transnational practices in the economic, social, and political dimensions. Interviewees make this argument most clearly when explaining changes in their life projects, which, though at one time were centered on the idea of returning to Mexico, now are primarily oriented toward staying in the United States.

Interestingly, this shift toward permanence on the northern side of the Mexican border has been accompanied by growing interest in the new communications technologies that allow for continuous interaction despite geographical distance. It is significant, for example, that in the homes of immigrants of indigenous origin, with educational levels of three years or less of primary school, we have found intensive use of computers connected to the internet, operated mainly by the immigrants' children born in the United States. These computers allow not only communication with friends and relatives in places of origin but also the creation of professional web pages to promote, for instance, the services of a musical group that can be hired for social occasions, as well as participation in blogs, exchange of videos via YouTube, and circulation of various kinds of information via Facebook and Twitter. Naturally, this intense virtual communication is accompanied by physical interactions among those who do cross the border for commercial, tourist, or family reasons. The proximity of the border, and especially of the city of Tijuana, is a key element in understanding the integration strategies deployed by Mexican immigrants in the Los Angeles region. Tijuana appears as a resource of great value in getting access to goods and services as divergent as health care, Mexican consumer goods, or simply forms of entertainment and recreation.

Beyond the means through which cross-border ties are maintained, it is important to inquire as to their nature and their impact on the processes of integration. In this sense, it is worth pointing out that in the cases observed, there does not seem to be a contradiction between the maintenance of strong transnational ties and economic, social, cultural, and political incorporation in Los Angeles. However, our research design does not allow us to predict whether, over the medium or long term, immigrants' ties with their hometowns will maintain the same vigor. On the one hand, aspects such as the increase in violence in Mexico and the reorientation of life projects toward the United States suggest the possibility of progressive distancing from the places of origin. On the other hand, the new forms of virtual communication and interaction point toward the construction of new transnational linkages.

In our examination of public policies related to the process of integration, an aspect that immediately stands out is the way immigration policy has ceased to be the exclusive preserve of the US federal government. Both state and local legislative bodies now attempt to exercise influence—whether positive or negative—over the lives of immigrants. As we have pointed out, the role of state and local governments in this respect stems partly from the absence of federal policies addressing immigrant integration.

In the course of our study, making use of information from the county and city of Los Angeles, we have documented a variety of policies with diverse impacts on the process of integration of our interviewees in particular and of Mexican immigrants in general. What is striking at first glance is the existence of a range of laws, some of which can be classified as pro-immigrant and others as anti-immigrant. However, a more detailed review of the policies in effect in Los Angeles shows that the majority of these initiatives facilitate the lives of the immigrants, their families, and their communities. Although the onset of fiscal crisis in the state of California led to a reduction in many social services offered to the immigrant population, our analysis still reveals the prevalence of laws that broaden immigrants' rights, such as those dealing with health, education, and employment.

It is important to stress, as we do in our chapter on this topic, that in the context of the whole United States, the region under study is generally less hostile toward immigrants than others. This helps to account for the existence of such state and local laws, and also for our interviewees' positive assessment of their settlement and integration in the region. It is equally important to emphasize that the public policies generated by local governments such as Los Angeles County and various cities of the Los Angeles region have also been made possible by the organizational capacity and mobilizations of both immigrants themselves and other organizations of civil society. In that sense, these policies come closer to the multiculturalist position and, therefore, are farther from the classic paradigm of assimilation.

In sum, in this book we have found that in spite of the great efforts made by Mexican immigrants to incorporate themselves into the economy, society, culture, and political life of Los Angeles (that is, their integration into US society), and in spite of the region's governmental bodies implementing public policies that favor this process (their integration by US society), still the majority of such immigrants achieve only limited or precarious integration, especially in the case of the undocumented. For this reason, achieving the status of legal permanent residents or naturalized citizens is a fundamental requirement for reaching full integration in which immigrants can improve their families' standard of living and also increase their participation in the welfare and progress of Los Angeles society.

Notes

INTRODUCTION

1. Gordon, *Assimilation in American Life.*
2. Portes and Zhou, "Should Immigrants Assimilate?"
3. Levitt and Glick-Schiller, "Conceptualizing Simultaneity."
4. Passel and Cohn, *Trends in Unauthorized Immigration;* Passel and Cohn, *Mexican Immigrants.*
5. Huntington, "The Hispanic Challenge."
6. US Census Bureau, "American Community Survey."

1. THEORETICAL PERSPECTIVES ON IMMIGRANT INTEGRATION

1. Huntington, "The Hispanic Challenge"; Huntington, *Who We Are?*
2. Martuccelli, *Sociologies de la modernité.*
3. Wieviorka, "L'intégration."
4. Schnapper, *Qu'est-ce que l'intégration?*, 16.
5. Pastor and Ortiz, *Immigrant Integration in Los Angeles*, 1.
6. Park and Burgess, *Introduction to the Science of Sociology*; Gamio, *The Life Story of the Mexican Immigrant;* Gamio, *Mexican Immigration to the United States.*
7. Schnapper, *Qu'est-ce que l'intégration?*, 2007.
8. Park and Burgess, *Introduction to the Science of Sociology*, 756–69.
9. Gordon, *Assimilation in American Life.*
10. Vigdor, *From Immigrants to Americans.*
11. Alba and Nee, *Remaking the American Mainstream.*
12. Alba and Nee, "Rethinking Assimilation Theory for a New Era of Immigration," *Remaking the American Mainstream;* Jiménez and Fitzgerald, "Mexican Assimilation"; Telles and Ortiz, *Generations of Exclusion.*

13. Alba and Nee, *Remaking the American Mainstream.*
14. Zhou, "Segmented Assimilation."
15. Portes and Zhou, "Should Immigrants Assimilate?"
16. Ibid., 82.
17. Brown and Bean, "Assimilation Models, Old and New."
18. Portes and Rumbaut, *Immigrant America.*
19. Brown and Bean, "Assimilation Models, Old and New"; Jiménez and Fitzgerald, "Mexican Assimilation."
20. Portes and Rumbaut, *Immigrant America.*
21. Schnapper, *Qu'est-ce que l'intégration?*
22. Touraine, *Pourrons-nous vivre ensemble?*
23. Taylor, *The Sources of the Self.*
24. Sartori, *La sociedad multiétnica.*
25. Ibid.
26. San Román, *Los muros de la separación.*
27. Wieviorka, "A World in Movement."
28. Glick-Schiller, Basch, and Szanton, "From Immigrant to Transmigrant"; Levitt, DeWind, and Vertovec, "International Perspectives on Transnational Migration."
29. Wihtol de Wenden, *La globalization humaine.*
30. Jiménez and Fitzgerald, "Mexican Assimilation."
31. Wieviorka, "A World in Movement."
32. Schnapper, *Qu'est-ce que l'intégration?*
33. Borjas, "Self-Selection and the Earnings of Immigrants."
34. Light, *Ethnic Enterprise in Americas;* Wilson and Portes, "Immigrant Enclaves"; Waldinger, "The Ethnic Enclave Debate Revisited"; Kaplan and Li, *Landscapes of the Ethnic Economy.*
35. Piore, *Birds of Passage.*
36. Vigdor, *From Immigrants to Americans,* 58–59.
37. Piore, *Birds of Passage.*
38. Valenzuela, "Compatriots or Competitors?"
39. Piore, *Birds of Passage.*
40. Portes and Rumbaut, *Immigrant America.*
41. Waldinger, "The Making of an Immigrant Niche."
42. Waldinger, "Immigrants and Minorities"; Zabin, *Mixtec Migrants in California Agriculture.*
43. Borjas, "Self-Selection and the Earnings of Immigrants."
44. Chiswick, "The Effect of Americanization on the Earnings of Foreign-Born Men."
45. Borjas, "Self-Selection and the Earnings of Immigrants."
46. Sassen, "New Trends in the Socio-Spatial Organization of the New York City Economy."
47. Myers and Woo, "Immigrant Trajectories into Homeownership."
48. Fix, Laglagaron, et al., *An Analytic Framework for Developing an Immigrant Integration Strategy for Los Angeles County;* Fix, McHugh, et al., *Los Angeles on the Leading Edge.*
49. Ibid.

50. Pastor and Ortiz, *Immigrant Integration in Los Angeles.*

51. Telles, "Mexican Americans and the American Nation."

52. Rumbaut, Massey, and Bean, "Linguistic Life Expectancies."

53. Durand and Martínez, "Los nuevos procesos de integración, matrimonios mixtos y migración México-Estados Unidos."

54. Montejano, "Who Is Samuel P. Huntington?"

55. Ibid.

56. Huntington, "The Hispanic Challenge."

57. Thomas and Znaniecki, *The Polish Peasant in Europe and America.*

58. Park and Burgess, *Introduction to the Science of Sociology,* 756–69.

59. Gordon, *Assimilation in American Life.*

60. Gamio, *The Life Story of the Mexican Immigrant.*

61. Wilson, *The Truly Disadvantaged.*

62. Young, *Justice and the Politics of Difference;* Taylor, *The Ethics of Authenticity;* Kymlicka, *The Rights of Minority Cultures.*

63. Barth, *Ethnic Groups and Boundaries.*

64. Telles and Ortiz, *Generations of Exclusion.*

65. Alba and Nee, *Remaking the American Mainstream.*

66. Brubaker, *Ethnicity without Groups.*

67. Ibid, 116–31.

68. Held et al., *Global Transformations.*

69. González, *Relaciones estado-diáspora.*

70. Sartori, *La sociedad multiétnica;* Huntington, "The Hispanic Challenge."

71. Soysal, *Limits of Citizenship;* Held and McGrew, *Globalization/Anti-Globalization.*

72. Taylor, *Multiculturalisme;* Soysal, *Limits of Citizenship;* Kymlicka, "Two Models of Pluralism and Tolerance."

73. Wihtol de Wenden and Hargreaves, "The Political Participation of Ethnic Minorities in Europe."

74. Blanco and Barbero González, *Pautas de asentamiento de la población inmigrante.*

75. Milkman, *Organizing Immigrants.*

76. Bada, Fox, and Selee, *Invisible no More.*

77. Ibid.

78. Meissner et al., *Immigration and America Future;* Pastor and Ortiz, *Immigrant Integration in Los Angeles.*

79. Calderón and Martínez, *La dimensión política de la migración mexicana,* 12.

80. Bloemraad, *Becoming a Citizen.*

2. MEXICAN IMMIGRATION AND THE DEVELOPMENT OF THE LOS ANGELES METROPOLITAN AREA

1. Passel and Cohn, *Trends in Unauthorized Immigration;* Passel and Cohn, *Mexican Immigrants.*

2. Passel, *Estimates of the Size and Characteristics of the Undocumented Population*, 2.

3. Passel and Cohn, *Trends in Unauthorized Immigration*.

4. US Department of Homeland Security, "Office of Immigration Statistics."

5. Ibid.

6. Light, *Deflecting Immigration*, 62.

7. Ibid.

8. Charles, *Won't You Be My Neighbor?*, 6.

9. Ibid., 6–7.

10. Davis, *City of Quartz*, 22.

11. Portes and Rumbaut, *Immigrant America*.

12. Waldinger and Bozorgmehr, "The Making of a Multicultural Metropolis," 7.

13. Ibid.

14. Davis, *City of Quartz*, 22.

15. Soja, *Postmetropolis*.

16. Griswold, *The Los Angeles Barrio*, 36–39.

17. Soja, *Postmetropolis*, 127.

18. Sánchez, *Becoming Mexican American*, 71.

19. Romo, *East Los Angeles*, 132–39.

20. Hoffman, "Stimulus to Repatriation"; Sánchez, *Becoming Mexican American*.

21. García y Griego, "The Bracero Policy Experiment," 116.

22. McWilliams, *North from Mexico*.

23. Soja, *Postmetropolis*.

24. Portes and Rumbaut, *Immigrant America*.

25. Waldinger and Bozorgmehr, "The Making of a Multicultural Metropolis," 10–11.

26. Soja, *Postmetropolis*, 140.

27. Scott, *New Industrial Spaces*; Storper and Walker, *The Capitalist Imperative*.

28. Piore and Sabel, *The Second Industrial Divide*.

29. Rocha, "Migrantes precarios"; Benner, *Work in the New Economy*; Bernhardt et al., *Confronting the Gloves-Off Economy*.

30. Waldinger and Bozorgmehr, "The Making of a Multicultural Metropolis," 10–11.

31. Alarcón, "Los inmigrantes mexicanos y el mercado de trabajo en Los Ángeles al inicio del siglo XXI," 182.

32. Charles, *Won't You Be My Neighbor?*, 10–11.

33. Ibid., 11–15.

34. Valenzuela, "Working on the Margins in Metropolitan Los Angeles."

35. Estrada and Hondagneu-Sotelo, "Intersectional Dignities"; Ramírez and Hondagneu-Sotelo, "Mexican Immigrant Gardeners"; Ibarra, *Migrantes en mercados de trabajo globales*; Levine, "El proceso de incorporación de los migrantes mexicanos a la vida y el trabajo en Los Ángeles, California."

36. Hondagneu-Sotelo, *Domestica*, 7–21.

37. Ibarra, *Migrantes en mercados de trabajo globales*.

38. Massey, Durand, and Malone, *Beyond Smoke and Mirrors*, 90.

39. Jimenez, *Humanitarian Crisis*.

40. Gamio, *The Life Story of the Mexican Immigrant*.

41. Zazueta and García y Griego, *Los trabajadores mexicanos en Estados Unidos*.

42. CONAPO, *Índices de intensidad migratoria*.

43. Ibid., 31.

44. Durand and Massey, *Clandestinos*.

45. CONAPO, *Índices de intensidad migratoria*.

46. Ibid.

47. Delgado, Márquez, and Rodríguez, "Organizaciones transnacionales de migrantes y desarrollo regional en Zacatecas," 165.

48. Moctezuma, "El circuito migratorio Sain El Alto, Zacatecas-Oakland, California."

49. Alarcón, "Los inmigrantes mexicanos y el mercado de trabajo en Los Ángeles al inicio del siglo XXI," 182.

50. Alarcón and Escala, "Transnational Philanthropy and Organizational Strategies."

51. Mines, *Developing a Community Tradition of Migration*, 74.

52. Nichols, *Santos, duraznos y vino*.

53. Moctezuma, *La transnacionalidad de los sujetos*.

54. Delgado, Márquez, and Rodríguez, "Organizaciones transnacionales de migrantes y desarrollo regional en Zacatecas."

55. Alarcón and Escala, "Transnational Philanthropy and Organizational Strategies."

56. IME, *Matrículas consulares*.

57. Arellano, *Orange County*.

58. Rivera-Salgado, "Transnational Political Strategies"; Zabin, *Mixtec Migrants in California Agriculture*; Fox and Rivera-Salgado, "Introducción."

59. Nagengast and Kearney, "Mixtec Identity, Political Consciousness, and Political Activism."

60. Rivera-Salgado and Escala, "Collective Identity and Organizational Strategies of Indigenous and Mestizo Mexican Migrants"; Fox and Rivera-Salgado, "Introducción."

61. Zabin, *Mixtec Migrants in California Agriculture*.

62. Kissam, "La migración entre México y Estados Unidos."

63. Runsten and Kearney, *A Survey of Oaxacan Village Networks in California Agriculture*; López and Runsten, "El trabajo de los mixtecos y zapotecos en California"; Cruz-Manjarrez, "Performance, Ethnicity and Migration."

64. Fox and Rivera-Salgado, "Introducción"; Escárcega and Varese, "La ruta mixteca"; Stephen, *Transborder Lives: Indigenous Oaxacans in Mexico*.

65. Kearney and Nagengast, *Anthropological Perspectives on Transnational Communities in Rural California*.

66. Rivera-Salgado and Escala, "Collective Identity and Organizational Strategies of Indigenous and Mestizo Mexican Migrants."

67. López, Escala, and Hinojosa-Ojeda, *Migrant Associations, Remittances and Regional Development between Los Angeles and Oaxaca*.

68. López and Runsten, "El trabajo de los mixtecos y zapotecos en California."

69. IME, *Matrículas consulares.*

70. Chávez, Rosas, and Zamudio, "La migración en el estado de Veracruz."

71. Pérez, "Las redes sociales de la migración emergente de Veracruz a los Estados Unidos"; Córdova, Núñez, and Skerritt, *Migración internacional, crisis agrícola y transformaciones culturales en la región central de Veracruz.*

72. Mestries, "Migración internacional y campesinado cafetalero en México."

73. Rosas, *Varones al son de la migración.*

74. Córdova, Núñez, and Skerritt, *Migración internacional, crisis agrícola y transformaciones culturales en la región central de Veracruz.*

75. Mestries, "Migración internacional y campesinado cafetalero en México."

76. Léonard, Quesnel, and del Rey, "De la comunidad territorial al archipiélago familiar."

77. Mestries, "Migración internacional y campesinado cafetalero en México."

78. Anguiano, "Rumbo al norte."

79. Pérez, "Las redes sociales de la migración emergente de Veracruz a los Estados Unidos."

80. Mestries, "Migración internacional y campesinado cafetalero en México."

81. IME, *Matrículas consulares.*

82. Mestries, "Migración internacional y campesinado cafetalero en México," 264.

83. Chávez, Rosas, and Zamudio, "La migración en el estado de Veracruz."

84. Anguiano, "Rumbo al norte."

85. Ibid.

86. Córdova, Núñez, and Skerritt, *Migración internacional.*

3. STATISTICAL ANALYSIS OF MEXICAN IMMIGRANTS' INTEGRATION IN THE METROPOLITAN LOS ANGELES AREA

1. This chapter is based on preliminary versions published in Alarcón and Ramírez-García, "Integración económica de los inmigrantes mexicanos en la Zona Metropolitana de Los Ángeles"; and Ramírez-García and Alarcón, "Integración en desventaja."

2. Alarcón, "U.S. Immigration Policy and the Mobility of Mexicans (1882–2005)."

3. Durand and Massey, *Clandestinos.*

4. Alba and Nee, *Remaking the American Mainstream;* Telles and Ortiz, *Generations of Exclusion;* Portes and Rumbaut, *Legacies;* Waldinger and Reichi, "Second-Generation Mexicans"; Huntington, "The Hispanic Challenge"; Levine, *Los nuevos pobres de Estados Unidos;* Tinley, "Migración de Guanajuato a Alabama"; Barrow and Rouse, "The Economic Value of Education by Race and Ethnicity."

5. Telles and Ortiz, *Generations of Exclusion,* 265.

6. Levine, *Los nuevos pobres de Estados Unidos.*

7. Barrow and Rouse, "The Economic Value of Education by Race and Ethnicity."

8. Huntington, "The Hispanic Challenge."

9. Portes and Rumbaut, *Immigrant America.*

10. Ibid.

11. Baron, "English Spoken Here?"

12. Alba and Nee, *Remaking the American Mainstream.*

13. Galindo, *Nosotros no cruzamos la frontera;* Baron, "English Spoken Here?"; Alba, "Bilingualism Persists, But English Still Dominates"; Pew Hispanic Center and Kaiser Family Foundation, "2002 National Survey of Latinos."

14. Huntington, "The Hispanic Challenge," 30.

15. Alba, "Bilingualism Persists, but English Still Dominates."

16. Alba and Nee, *Remaking the American Mainstream;* McManus, "Labor Market Effects of Language Enclaves."

17. Baron, "English Spoken Here?"; Alba and Nee, *Remaking the American Mainstream.*

18. Fix and Passel, *U.S. Immigration.*

19. Pew Hispanic Center and Kaiser Family Foundation, "2002 National Survey of Latinos."

20. US Census Bureau, "Current Population Survey."

21. Fix, McHugh, et al., *Los Angeles on the Leading Edge.*

22. Bernhardt et al., *Confronting the Gloves-Off Economy;* Rocha, "Migrantes precarios."

23. Myers and Woo, "Immigrant Trajectories into Homeownership."

24. Alba and Logan, "Assimilation and Stratification in the Homeownership Patterns of Racial and Ethnic Groups"; Mulder and Wagner, "First-Time Homeownership in the Family Life Course"; Painter et al., "Race, Immigrant Status, and Housing Tenure Choice."

25. Waldinger, "Ethnicity and Opportunity in the Plural City," 453.

26. Huntington, "The Hispanic Challenge," 30.

4. ECONOMIC INTEGRATION: MOBILITY, LABOR NICHES, AND LOW-END JOBS

1. Levitt and Glick Schiller, "Conceptualizing Simultaneity."

2. Waldinger, "The Making of an Immigrant Niche."

3. Sassen, "New Trends in the Socio-Spatial Organization of the New York City Economy," 60.

4. Castells and Portes, "World Underneath."

5. Alarcón, "The Free Circulation of Skilled Migrants in North America."

6. Waldinger, "The Ethnic Enclave Debate Revisited."

7. Myers and Woo, "Immigrant Trajectories into Homeownership"; Diaz McConnell and Marcelli, "Buying into the American Dream?

8. Fox and Rivera-Salgado, "Introducción," 17.

9. Rocha, "Migrantes precarios," 108.

10. Ramírez and Hondagneu-Sotelo, "Mexican Immigrant Gardeners."

11. Light, Bernard, and Kim, "Immigrant Incorporation in the Garment Industry of Los Angeles."

12. Estrada and Hondagneu-Sotelo, "Intersectional Dignities."

13. Myers and Woo, "Immigrant Trajectories into Homeownership."

14. Diaz and Marcelli, "Buying into the American Dream?"

15. Cornelius, "Impacts of the 1986 U.S. Immigration Law on Emigration from Rural Mexican Sending Communities"; Martin, "Harvest of Confusion."

16. Waldinger, "Ethnicity and Opportunity in the Plural City," 453.

5. SOCIAL INTEGRATION: BUILDING A FAMILY, A COMMUNITY, AND A LIFE

1. Fix, Laglagaron, et al., *An Analytic Framework for Developing an Immigrant Integration Strategy for Los Angeles County;* Fix, McHugh, et al., *Los Angeles on the Leading Edge.*

2. Pastor and Ortiz, *Immigrant Integration in Los Angeles.*

3. Fix, Laglagaron, et al., *An Analytic Framework for Developing an Immigrant Integration Strategy for Los Angeles County;* Fix, McHugh, et al., *Los Angeles on the Leading Edge.*

4. Fitzgerald and Alarcón, "Migration."

5. Passel, Cohn, and Gonzalez-Barrera, *Net Migration from Mexico Falls to Zero—and Perhaps Less.*

6. Durand and Martínez, "Los nuevos procesos de integración."

7. Ibid., 446.

8. Ibid., 447.

9. Telles, "Mexican Americans and the American Nation."

10. Fix, Laglagaron, et al., *An Analytic Framework for Developing an Immigrant Integration Strategy for Los Angeles County;* Fix, McHugh, et al., *Los Angeles on the Leading Edge,* 57.

11. Portes, Fernández-Kelly, and Light, "Life on the Edge," 13.

12. Ibid.

13. US Census Bureau, "American Community Survey."

14. Ibid.

15. Telles, "Mexican Americans and the American Nation."

16. There is a broad literature available on immigrant groups and associations, both in the United States and outside it. Probably the best account is Moya, "Immigrants and Associations."

17. Many works have closely examined this specific form of association among Mexican immigrants in the United States. See for instance Lanly and Valenzuela, *Clubes de migrantes oriundos mexicanos en los Estados Unidos,* and Merz, *Nuevas pautas para México,* among others.

18. There is an extensive bibliography on Oaxacan migration to California and to the United States in general, and on the associations these immigrants have built. An assessment of this literature can be found in Stephen, *Transborder Lives.*

19. There is a wealth of literature on Zacatecan associations in the United States. See Merz, *Nuevas pautas para México;* Fernández de Castro, García, and Vila, *El Programa 3x1 para migrantes;* and Bada, Fox, and Selee, *Context Matters,* among others.

20. The nexus of migration, organizational forms, and sports activity has recently been examined by a number of different analysts. See, for instance, Fox and Rivera-Salgado, "Introducción"; Alonso, "Inmigrantes extranjeros en Barcelona"; Llopis and Moncusí, "'El deporte une bastantísimo aquí'"; and Alonso and Escala, "Introducción."

21. Somerville, Durana, and Terrazas, "Hometown Associations."

22. Escala, Bada, and Rivera-Salgado, "Mexican Migrant Civic and Political Participation in the United States"; Bada et al., *Context Matters.*

23. Fix, Laglagaron, et al., *An Analytic Framework for Developing an Immigrant Integration Strategy for Los Angeles County;* Fix, McHugh, et al., *Los Angeles on the Leading Edge.*

24. Waters, *Black Identities.*

25. Ibid., 332.

26. Pastor and Ortiz, *Immigrant Integration in Los Angeles.*

6. CULTURAL INTEGRATION: REDEFINING IDENTITIES IN A DIVERSE CITY

1. García, *Mexican Americans,* 295.

2. Soja, *Postmetropolis.*

3. González, "Chicano History." Note should be taken of the important work done by Chicano historians such as Rodolfo Acuña, Alberto Camarillo, Richard Griswold del Castillo, George Sánchez, and Juan Gómez-Quiñonez, all of whom contributed to winning a place for the population of Mexican origin in the history of the United States.

4. Romo, *East Los Angeles,* vii.

5. Sánchez, *Becoming Mexican American.*

6. Odgers, *Identités frontalières,* 39–50.

7. Soja, *Postmetropolis.*

8. Telles and Ortiz, *Generations of Exclusion.*

9. Sánchez, *Becoming Mexican American,* 71.

10. Waldinger and Bozorgmehr, "The Making of a Multicultural Metropolis"; Charles, "Residential Segregation in Los Angeles."

11. Charles, "Residential Segregation in Los Angeles."

12. US Census Bureau, "American Community Survey."

13. Charles, *Won't You Be My Neighbor?,* 5.

14. Alarcón, "Los inmigrantes mexicanos y el mercado de trabajo en Los Ángeles al inicio del siglo XXI," 182.

15. *"Guelaguetza"* is a Zapotec word meaning offering, or gift, which alludes to reciprocity or mutual aid among residents of an area.

16. Escala, "Migración, formas organizativas y espacio público."

17. Ibid.

18. During our fieldwork in Los Angeles, we had the opportunity to attend several rehearsals and performances of Guish-Bac.

19. Loza, "From Veracruz to Los Angeles"; Cardona, "Los actores culturales entre la tentación comunitaria y el mercado global."

20. Experience LA, "Movimiento Jaranero de California."

21. Among our interviewees were several who formed a group playing tropical music at weddings, baptisms, and similar events. This allowed the members—mostly workers in textile factories—to earn extra income as musicians.

22. Hirschman, "The Role of Religion in the Origins and Adaptation of Immigrant Groups in the United States"; Warner and Wittner, *Gathering in Diaspora*.

23. Levitt, "Routes and Roots"; Rivera, "Cuando los Santos también migran."

24. Odgers, "Construcción del espacio y religión en la experiencia de la movilidad."

25. The term *"bíblicas no evangélicas"* (non-evangelical Bible churches) is used in the Censo Nacional de Población to describe Jehovah's Witnesses, Seventh Day Adventists, and Mormons. De la Torre, Gutiérrez, and Aguilar, "Raíces en movimiento."

26. Ibid.; Hernández and Rivera, *Regiones y religiones en México*.

27. The term *"iglesias cristianas"* is commonly used to denote evangelical churches, many of them Pentecostal.

28. Quinones, "A Church is Reborn."

29. Ibid.

30. Even though Veracruz migration began to intensify only recently (in the year 2000), in 2008 we were able to find at least four Veracruzan clubs in continuous operation within the Los Angeles region. They were linked through the Veracruzan Federation and maintained sporadic communication with other Veracruzan clubs outside the Los Angeles area. (Interviews with leaders of the Federación Veracruzana, Fundación Yanga, and Club Porteños.)

7. POLITICAL INTEGRATION: FROM LIFE IN THE MARGINS TO THE PURSUIT OF RECOGNITION

1. Bloemraad, *Becoming a Citizen*.

2. Glazer, "Governmental and Nongovernmental Roles in the Absorption of Immigrants in the United States," 60.

3. Brubaker, *Immigration and the Politics of Citizenship in Europe and North America;* Kymlicka, *Ciudadanía multicultural*.

4. Gamio, *Mexican Immigration to the United States,* 157.

5. Portes and Rumbaut, *Immigrant America*.

6. Fix, Laglagaron, et al., *An Analytic Framework for Developing an Immigrant Integration Strategy for Los Angeles County;* Fix, McHugh, et al., *Los Angeles on the Leading Edge*.

7. Bada, Fox, and Selee, *Invisible no More,* 36.

8. Ibid., 36.

9. Bakker and Smith, "El Rey del Tomate."

10. Fox and Rivera-Salgado, "Introducción."

11. Martínez, "Los derechos políticos de los migrantes mexicanos"; Rivera-Salgado, "Mexican Migrants and the Mexican Political System."

12. Rivera-Salgado, "Mexican Migrants and the Mexican Political System."

13. Ibid.

14. Bada, Fox, and Selee, *Invisible no More,* 36; Escala, Bada, and Rivera, "Mexican Migrant Civic and Political Participation in the United States."

15. Fix, Laglagaron, et al., *An Analytic Framework for Developing an Immigrant Integration Strategy for Los Angeles County;* Fix, McHugh, et al., *Los Angeles on the Leading Edge.*

16. Pastor and Ortiz, *Immigrant Integration in Los Angeles.*

8. PUBLIC POLICIES AND MEXICAN IMMIGRANT INTEGRATION IN THE CITY AND COUNTY OF LOS ANGELES

1. Varsanyi, *Taking Local Control.*

2. National Conference of State Legislatures, "State Laws Related to Immigration and Immigrants."

3. Progressive States Network, *The Anti-Immigrant Movement That Failed.*

4. Schneider and Ingram, "Social Construction of Target Populations," 334.

5. Schneider and Ingram, *Policy Design for Democracy,* 334.

6. These were their affiliations at the time of the *Media Matters* report of 2008. Both Dobbs and Beck later moved to Fox.

7. Media Matters Action Network, "Fear and Loathing in Prime Time."

8. Stelter and Carter, "Lou Dobbs Abruptly Quits CNN."

9. Southern Policy Law Center, "Intelligence Nativists to 'Patriots'."

10. Jimenez, *Humanitarian Crisis.*

11. The information and data provided in this section come from the official internet page of Los Angeles County, http://www.lacounty.gov.

12. Coalition for Humane Immigrant Rights of Los Angeles, "Local Law Enforcement and Immigration"; Fitzgerald and Alarcón, "Migration."

13. Immigration and Customs Enforcement, "Fiscal Year 2008 Annual Report."

14. Coalition for Humane Immigrant Rights of Los Angeles, "Local Law Enforcement and Immigration: The 287(g) Program in Southern California."

15. Coalition for Humane Immigrant Rights of Los Angeles, "Local Law Enforcement and Immigration: Special Order 40."

16. Pendleton, *Local Police Enforcement of Immigration Laws and Its Effects on Victims of Domestic Violence.*

17. Coalition for Humane Immigrant Rights of Los Angeles, "Local Law Enforcement and Immigration: Special Order 40."

18. California Budget Project, "The Governor's Proposed Cuts to the SSI/SSP Program and CAPI Would Affect More than 1.3 Million Californians."

19. Department of Public Social Services, "General Relief Policy."

20. Los Angeles County, "Board of Supervisors Policy Manual."

21. Los Angeles County, "Hate Crime Report 2008."

22. Los Angeles County, "Board of Supervisors Policy Manual."

23. Los Angeles County, Human Relations Commission, "Hate Crime Report 2008."

24. US Department of Homeland Security, "E-Verify."

25. Ibid.

26. For an extensive discussion of the problems that the E-Verify program presents for migrant workers, see Coalition for Humane Immigrant Rights of Los Angeles, "E-Verification and Employer Sanctions Laws."

27. Simmons, "Lancaster Requires Businesses to Do Immigration Checks on New Hires."

28. Santa Ana, *Brown Tide Rising;* Chavez, *The Latino Threat.*

29. "Why Illegal Immigration Isn't to Blame for the State Budget Crisis."

30. Haydamack, Flaming, and Joassart, *Hopeful Workers, Marginal Jobs.*

31. Ibid.

32. Pastor and Ortiz, *Immigrant Integration in Los Angeles.*

33. Centers for Disease Control and Prevention, "Work-Related Injury Deaths Among Hispanics–United States, 1992–2006."

34. Gorman, "Street Vendors Feel the Heat."

35. MacDonald, "The Reclamation of Skid Row."

36. Garrett, "Taco Trucks Can Stay Parked."

37. UCLA, "UCLA School of Law Clinical Program Wins Case Challenging Validity of Los Angeles City Ordinance Implemented against Taco Trucks."

38. Valenzuela et al., *On the Corner.*

39. Ibid.

40. Fujioka, "Foreign Consulate Annual Review Survey."

41. Gorman, "Day Laborer Rules OKd."

42. Clean Carwash Campaign, home page.

43. Nazario and Smith, "Inspectors Find Dirt on Books at Southern California Carwashes."

44. Fortuny, Capps, and Passel, "The Characteristics of the Unauthorized Immigrants in California, Los Angeles County, and the United States."

45. Clean Carwash Campaign, home page.

46. "Criminal Charges Filed against Car Wash Owners."

47. Clean Carwash Campaign, home page.

48. Clean Carwash Los Angeles Organization, "Carwash Workers Organizing Committee of the United Steelworkers."

49. Nazario and Smith, "Inspectors Find Dirt on Books at Southern California Carwashes."

50. Clean Carwash Campaign, home page.

51. Human Rights Center and International Human Rights Clinic, *Left Out;* Hondagneu-Sotelo, *Domestica.*

52. DiNovella, "First Domestic Workers' Bill of Rights Passes."

53. Villaraigosa, "The Real Minutemen."

54. Bernhardt et al., *Broken Laws, Unprotected Workers.*

55. Gorman, "Labor Advocates Push for Law Making Wage Theft a Criminal Offense in L.A."

56. Government Accountability Office, "Diverse Federal and State Efforts to Support Adult English Language Learning Could Benefit from More Coordination."

57. California Adult Schools, "Adult Education Programs."

58. Alarcón, "Proposition 187"; Santa Ana, *Brown Tide Rising;* University of Southern California, "Proposition 187."

59. American Civil Liberties Union, "California's Anti-Immigrant Proposition 187 Is Voided, Ending State's Five Year Battle with ACLU, Rights Groups."

60. English Language in Public Schools, "Proposition 227."

61. Rossell, The Near End of Bilingual Education."

62. Brock et al., *Effects of the Implementation of Proposition 227 on the Education of English Learners, K–12.*

63. California Advance Legislative Service, "Immigration Law."

64. See the reports published in the *Chicago Tribune* about the undocumented student at the University of Illinois in Chicago who won a decision that he would not be deported as long as he was studying there (e.g., Olivo, "Rigo Padilla Deportation Is Stayed").

65. Los Angeles County, Federation of Labor, "LA council Votes Unanimously for Resolution Supporting Carwash Workers' Efforts to Clean up Industry."

66. Office of the City Clerk, "Ordinance No. 17585."

67. Kragh, "Forging a Common Culture."

CONCLUSION

1. Gamio, *The Life Story of the Mexican Immigrant.*
2. Huntington, "The Hispanic Challenge."
3. Portes and Zhou, "Should Immigrants Assimilate?"
4. Ibid.

Bibliography

Alarcón, Rafael. "The Free Circulation of Skilled Migrants in North America." In *Migration without Borders: Essays on the Free Movement of People,* edited by Antoine Pécoud and Paul de Guchteneire, 243–57. New York: UNESCO and Berghahn, 2007.

———. "Los inmigrantes mexicanos y el mercado de trabajo en Los Ángeles al inicio del siglo XXI." In *Orbis/Urbis Latino: Los hispanos en las ciudades de los Estados Unidos,* edited by Cardenio Bedoya, Flavia Belpoliti, and Marc Zimmerman, 182–92. Houston: Global Casa/Lacasa Publications, University of Houston, 2008.

———. "Proposition 187: An Effective Measure to Deter Undocumented Migration to California?" Report prepared for Multicultural Education, Training and Advocacy, San Francisco, California, October 1994.

———. "U.S. Immigration Policy and the Mobility of Mexicans (1882–2005)." *Migraciones Internacionales* 6 (2011): 185–218.

Alarcón, Rafael, Alejandro Díaz Bautista, Rodolfo Cruz, Gabriel González-König, Antonio Izquierdo, Guillermo Yrizar, and René Zenteno. "La crisis financiera en Estados Unidos y su impacto en la migración mexicana." *Migraciones Internacionales* 5 (2009): 193–210.

Alarcón, Rafael, and Luis Escala Rabadán. "Transnational Philanthropy and Organizational Strategies: The Challenge of Mexican Hometown Associations in the United States." In *New Perspectives on Remittances from Mexicans and Central Americans in the United States,* edited by Germán Zárate Hoyos, 130–58. Kassel, Germany: Kassel University Press, 2007.

Alarcón, Rafael, and Telésforo Ramírez-García. "Integración económica de los inmigrantes mexicanos en la Zona Metropolitana de Los Ángeles." *Papeles de Población* 17 (2011): 73–103.

Alba, Francisco. "Migración internacional: Consolidación de patrones emergentes." *Demos* 13 (2000): 10–11.

Alba, Richard. "Bilingualism Persists, but English Still Dominates." Migration Policy Institute, 2005. Accessed August 15, 2011. http://www.migrationpolicy.org/article/bilingualism-persists-english-still-dominates.

Alba, Richard, and John Logan. "Assimilation and Stratification in the Home-ownership Patterns of Racial and Ethnic Groups." *International Migration Review* 26 (1992): 1314–41.

Alba, Richard, and Victor Nee. "Rethinking Assimilation Theory for a New Era of Immigration." *International Migration Review* 31 (1997): 826–75.

———. *Remaking the American Mainstream: Assimilation and Contemporary Immigration*. Cambridge: Harvard University Press, 2005.

Alonso Meneses, Guillermo. "Inmigrantes extranjeros en Barcelona." In *Migración internacional e identidades cambiantes,* edited by María Eugenia Anguiano Téllez and Miguel Hernández Madrid. Zamora, Mexico: El Colegio de Michoacán, El Colegio de la Frontera Norte, 2002.

Alonso Meneses, Guillermo, and Luis Escala Rabadán. "Introducción." In *Off-side/Fuera de lugar: Futbol y migraciones en el mundo contemporáneo,* edited by Guillermo Alonso Meneses and and Luis Escala Rabadán. Tijuana, Mexico: El Colegio de la Frontera Norte, CLAVE Editorial, 2012.

American Civil Liberties Union. "California's Anti-Immigrant Proposition 187 Is Voided, Ending State's Five Year Battle with ACLU, Rights Groups," July 1999. Accessed November 18, 2000. https://www.aclu.org/immigrants-rights/cas-anti-immigrant-proposition-187-voided-ending-states-five-year-battle-aclu-righ.

Anguiano Téllez, María Eugenia. "Rumbo al norte: Nuevos destinos de la emigración veracruzana." *Migraciones Internacionales* 3 (2005): 82–110.

Arango, Joaquín. "Las migraciones internacionales en un mundo globalizado." In *Inmigración en Canarias: Contexto, tendencias y retos,* edited by Antonio González Viéitez, 11–22. Madrid: Fundación Pedro García Cabrera, 2007.

Arellano, Gustavo. *Orange County: A Personal History*. New York: Scribner, 2008.

Ariza, Marina, and Alejandro Portes, eds. *El país transnacional*. Mexico City: Universidad Nacional Autónoma de México, 2007.

Bada, Xóchitl. "Mexican Migrants: The Attractions and Realities of the United States." *Latin American Research Review* 45 (2010): 236–44.

Bada, Xóchitl, Jonathan Fox, R. Donnelly, and Andrew Selee. *Context Matters: Latino Immigrant Civic Engagement in Nine U.S. Cities*. Washington, DC: Woodrow Wilson International Center for Scholars, 2010.

Bada, Xóchitl, Jonathan Fox, and Andrew Selee. *Invisible no More: Mexican Migrant Civic Participation in the United States*. Washington, DC: Woodrow Wilson International Center for Scholars, 2006.

Bakker, Matt, and Michael Peter Smith. "El Rey del Tomate: Migrant Political Transnationalism and Democratization in Mexico." *Migraciones Internacionales* 2 (2003): 59–83.

Balbo, Marcello, ed. *International Migrants and the City: Bangkok, Berlin, Dakar, Karachi, Johannesburg, Naples, São Paulo, Tijuana, Vancouver,*

Vladivostok, Venecia. Venice: UNHABITAT-United Nations, Università Iuav di Venezia, 2005.

Baron, Dennis. "English Spoken Here? What the 2000 Census Tells Us about Language in the USA." *Essays on Language, Reading, Writing, and Technology*, 2007. Accessed January 13, 2010. http://www.english.illinois.edu/-people-/faculty/debaron/essayset.html.

Barrow, Lisa, and Cecilia Elena Rouse. "The Economic Value of Education by Race and Ethnicity." *Economic Perspectives* 30 (2006): 14–27.

Barth, Frederik. *Ethnic Groups and Boundaries: The Social Organization of Culture Difference*. Oslo, Norway: Universitetsforlaget, 1969.

Bauman, Zygmunt. *Liquid Times: Living in an Age of Uncertainty*. Cambridge: University of Cambridge, 2006.

Benner, Chris. *Work in the New Economy: Flexible Labor Markets in Silicon Valley*. Oxford: Blackwell, 2002.

Bernhardt, Annette, Heather Boushey, Laura Dresser, and Chris Tilly, eds. *Confronting the Gloves-Off Economy: America's Broken Labor Standards and How to Fix Them*. Champaign, IL: Labor and Employment Relations Association, 2008. Accessed October, 2010. http://nelp.3cdn.net/of16d12cb9c05e6aa4_bvm6i2w2o.pdf.

Bernhardt, Annette, Ruth Milkman, Nik Theodore, Douglas Heckathorn, Mirabai Auer, James DeFilippis, Ana Luz González, Victor Narro, Jason Perelshteyn, Diana Polson, and Michael Spiller. *Broken Laws, Unprotected Workers: Violations of Employment and Labor Laws in America's Cities*. Chicago, Los Angeles, and New York: Center for Urban Economic Development, National Employment Law Project, and UCLA Institute for Research on Labor and Employment, 2009. Accessed January, 2010. http://www.nelp.org/page/-/brokenlaws/BrokenLawsReport2009.pdf?nocdn = 1.

Blanco, Cristina, and Iker Barbero González, eds. *Pautas de asentamiento de la población inmigrante: Implicaciones y retos socio-jurídicos*. Madrid: Dykinson, 2009.

Bloemraad, Irene. *Becoming a Citizen: Incorporating Immigrants and Refugees in the United States and Canada*. Berkeley: University of California Press, 2006.

Bloemraad, Irene, and Reed Ueda. "Naturalization and Nationality." In *Companion to American Immigration*, edited by Reed Ueda, 36–57. Oxford: Blackwell, 2006.

Borjas, George. "Self-Selection and the Earnings of Immigrants: Reply." *American Economic Review* 80 (1990): 305–8.

———. "The Analytics of the Wage Effect of Immigration." Working Paper/NBER Working Paper Series, National Bureau of Economic Research, Cambridge, MA, 2009. Accessed December, 2009. http://www.nber.org/papers/w14796.pdf.

Brock, Leslie, Danielle Delancey, Phil Esra, Amy Merickel, Thomas Parrish, María Pérez, Miguel Socias, Robert Linquanti, Cecilia Speroni, and Angeline Spain. *Effects of the Implementation of Proposition 227 on the Education of English Learners, K–12: Findings from a Five-Year Evaluation*, Washington, DC: American Institutes for Research, WestEd, 2006. Accessed March, 2008. http://www.wested.org/online_pubs/227Reportb.pdf.

Brown, Susan, and Frank Bean. "Assimilation Models, Old and New: Explaning a Long-Term Process." Migration Policy Institute, 2006. Accessed February 13, 2008. http://www.migrationinformation.org/Feature/display.cfm?id = 442.

Brubaker, W. Rogers. *Ethnicity without Groups*. Cambridge: Harvard University Press, 2004.

———. "The Return of Assimilation? Changing Perspectives on Immigration and Its Sequels in France, Germany and the United States." *Ethnic and Racial Studies* 24 (2001): 531–48.

———, ed. *Immigration and the Politics of Citizenship in Europe and North America*. Lanham: University Press of America, 1992.

Cabrera Hernández, José, Andrew Hall, Jessica de Anda, David Rocha Romero, and Raúl Saldaña. "Coping with Hard Times in El Norte." In *Recession without Borders: Mexican Migrants Confront the Economic Downturn*, edited by David Fitzgerald, Rafael Alarcón, and Leah Muse-Orlinoff, 95–110. London: Lynne Rienner, 2011.

Calderón Chelius, Leticia, and Jesús Martínez Saldaña. *La dimensión política de la migración mexicana: Migraciones internacionales*. Mexico City: Instituto Mora, 2002.

California Adult Schools. "Adult Education Programs." Accessed July 13, 2012. http://californiaadultschools.org/cas/programs.

California Advance Legislative Service. "Immigration Law. Education. California Extends In-State Tuition Benefits to Undocumented Aliens." *Harvard Law Review* 115 (2002): 1548–54.

California Budget Project. "The Governor's Proposed Cuts to the SSI/SSP Program and CAPI Would Affect More than 1.3 Million Californians." Accessed March 14, 2010. http://www.cbp.org/documents/090204_SSISSP_County.pdf.

Cardona, Ishtar. "Los actores culturales entre la tentación comunitaria y el mercado global: El surgimiento del Son Jarocho." *Política y Cultura* 26 (2006): 213–32.

Castells, Manuel. *La era de la información*. Vol. 1: *La sociedad red*. Mexico City: Siglo XXI, 2002.

———. *La era de la información*. Vol. 2: *El poder de la identidad*. Mexico City: Siglo XXI, 2001.

———. *La era de la información*. Vol. 3: *Fin de milenio*. Mexico City: Siglo XXI, 2001.

———. *The Rise of the Network Society*. Cambridge: Blackwell, 1996.

Castells, Manuel, and Alejandro Portes. "World Underneath: The Origins, Dynamics, and Effects of the Informal Economy." In *The Informal Economy: Studies in Advanced and Less Developed Countries*, edited by Alejandro Portes, Manuel Castells, and Lauren Benton, 11–37. Baltimore: Johns Hopkins University Press, 1989.

Centers for Disease Control and Prevention. "Work-Related Injury Deaths among Hispanics: United States, 1992–2006." Accessed December 12, 2009. http://www.cdc.gov/mmwr/preview/mmwrhtml/mm5722a1.htm.

Chaloff, Jonathan, and George Lemaître. "Managing Highly-Skilled Labour Migration: A Comparative Analysis of Migration Policies and Challenges in

OECD Countries." *OECD Social Employment and Migration Working Papers* 79 (2009): 2–54. Accessed December 15, 2009. doi: 10.1787/1815199x.

Charles, Camille Zubrinsky. "Residential Segregation in Los Angeles." In *Prismatic Metropolis: Inequality in Los Angeles*, edited by Lawrence Bobo, Melvil L. Oliver, James H. Johnson Jr., and Abel Valenzuela Jr., 167–219. New York: Russell Sage Foundation, 2000.

———. *Won't You Be My Neighbor? Race, Class and Residence in Los Angeles*. New York: Russell Sage Foundation, 2006.

Chávez, Ana Margarita, Carolina A. Rosas, and Patricia Zamudio. "La migración en el estado de Veracruz, una visión desde sus municipios." In *Nación, estado, comunidad: Consolidación y emergencia en la emigración mexicana*, edited by Agustín Escobar Latapí, 295–331. Buenos Aires: CIESAS/Antropología, 2007.

Chavez, Leo. *The Latino Threat: Constructing Immigrants, Citizens and the Nation*. Stanford: Stanford University Press, 2008.

Chiswick, Barry. "The Effect of Americanization on the Earnings of Foreign-Born Men." *Journal of Political Economy* 86 (1978): 897–921.

Clean Carwash Campaign. Accessed December, 2009. http://www.cleancarwashcampaign.org/?action = cat&categoryID = b18ebe72–95a6–4272–%20 9446–6e5e92bd0011.

———. "Carwash Worker Law Renewal Signed Into Law." Accessed December 1, 2009. http://laborweb.aflcio.org/sites/Open5/carwash/index.cfm?action = article&articleID = 052c7088–0906–428a-a3b4-e6b84304fd05.

———. "CLEAN members." Accessed December 12, 2009. http://laborweb.aflcio.org/sites/Open5/carwash/index.cfm?action = cat&categoryID = 5abd8d03-bff7–4e5e-a7d1–1abcd6edf4b3.

———. "Report: Cleaning up the Carwash Industry." Accessed December 1, 2009. http://laborweb.aflcio.org/sites/Open5/carwash/index.cfm?action = article&articleID = ae961 5a4–6be8–47be-b29e-5b78b353dca3.

Clean Carwash Los Angeles Organization. "Carwash Workers Organizing Committee of the United Steelworkers." Accessed December 12, 2010. http://cleancarwashla.org/.

Coalition for Humane Immigrant Rights of Los Angeles. "Local Law Enforcement and Immigration: The 287(g) Program in Southern California." 2008. Accessed December 1, 2009. http://chirla.org/files/287g%20Factsheet%2011–24–08.pdf.

———. "Local Law Enforcement and Immigration: Special Order 40." 2008. Accessed December 1, 2009. http://chirla.org/files/Factsheet%20Special%20 Order%2040%2011.20.08.pdf.

———. "E-Verification and Employer Sanctions Laws: Impacts on Employers and Workers." Accessed January 12, 2010. http://chirla.org/files/E-VerifyPolicy Report-CHIRLA-Dec102008.pdf.

Conjunto Jardín. "The group: About." Accessed July 12, 2012. http://www. conjuntojardin.com/thegroup/about/.

Consejo Nacional de Población (CONAPO). "Índices de intensidad migratoria, México-Estados Unidos, 2000." Accessed August 15, 2011. http://www. conapo.gob.mx/es/CONAPO/Indices_de_Intensidad_Migratoria_Mexico-Estados_Unidos_2000.

Córdova Plaza, Rosío, Cristina Núñez, and David Skerritt, eds. *Migración internacional, crisis agrícola y transformaciones culturales en la región central de Veracruz.* Veracruz, Mexico: CEMCA/Universidad Veracruzana/Plaza y Valdés/Conacyt, 2008.

Cornelius, Wayne. "Impacts of the 1986 U.S. Immigration Law on Emigration from Rural Mexican Sending Communities." In *Undocumented Migration to the United States: IRCA and the Experience of the 1980s,* edited by Frank Bean, Barry Edmonston, and Jeffrey Passel, 227–49. Washington, DC: Rand Corporation/Urban Institute Press, 1990.

County of Los Angeles. Government/Public Information—Records. Accessed December 1, 2009. http://www.lacounty.gov/.

County of Los Angeles, Community and Senior Services. "Racial Hate Crimes Down, Homophobic and Religious Crimes Rise in 2008." Accessed February 1, 2010. http://lahumanrelations.org/hatecrime/data/2008%20Hate%20Crime%20Press%20Release.pdf.

"Criminal Charges Filed against Car Wash Owners." *Los Angeles Times,* February 10, 2009. Accessed December 2, 2009. http://latimesblogs.latimes.com/lanow/2009/02/los-angeles-cit.html.

Cruz-Manjarrez, Adriana. "Performance, Ethnicity and Migration: Dance and Music in the Continuation of Ethnic Identity among Immigrant Zapotecs from the Oaxaca Highland Village of Villa Hidalgo, Yalalag to Los Angeles." Master's thesis, University of California Los Angeles/World Cultures, 2001.

Davis, Mike. *City of Quartz: Excavating the Future in Los Angeles.* New York: Vintage, 1992.

De la Torre, Renée, and Cristina Gutiérrez Zúñiga. "Territorios de la diversidad religiosa hoy." In *Atlas de la diversidad religiosa en México,* edited by Renée De la Torre and Cristina Gutiérrez Zúñiga, 35–183 Zapopan, Mexico: El Colegio de Jalisco, El Colegio de la Frontera Norte, Centro de Investigaciones y Estudios Superiores en Antropología Social, 2007.

Delgado Wise, Raúl, Humberto Márquez Covarrubias, and Héctor Rodríguez Ramírez. "Organizaciones transnacionales de migrantes y desarrollo regional en Zacatecas." *Migraciones Internacionales* 4 (2004): 159–81.

Department of Public Social Services. "General Relief Policy," 2009. Accessed July 12, 2010. http://dpss.lacounty.gov/ dpss/GR/pdf/general_relief_policy.pdf.

Diaz McConnell, Eileen, and Enrico A. Marcelli. "Buying into the American Dream? Mexican Immigrants, Legal Status and Homeownership in Los Angeles County." *Social Science Quarterly* 1 (2007): 199–221.

DiNovella, Elizabeth. "First Domestic Workers' Bill of Rights Passes." Accessed July 13, 2012. http://www.yesmagazine.org/new-economy/first-domestic-workers-bill-of-rightspasses-in-new-york.

Durand, Jorge, and Enrique Martínez Curiel. "Los nuevos procesos de integración, matrimonios mixtos y migración México-Estados Unidos: Nuevas tendencias." In *Fronteras fragmentadas: Género, familia e identidades en la migración,* edited by Gail Mummert, 437–49. Zamora, Mexico: El Colegio de Michoacán, 1999.

Durand, Jorge, and Douglas S. Massey. *Clandestinos: Migración México-Estados Unidos en los albores del siglo XXI.* Mexico: Miguel Ángel Porrúa, 2003.

EFFNATIS 2001. "Final Report," 2001. Accessed May 29, 2010. http://www.efms.uni-bamberg.de/pdf/finalreportk.pdf.

Egelko, Bob. "Group's Leader Urges New Strategy on Immigrant Rights." *San Francisco Chronicle,* November 27, 2009. Accessed November 29, 2009. http://www.sfgate.com/news/article/Group-s-leader-urges-new-strategy-on-immigrant-3280347.php.

English Language in Public Schools. "Proposition 227," 1988. Accessed December 13, 1987. http://primary98.sos.ca.gov/VoterGuide/Propositions/227text.htm.

Escala Rabadán, Luis. "Migración, formas organizativas y espacio público: La celebración de la Guelaguetza en San Diego." Paper presented at Seminario Interno de Estudios Sociales of El Colegio de la Frontera Norte, December 2008.

Escala Rabadán, Luis, Xóchitl Bada, and Gaspar Rivera-Salgado. "Mexican Migrant Civic and Political Participation in the United States: The Case of Hometown Associations in Los Angeles and Chicago." *Norteamérica* 2 (2006): 127–72.

Escárcega, Sylvia, and Stefano Varese. "Una mirada retrospectiva a la migración transnacional mixteca." In *La ruta mixteca: El impacto etnopolítico de la migración trasnacional de los pueblos indígenas de México,* edited by Sylvia Escárcega and Stefano Varese, 15–40. Mexico City: EIICH-Universidad Nacional Autónoma de México, 2004.

Estrada, Emir, and Pierrette Hondagneu-Sotelo. "Intersectional Dignities: Latino Immigrant Street Vendor Youth in Los Angeles." *Journal of Contemporary Ethnography* 1 (2011): 102–31.

Experience LA. "Movimiento Jaranero de California," 2012. Accessed July 12, 2012. http://www.experiencela.com/calendar/eventmore.%20asp?key = 28930.

Fernández de Castro, Rafael, Rodolfo García Zamora, and Ana Vila Freyer, eds. *El Programa 3x1 para migrantes: ¿Primera política transnacional en México?* Mexico: Instituto Tecnológico Autónomo de México/Universidad Autónoma de Zacatecas/Miguel Ángel Porrúa, 2006.

Fitzgerald, David, and Rafael Alarcón. "Migration: Policies and Politics." In *Mexico and the United States: Confronting the 21st Century,* edited by Peter H. Smith and Andrew Selee, 113–138. London: Lynne Rienner, 2013.

Fix, Michael, and Jeffrey Passel. "U.S. Immigration: Trends and Implications for Schools." New Orleans: No Child Left Behind Implementation Institute/The Urban Institute. Accessed May 13, 2007. www.urban.org/ UploadedPDF/410654_NABEPresentation.pdf.

Fix, Michael, Laureen Laglagaron, Aaron Matteo Terrazas, and Margie McHugh. *An Analytic Framework for Developing an Immigrant Integration Strategy for Los Angeles County.* Los Angeles: National Center on Immigrant Integration Policy/Migration Policy Institute, 2007.

Fix, Michael, Margie McHugh, Aaron Matteo Terrazas, and Laureen Laglagaron. *Los Angeles on the Leading Edge: Immigrant Integration Indicators and Their Policy Implications.* Los Angeles: National Center on Immigrant Integration Policy/Migration Policy Institute, 2008.

Flores, Edward, Gary Painter, and Harry Pachon. "¿Qué Pasa? Are English Language Learning Students Remaining in English Learning Classes Too Long?" Tomás Rivera Policy Institute. Accessed December 14, 2009. http://www.trpi.org/PDFs/ ell_report.pdf.

Fortuny, Karina, Randy Capps, and Jeffrey Passel. "The Characteristics of the Unauthorized Immigrants in California, Los Angeles County, and the United States." Urban Institute, 2007. http://www.urban.org/research/publication/characteristics-unauthorized-immigrants-california-los-angeles-county-and-united-states/view/full_report.

Fox, Jonathan, Andrew Selee, and Xóchitl Bada. "Conclusions." In *Invisible no More: Migrant Civic Participation in the United States,* edited by Xóchitl Bada, Jonathan Fox, and Andrew Selee, 35–40. Washington DC: Center for Global/International and Regional Studies/Universidad de California Santa Cruz, 2006.

Fox, Jonathan, and Gaspar Rivera-Salgado. "Introducción." In *Indígenas mexicanos migrantes en los Estados Unidos,* edited by Jonathan Fox and Gaspar Rivera-Salgado, 9–74. Mexico City: H. Cámara de Diputados LIX Legislatura/Universidad de California Santa Cruz/Universidad Autónoma de Zacatecas/Miguel Ángel Porrúa, 2004.

———, eds. *Indígenas migrantes mexicanos en los Estados Unidos.* Mexico City: Porrúa/Universidad Autónoma de Zacatecas/Universidad de California, 2004.

Frey, William, and Dowell Myers. "CensusScope." Accessed March 15, 2012. http://www.censusscope.org/us/s6/rank_dissimilarity_white_other.html.

Fujioka, William. "Foreign Consulate Annual Review Survey." Accessed December 8, 2009. http://file.lacounty. gov/bc/q4_2009/cms1_140034.pdf.

Galicia Bretón-Mora, Fabiola. "Inserción laboral de inmigrantes calificados de Zacatecas, Oaxaca y Veracruz en Los Ángeles, California." PhD diss., El Colegio de la Frontera Norte, 2012.

Galindo, Carlos. *Nosotros no cruzamos la frontera: Los hijos de estadounidenses de los inmigrantes mexicanos.* Mexico City: CONAPO, 2009.

Gamio, Manuel. *The Life Story of the Mexican Immigrant: Autobiographic Documents Collected by Manuel Gamio, 1931.* New York: Dover, 1971 [1931].

———. *Mexican Immigration to the United States: A Study of Human Migration and Adjustment.* New York: Dover, 1971 [1930].

García, Mario T. *Mexican Americans.* New Haven: Yale University Press, 1989.

García y Griego, Larry Manuel. "The Bracero Policy Experiment: U.S.-Mexican Responses to Mexican Labor Migration, 1942–1955." PhD diss., University of California, Los Angeles, 1988.

Garrett, Therolf. "Taco Trucks Can Stay Parked." *Los Angeles Times,* August 28, 2008. Accessed December 10, 2010. http://articles.latimes.com/2008/aug/28/local/me-tacos28.

Giddens, Anthony. *Runaway World: How Globalization Is Reshaping Our Lives.* London: Profile, 1999.

Giménez, Gilberto. "Paradigmas de identidad." In *Sociología de la identidad,* edited by Aquiles Chihu. Mexico City: Universidad Autónoma Metropolitana, 2002.

———. "Culturas e identidades." *Revista Mexicana de Sociología* 66 (2004): 77–99.

Glazer, Nathan. "Governmental and Nongovernmental Roles in the Absorption of Immigrants in the United States." In *Paths to Inclusion: The Integration of Migrants in the United States and Germany,* edited by Peter H. Schuck and Rainer Münz, 59–82. New York: Berghahn, 1998.

Glick-Schiller, Nina, Linda Basch, and Cristina Szanton. "From Immigrant to Transmigrant: Theorizing Transnational Migration." *Anthropological Quarterly* 68 (1995): 48–63.

Goffman, Erving. *Stigma: Notes on the Management of Spoiled Identity.* New York: Prentice Hall, 1963.

Goldring, Luin. "Blurring Borders: Constructing Transnational Community in the Process of Mexico-U.S. Migration." *Research in Community Sociology* 6 (1996): 69–104.

González, Gilbert G. "Chicano History: Transcending Cultural Models." *Pacific Historical Review* 4 (1994): 469–97.

González Gutiérrez, Carlos, ed. *Relaciones estado-diáspora: Aproximaciones desde cuatro continentes.* Mexico City: Miguel Ángel Porrúa/Secretaría de Relaciones Exteriores/Universidad Autónoma de Zacatecas, 2006.

Gordon, Milton. *Assimilation in American Life: The Role of Race, Religion and National Origins.* New York: Oxford University Press, 1964.

Gorman, Anna. "Day Laborer Rules OKd: Los Angeles Seeks to Have Home Improvement Stores Create Centers for Workers." *Los Angeles Times,* August 15, 2008. Accessed June 28, 2011. http://articles.latimes.com/2008/aug/14/local/me-homedepot14.

———. "Labor Advocates Push for Law Making Wage Theft a Criminal Offense in L.A." *Los Angeles Times,* October 27, 2009. Accessed June 28, 2011. http://latimesblogs.latimes.com/lanow/2009/10/labor-advocates-push-for-wage-theft-law.html.

———. "Street Vendors Feel the Heat." *Los Angeles Times,* April 1, 2007. Accessed June 28, 2011. http://articles.latimes.com/2007/apr/01/local/me-vendors1.

Government Accountability Office (GAO). "Diverse Federal and State Efforts to Support Adult English Language Learning Could Benefit from More Coordination," July 29, 2009. Accessed October 27, 2009. http://www.gao.gov/products/ GAO-09-575.

Greenhouse, Steven. "Carwashes Violating Wage Laws, State Finds." *New York Times,* August 15, 2008. Accessed September 13, 2008. http://www.nytimes.com/2008/08/16/nyregion/16carwash.html.

Griswold del Castillo, Richard. *The Los Angeles Barrio, 1850–1890: A Social History,* Berkeley: University of California Press, 1979.

Harris, Kamala D. "Brown Sues Los Angeles Car Wash Company for Workers Rights Violations." *Office of the Attorney General.* Accessed December 19, 2009. http://ag.ca.gov/newsalerts/print_release.php?id = 1841.

Haydamack, Brent, Daniel Flaming, and Pascale Joassart. *Hopeful Workers, Marginal Jobs: L.A.'s Off-the-Books Labor Force*. Los Angeles: Economic Roundtable, 2005.

Held, David, and Anthony McGrew. *Globalization/Anti-Globalization: Beyond the Great Divide*. Cambridge, UK: Polity Press, 2007.

Held, David, Anthony McGrew, David Goldblatt, and Jonathan Perraton. *Global Transformations: Politics, Economics and Culture*. Palo Alto: Stanford University Press, 1999.

Hernández, Alberto, and Carolina Rivera, eds. *Regiones y religiones en México: Estudios de la transformación sociorreligiosa*. Michoacán, Mexico: El Colegio de la Frontera Norte/CIESAS/El Colegio de Michoacán, 2009.

Hirschman, Charles. "The Role of Religion in the Origins and Adaptation of Immigrant Groups in the United States." *International Migration Review* 38 (2004): 1206–33.

Hoffman, Abraham. "Stimulus to Repatriation: The 1931 Federal Deportation Drive and the Los Angeles Mexican Community." *Pacific Historical Review* 2 (1973): 205–19.

Hondagneu-Sotelo, Pierrette. *Domestica: Immigrant Workers Clearing and Caring in the Shadows of Affluence*. Berkeley: University of California Press, 2001.

Human Rights Center and International Human Rights Clinic. *Left Out: Assessing the Rights of Migrant Domestic Workers in the United States, Seeking Alternatives*. Berkeley: Human Rights Center/International Human Rights Clinic/Boalt Hall School of Law.

Huntington, Samuel. "The Hispanic Challenge." *Foreign Policy*, March 1, 2004. Accessed May 14, 2009. http://www.foreignpolicy.com/articles/2004/03/01/the_hispanic_challenge.

———. *Who We Are? The Challenges to America's National Identity*. New York: Simon and Schuster, 2004.

Ibarra Escobar, Guillermo. *Migrantes en mercados de trabajo globales: Mexicanos y sinaloenses en Los Ángeles*. Culiacán, Mexico: Universidad Autónoma de Sinaloa, 2005.

Immigrant Legal Resource Center. "California Dream Act Resources," November 22, 2011. Accessed March 15, 2012. http://www.ilrc.org/ news-events/california-dream-act-resources.

Immigration and Customs Enforcement (ICE). "Fiscal Year 2008 Annual Report." Accessed July 13, 2012. http://cdm16064.contentdm.oclc.org/cdm/ref/collection/p266901coll4/id/2170.

Instituto de los Mexicanos en el Exterior (IME). *Matrículas consulares: Estadísticas de mexicanos en el exterior 2007*. Accessed July 1, 2011. http://www.ime.gob.mx/index.php?option = com_content&view = article&id = 19&Itemid = 507&lang = es.

———. *Matrículas consulares: Estadísticas de mexicanos en el exterior 2010*. Accessed July 1, 2011. http://www.ime.gob.mx/index.php?option = com_content&view = article&id = 19&Itemid = 507&lang = es.

Jimenez, Maria. *Humanitarian Crisis: Migrant Deaths at the U.S.-Mexico Border*. San Francisco: American Civil Liberties Union of San Diego and Imperial Counties/Mexico's National Commission of Human Rights, 2009.

Jiménez, Tomás, and David Fitzgerald. "Mexican Assimilation: A Temporal and Spatial Reorientation." *Du Bois Review: Social Science Research on Race* 4 (2007): 337–54. Accessed August 15, 2011. doi: 10.1017/S1742058X07070191.

Kaplan, D. H., and W. Li. *Landscapes of the Ethnic Economy*. Plymouth, UK: Rowman and Littlefield, 2006.

Kearney, Michael, and Carole Nagengast. *Anthropological Perspectives on Transnational Communities in Rural California*. Davis, CA: Institute for Rural Studies, 1989.

Kissam, Ed. "La migración entre México y Estados Unidos, implicaciones para el desarrollo de una colaboración bilateral en educación de adultos." In *Educación de adultos*, edited by Manuel Servín Massieu, 2–9. Mexico, 1993.

Kragh, Erin. "Forging a Common Culture: Integrating California's Illegal Immigrant Population." *Boston Third World Law Journal* 2 (2004). Accessed March 23, 2008. http://lawdigitalcommons.bc.edu/twlj/vol24/iss2/4/.

Kymlicka, Will. *The Rights of Minority Cultures*. Oxford: Oxford University Press, 1995.

———. "Two Models of Pluralism and Tolerance." In *Toleration*, edited by D. Heyd, 81–105. Princeton: Princeton University Press, 1996.

———. *Ciudadanía multicultural: Una teoría liberal de los derechos de las minorías*. Buenos Aires: Paidós, 2006.

Lanly, Guillaume, and Basilia Valenzuela, eds. *Clubes de migrantes oriundos mexicanos en los Estados Unidos: La política transnacional de la nueva sociedad civil migrante*. Guadalajara: Universidad de Guadalajara, 2004.

Léonard, Éric, André Quesnel, and Alberto del Rey. "De la comunidad territorial al archipiélago familiar: Movilidad, contractualización de las relaciones inter-generacionales y desarrollo local en el sur del estado de Veracruz." *Estudios Sociológicos* 66 (2004): 557–89.

Levine, Elaine. *Los nuevos pobres de Estados Unidos: Los hispanos*. Mexico City: Universidad Nacional Autónoma de México/Miguel Ángel Porrúa, 2001.

———. "El proceso de incorporación de los migrantes mexicanos a la vida y el trabajo en Los Ángeles, California." *Migraciones Internacionales* 2 (2005): 108–36.

Levitt, Peggy. "Routes and Roots: Understanding the Lives of the Second Generation Transnationally." *Journal of Ethnic and Migration Studies* 7 (2009): 1225–42.

Levitt, Peggy, Josh DeWind, and Steven Vertovec. "International Perspectives on Transnational Migration: An Introduction." *International Migration Review* 3 (2003): 565–75.

Levitt, Peggy, and Nina Glick-Schiller. "Conceptualizing Simultaneity: A Transnational Social Field Perspective on Society." *International Migration Review* 38 (2004): 1002–39.

Light, Ivan Hubert. *Ethnic Enterprise in Americas: Bussiness and Welfare among Chinese, Japanese and Blacks*. Berkeley: University of California Press, 1972.

———. *Deflecting Immigration: Networks, Markets and Regulation in Los Angeles*. New York: Russell Sage Foundation, 2006.

Light, Ivan, Richard B. Bernard, and Rebecca Kim. "Immigrant Incorporation in the Garment Industry of Los Angeles." *International Migration Review* 1 (1999): 5–25.

Llopis, Ramón, and Albert Moncusí. "'El deporte une bastantísimo aquí': Las ligas de futbol de la asociación de latinoamericanos y ecuatorianos en Valencia." In *La migración ecuatoriana: Transnacionalismo, redes e identidades,* edited by Gioconda Herrera, María Carrillo, and Alicia Torres, 493–512. Quito: FLACSO, 2005.

López, Felipe, Luis Escala Rabadán, and Raúl Hinojosa-Ojeda. *Migrant Associations, Remittances and Regional Development between Los Angeles and Oaxaca.* Los Angeles: University of California, North American Integration and Development Center, 2001.

López, Felipe, and David Runsten. "El trabajo de los mixtecos y zapotecos en California: Experiencia rural y urbana." In *Indígenas mexicanos migrantes en los Estados Unidos,* edited by Jonathan Fox and Gaspar Rivera, 277–309. Mexico City: Cámara de Diputados/Universidad de California/Universidad Autónoma de Zacatecas/Miguel Ángel Porrúa, 2004.

Los Angeles County. "Board of Supervisors Policy Manual," February 26, 2009. Accessed March 3, 2009. http://countypolicy.co.la.ca.us/.

Los Angeles County, Federation of Labor (AFL-CIO). "LA Council Votes Unanimously for Resolution Supporting Carwash Workers' Efforts to Clean up Industry." Accessed July 30, 2009. http://launionaflcio.org/2008/6467/2008–08–07la-city-council-votes-unanimously-for-resolution-supporting-carwash-workers-efforts-to-clean-up-industry.html.

Los Angeles County, Human Relations Commission. "Hate Crime Report 2008." Accessed Decembr 1, 2009. http://lahumanrelations.org/hatecrime/data/2008%20Hate%20Crime%20Report%2011–12–09_08–09.pdf.

———. "Network Member Organizations," 2011. Accessed December 1, 2009. http://lahumanrelations.org/programs/network/members.htm.

Los Angeles Downtown Industrial District. "Safer Cities Initiative Reduces Crime on Skid Row," 2006. *Newsletter.* Accessed May 15, 2008. http://www.centralcityeast.org/news/newsletters/ nl_4th2006.pdf.

Lowestein, Roger. "The Immigration Equation." *New York Times Magazine,* July 9, 2006. Accessed December 9, 2009. http://www.nytimes.com/2006/07/09/magazine/09IMM.html?ex = 1310097600&en = 45962e550ceea8df&ei = 5088&partner = rssnyt&e mc = rss.

Loza, Steven. "From Veracruz to Los Angeles: The Reinterpretation of the Son Jarocho." *Latin American Music Review* 2 (1992): 179–94.

MacDonald, Heather. "The Reclamation of Skid Row." *City Journal* 4 (2007): 15–16. http://www.city-journal.org/html/17_4_skid_row.html.

Martin, Philip L. "Harvest of Confusion: Immigration Reform and California Agriculture." *International Migration Review* 1 (1990): 69–95.

Martínez Saldaña, Jesús. "Los derechos políticos de los migrantes mexicanos: Oportunidades y desafíos." In *Invisible no More: Mexican Migrant Civic Participation in the United States,* edited by Xóchitl Bada, Jonathan Fox, and Andrew Selee, 45–46. Washington, DC: Woodrow Wilson International Center for Scholars, 2006.

Martuccelli, Danilo. *Sociologies de la modernité: L'itinéraire du XXème siècle.* Paris: Gallimard, 1999.

Massey, Douglas, Jorge Durand, and Nolan Malone. *Beyond Smoke and Mirrors: Mexican Immigration in an Era of Economic Integration.* New York: Russell Sage Foundation, 2000.

McManus, W. S. "Labor Market Effects of Language Enclaves: Hispanic Men in the United States." *Journal of Human Resources* 25 (1990): 228–52.

McWilliams, Carey. *North from Mexico: The Spanish- Speaking People of the United States,* 1948. New York: Praeger, 1990.

Media Matters Action Network. "Fear and Loathing in Prime Time: Immigration Myths and Cable News 2008." Accessed November 12, 2009. http://mediamattersaction.org/reports/fearandloathing/online_version.

Meissner, Doris, Deborah W. Meyers, Demetrious G. Papadimetriou, and Michael Fix. *Immigration and America Future: A New Chapter.* Washington, DC: Migration Policy Institute, 2006.

Merkel, Angela. "El multiculturalismo en Alemania: Un fracaso total." *BBC,* October 16, 2010. Accessed Jun 17, 2011. http://www.bbc.co.uk/mundo/noticias/2010/10/101016_angela_merkel_muticulturalismo_falla_alemania_med.shtml.

Merz, Barbara, ed. *Nuevas pautas para México: Observaciones sobre remesas, donaciones filantrópicas y desarrollo equitativo.* Cambridge: Harvard University Press, 2005.

Mestries Benquet, Francis. "Crisis cafetalera y migración internacional en Veracruz." *Migraciones Internacionales* 2 (2003): 121–48.

———. "Migración internacional y campesinado cafetalero en México: Fases, circuitos y trayectorias migratorias." *Análisis Económico* 46 (2006): 263–89.

Milkman, Ruth, ed. *Organizing Immigrants: The Challenge for Unions in Contemporary California.* Ithaca: ILR Press/Cornell University Press, 2000.

Mines, Richard. *Developing a Community Tradition of Migration: A Field Study in Rural Zacatecas, Mexico, and California Settlement Areas.* San Diego: University of California, 1981.

Moctezuma Longoria, Miguel. "El circuito migratorio Sain El Alto, Zacatecas-Oakland, California." PhD diss., El Colegio de la Frontera Norte, 1999.

———. *La transnacionalidad de los sujetos: Dimensiones, metodologías y prácticas convergentes de los migrantes mexicanos en Estados Unidos.* Mexico City: Universidad Autónoma de Zacatecas/Miguel Angel Porrúa, 2011.

Montejano, David. "Who Is Samuel P. Huntington?" *Texas Observer,* August 12, 2004. Accessed March 9, 2010. http://www.texasobserver.org/archives/item/14331-1727-who-is-samuel-p-huntington-the-intelligence-failure-of-a-harvard-professor.

Moya, José. "Immigrants and Associations: A Global and Historical Perspective." *Journal of Ethnic and Migration Studies* 5 (2005): 833–64.

Mulder, Clara H. and Wagner, Michael. "First-Time Homeownership in the Family Life Course: A West German-Dutch Comparison." *Urban Studies* 4 (1998): 687–713.

Música Tradicional Mexicana. "Encuentro de Jaraneros, 1996–2011." Accessed July 12, 2012. http://macuala.blogspot.mx/2011/01/encuentro-de-jaraneros .html.

Myers, Dowell, and Seong Woo Lee. "Immigrant Trajectories into Homeownership: A Temporal Analysis of Residential Assimilation." *International Migration Review* 32 (1998): 593–625.

Nagengast, Carole, and Michael Kearney. "Mixtec Identity, Political Consciousness, and Political Activism." *Latin American Research Review* 2 (1990): 61–91.

National Conference of State Legislatures. "State Laws Related to Immigration and Immigrants." 2009. Accessed December 13, 2009. http://www.ncsl.org/ research/immigration/state-laws-related-to-immigration-and-immigrants. aspx.

Nazario, Sonia, and Doug Smith. "Inspectors Find Dirt on Books at Southern California Carwashes." *Los Angeles Times,* March 23, 2008. Accessed December 1, 2008. http://www.latimes.com/news/local/la-me-carwash-220308,0,4406839. story.

Nichols, Sandra L. *Santos, duraznos y vino: Migrantes mexicanos y la transformación de Los Haro, Zacatecas, y Napa, California.* Mexico City: Universidad Autónoma de Zacatecas/Miguel Ángel Porrúa, 2006.

Odgers Ortiz, Olga. *Identités frontalières: Immigrés mexicains aux États-Unis.* Paris: L'Harmattan, 2002.

———. "Construcción del espacio y religión en la experiencia de la movilidad: Los Santos Patronos como vínculos espaciales en la migración México/Estados Unidos." *Migraciones Internacionales* 3 (2008): 5–23.

Office of the City Clerk. "Ordinance No. 17585," March 12, 2004. Accessed March 28, 2008. http://clkrep.lacity.org/onlinedocs/2002/02-0399_ ORD_175853_04-24-2004.pdf.

Office of Vocational and Adult Education (OVAE). "Promoción de la enseñanza del idioma inglés." Accessed December 2, 2009. http://www2.ed.gov/about/ offices/list/ovae/pi/AdultEd/englit.html.

Olivo, Antonio. "Rigo Padilla Deportastion Is Stayed." *Chicago Tribune,* December 11, 2009. Accessed December 14, 2009. http://www.chicagotribune.com/news/chi-uic-student-deportationdec11,0,7785361.story.

Painter, Gary, Gabriel Stuart, and Dowell Myers. "Race, Immigrant Status, and Housing Tenure Choice." *Journal of Urban Economics* 1 (2001): 150–67.

Papademetriou, Demetrios G., and Aaron Terrazas. *Immigrants and the Current Economic Crisis: Research Evidence, Policy Challenges, and Implications.* Washington, DC: Migration Policy Institute, 2009.

Park, Robert, and Ernest W. Burgess. *Introduction to the Science of Sociology.* New York: Greenwood Press, 1927.

Passel, Jeffrey. *Estimates of the Size and Characteristics of the Undocumented Population.* Washington, DC: Pew Hispanic Center, 2005.

Passel, Jeffrey, and D'Vera Cohn. *Trends in Unauthorized Immigration: Undocumented Inflow Now Trails Legal Inflow.* Washington, DC: Pew Hispanic Center, 2008.

————. *Mexican Immigrants: How Many Come? How Many Leave?* Washington, DC: Pew Hispanic Center, 2009.

Passel, Jeffrey, D'Vera Cohn, and Ana Gonzalez-Barrera. *Net Migration from Mexico Falls to Zero—and Perhaps Less.* Washington, DC: Pew Hispanic Center, 2012.

Pastor, Manuel, and Rhonda Ortiz. *Immigrant Integration in Los Angeles: Strategic Directions for Funders.* Los Angeles: University of Southern California, 2009.

Pendleton, Gail. *Local Police Enforcement of Immigration Laws and Its Effects on Victims of Domestic Violence.* Chicago: ABA Commission on Domestic Violence, 2008.

Pérez Monterosas, Mario. "Las redes sociales de la migración emergente de Veracruz a los Estados Unidos." *Migraciones Internacionales* 1 (2003): 136–60.

Pew Hispanic Center and Kaiser Family Foundation. "2002 National Survey of Latinos: Summary of Findings." Washington, DC. Accessed January 10, 2010. http://pewhispanic.org/files/reports/15.pdf.

Piore, Michael J. *Birds of Passage: Migrant Labor and Industrial Societies.* Cambridge: Cambridge University Press, 1979.

Piore, Michael J., and Charles Sabel. *The Second Industrial Divide: Possibilities for Prosperity.* New York: Basic Books, 1984.

Portes, Alejandro, Patricia Fernández-Kelly, and Ivan Light. "Life on the Edge: Immigrants Confront the American Health System." *Ethnic and Racial Studies* 1 (2012): 3–22.

Portes, Alejandro, and Rubén G. Rumbaut. *Legacies: The Story of the Immigrant Second Generation.* Berkeley: University of California Press, 2001.

————. *Immigrant America: A Portrait.* Berkeley: University of California Press, 2006.

Portes, Alejandro, and Min Zhou. "The New Second Generation: Segmented Assimilation and Its Variants." *Annals of the American Academy of Political and Social Science* 530 (1993): 74–97.

————. "Should Immigrants Assimilate?" *Public Interest* 116 (1994): 18–33.

Progressive States Network. *The Anti-Immigrant Movement That Failed.* New York: Progressive States Network, 2008. Accessed November 17, 2009. http://www.progressivestates.org/files/reports/immigrationSept08.pdf.

Project Vote Smart 2008. "SB 1301: Extending Student Financial Aid Eligibility." Accessed July 13, 2012. http://votesmart.org/bill/8041/22370/16749/nell-soto-did-not-vote-sb-1301-extending-student-financial-aid-eligibility#.VIKBpNLF_WI.

Quinones, Sam. "A Church Is Reborn." *Los Angeles Times,* February 10, 2008. Accessed November 17, 2009. http://articles.latimes.com/2008/feb/10/local/me-oaxacans10.

Ramírez, Hernan, and Pierrette Hondagneu-Sotelo. "Mexican Immigrant Gardeners: Entrepreneurs or Exploited Workers?" *Social Problems* 1 (2009): 70–88.

Ramírez-García, Telésforo, and Rafael Alarcón. "Integración en desventaja: Los inmigrantes mexicanos en Los Ángeles al inicio del siglo XXI." In *Colección de ensayos sobre población y derechos humanos en América Latina,* edited by Jorge Martínez Pizarro, 135–65. Rio de Janeiro: Asociación Latinoamericana de Población, 2011.

Rivera-Salgado, Gaspar. "Transnational Political Strategies: The Case of Mexican Indigenous Migrants." In *Immigration Research for a New Century: Multidisciplinary Perspectives,* edited by Nancy Foner, Ruben Rumaut, and Steven Gold, 134–56. New York: Russell Sage Foundation, 2000.

———. "Cross-Border Grassroots Organizations and the Indigenous Migrant Experience." In *Cross-Border Dialogues: U.S.-Mexico Social Movement Networking,* edited by David Brooks and Jonathan Fox, 259–74. La Jolla: University of California San Diego/Center for U.S.-Mexican Studies, 2002.

———. "Mexican Migrants and the Mexican Political System." In *Invisible no More: Mexican Migrant Civic Participation in the United States,* edited by Xóchitl Bada, Jonathan Fox, and Andrew Selee, 31–34. Washington, DC: Mexico Institute/Woodrow Wilson International Center for Scholars, 2006.

———. "Mexican Migrant Organizations." In *Invisible no More: Mexican Migrant Civic Participation in the United States,* edited by Xóchitl Bada, Jonathan Fox, and Andrew Selee, 5–8. Washington, DC: Mexico Institute, 2006b.

Rivera-Salgado, Gaspar, and Luis Escala Rabadán. "Collective Identity and Organizational Strategies of Indigenous and Mestizo Mexican Migrants." In *Indigenous Mexican Migrants in the United States,* edited by Jonathan Fox and Gaspar Rivera-Salgado, 145–78. San Diego: University of California, 2004.

Rivera Sánchez, Liliana. "Cuando los Santos también migran: Conflictos transnacionales por el espacio y la pertenencia." *Migraciones Internacionales* 4 (2006): 35–59.

Rocha Romero, David. "Migrantes precarios: Inmigrantes mexicanos en la subcontratación en Estados Unidos." *Norteamérica* 1 (2011): 95–126.

Romo, Ricardo. *East Los Angeles: History of a Barrio.* Austin: University of Texas Press, 1983.

Rosas, Carolina. *Varones al son de la migración: Migración internacional y masculinidades de Veracruz a Chicago.* Mexico City: El Colegio de México, 2008.

Rossell, Christine. "The Near End of Bilingual Education: In the Wake of California's Propo 227." *Education Next* 4 (2003). Accessed August 15, 2013. http://educationnext.org/thenearendofbilingualeducation/.

Rumbaut, Ruben, Douglas Massey, and Frank Bean. "Linguistic Life Expectancies: Immigrant Language Retention in Southern California." *Population and Development Review* 3 (2006): 447–60.

Runsten, David, and Michael Kearney. *A Survey of Oaxacan Village Networks in California Agriculture.* Davis: California Institute for Rural Studies, 1994.

Sánchez, George. *Becoming Mexican American: Ethnicity, Culture and Identity in Chicano Los Angeles, 1900–1945.* Oxford: Oxford University Press, 1993.

San Román, Teresa. *Los muros de la separación: Ensayo sobre alterofobia y filantropía.* Madrid: Tecnos, 1996.

Santa Ana, Otto. *Brown Tide Rising: Metaphors of Latinos in Contemporary American Public Discourse.* Austin: University of Texas Press, 2002.

Sartori, Giovanni. *La sociedad multiétnica: Pluralismo, multiculturalismo y extranjeros.* Madrid: Taurus, 2001.

Sassen, Saskia. *The Mobility of Labor and Capital: A Study in International Investment and Labor Flow.* Cambridge: Cambridge University Press, 1988.

———. "New Trends in the Socio-Spatial Organization of the New York City Economy." In *Economic Restructuring and Political Response,* edited by R. A. Beauregard, 69–114. Newbury Park: Sage, 1989.

———. *The Global City: New York, London, Tokyo.* Princeton: Princeton University, 1991.

———. *Globalization and Its Discontents: Essays on the New Mobility of People and Money.* New York: New Press, 1998.

———. *Contrageografías de la globalización: Género y ciudadanía en los circuitos transfonterizos.* Madrid: Queimada Gráficas Imprenta, 2003.

Scott, Allen. *New Industrial Spaces.* London: Pion, 1988.

———, ed. *Global City-Regions: Trends, Theory, Policy.* Oxford: Oxford University Press, 2001.

Schnapper, Dominique. *Qu'est-ce que l'intégration?* Paris: Gallimard, 2007.

Schneider, Anne, and Helen Ingram. "Social Construction of Target Populations: Implications for Politics and Policy." *American Political Review* 2 (1993): 334–47.

———. *Policy Design for Democracy.* Lawrence: University of Kansas Press, 1997.

Simmons, Ann M. "Lancaster Requires Businesses to Do Immigration Checks on New Hires." *Los Angeles Times,* December 26, 2009. Accessed December 28, 2009. http://latimesblogs.latimes.com/lanow/2009/12/lancaster-requires-businesses-to-do-immigration-checks-on-new-hires.html.

Smith, Michael, and Luis Guarnizo, eds. *Transnationalism from Below.* New Brunswick: Transaction, 1998.

Soja, Edward W. *Postmetropolis: Critical Studies of Cities and Regions.* Oxford: Blackwell, 2000.

Somerville, Will, Jamie Durana, and Aarón Mateo Terrazas. "Hometown Associations: An Untapped Resource for Immigrant Integration." *MPI Insight,* July 2008.

Southern Policy Law Center. "Intelligence Nativists to 'Patriots': Nativist Vigilantes Adopt 'Patriot' Movement Ideas," Autumn 2009. Accessed November 12, 2009. http://www.splcenter.org/intel/intelreport/article.jsp?aid = 1094.

Soysal, Yasemin. *Limits of Citizenship: Migrants and Postnational Membership in Europe.* Chicago: University of Chicago Press, 1994.

Stelter, Brian, and Bill Carter. "Lou Dobbs Abruptly Quits CNN." *New York Times,* November 11, 2009. Accessed December 7, 2009. http://www.nytimes.com/2009/11/12/business/media/12dobbs.html.

Stephen, Lynn. *Transborder Lives: Indigenous Oaxacans in Mexico, California and Oregon.* Durham: Duke University Press, 2007.

Storper, Michael, and Richard Walker. *The Capitalist Imperative: Territory, Technology and Industrial Growth.* Oxford: Basil Blackwell, 1989.

Susser, Ida. "The Separation of Mothers and Children." In *The Dual City*, edited by J.H. Mollenkopf and Manuel Castells. New York: Russell Sage Foundation, 1991.

Taylor, Charles. *The Sources of the Self: The Making of Modern Identity*. Cambridge: Harvard University Press, 1989.

———. *The Ethics of Authenticity*. Cambridge: Harvard University Press, 1991.

———. *Multiculturalisme: Différence en démocratie*. Flammarion, France: Flammarion Press, 1992.

Telles, Edward. "Mexican Americans and the American Nation: A Response to Professor Huntington." *Aztlan: A Journal of Chicano Studies* 2 (2006): 7–23.

———. *Race in Another America: The Significance of Skin Color in Brazil*. Princeton: Princeton University Press, 2004.

Telles, Edward, and Vilma Ortiz. *Generations of Exclusion: Mexican Americans, Assimilation and Race*. New York: Russell Sage Foundation, 2008.

Thomas, William I., and Florian Znaniecki. *The Polish Peasant in Europe and America: A Classic Work in Immigration History*. Champaign: University of Illinois Press, 1996.

Tinley, Alicia. "Migración de Guanajuato a Alabama: Experiencias escolares de cuatro familias mexicanas." *Sociológica* 60 (2006): 143–72.

Touraine, Alain. *Pourrons-nous vivre ensemble? Egaux et different*. Paris: Fayard, 1997.

University of California, Los Angeles (UCLA), International Institute. "Los nuevos caminos del movimiento jaranero."Accessed July 12, 2012. http://web.international.ucla.edu/institute/event/8177?AspxAutoDetectCookieSupport = 1.

———. "Estimated Average Costs." Accessed October 27, 2010. http://www.universityofcalifornia.edu/admissions/paying-for-uc/cost/index.html.

———. "UCLA School of Law Clinical Program Wins Case Challenging Validity of Los Angeles City Ordinance Implemented against Taco Trucks." Accessed December 1, 2009. http://www.law.ucla.edu/home/News/Detail.aspx?page = 20&recordid = 2325.

University of Southern California. "Proposition 187." Accessed November 15, 2008. http://www.usc.edu/libraries/archives/ethnicstudies/historicdocs/prop187.txt.

US Department of Homeland Security. "E-Verify." Accessed December 18, 2011. http://www.dhs.gov/files/programs/gc_1185221678150.shtm.

———. "Office of Immigration Statistics," 2006. Accessed August 15, 2011. http://www.dhs.gov/immigration-statistics, 2006.

US Census Bureau. "American Community Survey," 2007. Accessed November 13, 2009. http://www.census.gov/acs/www/data_documentation/2007_release/.

———. "Current Population Survey, Annual Social and Economic Supplement," March 2007. Accessed December 18, 2009. http://www.census.gov/cps/data/.

Valenzuela, Abel, Jr. "Compatriots or Competitors? A Study of Job Competition between the Foreign-Born and Native in Los Angeles, 1970–1980."

Working paper. Berkeley: University of California, Chicano/Latino Policy Project, 1993.

———. "Working on the Margins in Metropolitan Los Angeles: Immigrant Day-Labor Work." *Migraciones Internacionales* 2 (2002): 6–28.

Valenzuela, Abel Jr., Nik Theodore, Edwin Meléndez, and Ana Luz González. *On the Corner: Day Labor in the U.S.* Los Angeles: UCLA Center for the Study of Urban Poverty, 2006.

Vargas y Campos, Gloria. "El problema del bracero mexicano." Master's thesis, Universidad Nacional Autónoma de México, 1964.

Varsanyi, Monica, ed. *Taking Local Control: Immigration Policy Activism in U.S. Cities and States.* Stanford: Stanford University Press, 2010.

Vigdor, Jacob. *From Immigrants to Americans: The Rise and Fall of Fitting In.* New York: Manhattan Institute, 2009.

Villaraigosa, Antonio. "The Real Minutemen: Remarks to the UCLA Anderson Forecast Conference." Paper presented at UCLA, Los Angeles, December 4, 2005. Accessed December 6, 2009. http://clkrep.lacity.org/onlinedocs/2009 /09-2642_ca_11-25-09.pdf.

Waldinger, Roger. "Black/Immigrant Competition Re-Assessed: New Evidence from Los Angeles." *Sociological Perspectives* 3 (1997): 365–86.

———. "The Ethnic Enclave Debate Revisited." *International Journal of Urban and Regional Research* 3 (1993): 444–52.

———. "Ethnicity and Opportunity in the Plural City." In *Ethnic Los Angeles,* edited by Roger Waldinger and Mehdi Bozorgmehr, 445–70. New York: Russell Sage Foundation, 1996.

———. "Immigrants and Minorities: Conflict in the Job Markets." *Dissent* 4 (1987): 519–22.

———. "The Making of an Immigrant Niche." *International Migration Review* 105 (1994): 3–30.

Waldinger, Roger, and Mehdi Bozorgmehr. "The Making of a Multicultural Metropolis." In *Ethnic Los Angeles,* edited by Roger Waldinger and Mehdi Bozorgmehr, 3–37. New York: Russell Sage Foundation, 1996.

Waldinger, Roger, and Renee Reichi. "Second-Generation Mexicans: Getting Ahead or Falling Behind?" *Migration Information Source.* Migration Policy Institute, 2006. http://www.migrationpolicy.org/article/second-generation-mexicans-getting-ahead-or-falling-behind.

Walzer, Michael. *What It Means to Be American; Essays on the American Experience.* New York: Marsilio, 1992.

Warner, Stephen, and Judith Wittner. *Gathering in Diaspora: Religious Communities and the New Migration.* Philadelphia: Temple University Press, 1998.

Waters, Mary. *Black Identities: West Indian Immigrant Dreams and American Realities.* New York: Russell Sage Foundation, 1999.

"Why Illegal Immigration Isn't to Blame for the State Budget Crisis." *Los Angeles Times,* December 22, 2009. Accessed December 23, 2009. http://articles. latimes.com/2009/dec/22/opinion/la-ed-schwarzenegger23-2009dec23.

Wieviorka, Michel. "Is Multiculturalism the Solution?" *Ethnic and Racial Studies* 21 (1998): 881–910.

———. "L'intégration: Un concept en difficulté." *Cahiers Internationaux de Sociologie* 125 (2008): 221–40.

———. "A World in Movement." *Migraciones Internacionales* 6 (2011): 45–60.

Wihtol de Wenden, Catherine. *La globalization humaine.* Paris: Presses Universitaires de France, 2009.

———. *La question migratoire au XXIe siècle: Migrants, réfugiés et relations internationales.* Paris: Presses de Sciences Politiques, 2010.

Wihtol de Wenden, Catherine, and Alec G. Hargreaves. "The Political Participation of Ethnic Minorities in Europe: A Framework for Analysis." *New Community* 20 (1993): 1–8.

Wilson, K. L., and Alejandro Portes. "Immigrant Enclaves: An Analysis of the Labour Market Experiences of Cubans in Miami." *American Journal of Sociology* 82 (1980): 295–319.

Wilson, William Julius. *The Truly Disadvantaged.* Chicago: University of Chicago Press, 1987.

Wimmer, Andreas, and Nina Glick-Schiller. "Methodological Nationalism and Beyond: Nation-State Building, Migration and the Social Sciences." *Global Networks* 4 (2002): 301–34.

Wolfe, Alan. "Native Son: Samuel Huntington Defends the Homeland." *Foreign Affairs* 3 (2004): 120–25.

Wright, Richard, and Mark Ellis. "The Ethnic and Gender Division of Labor Compared among Immigrants to Los Angeles." *International Journal of Urban and Regional Research* 3 (2000): 583–600.

Young, Iris Marion. *Justice and the Politics of Difference.* Princeton: Princeton University Press, 1990.

Zabin, Carol. *Mixtec Migrants in California Agriculture: A New Cycle of Poverty.* Davis: California Institute for Rural Studies, 1993.

Zazueta, Carlos, and Manuel García y Griego. *Los trabajadores mexicanos en Estados Unidos: Resultados de la Encuesta Nacional de Emigración a la Frontera Norte del país y a los Estados Unidos.* Mexico City: Centro Nacional de Información y Estadísticas del Trabajo/Secretaría del Trabajo y Previsión Social, 1982.

Zhou, Min. "Segmented Assimilation: Issues, Controversies and Recent Research on the New Second Generation." *International Migration Review* 4 (1997): 975–1008.

Index

www.ingramcontent.com/pod-product-compliance
Lightning Source LLC
Chambersburg PA
CBHW020844270326
41928CB00006B/537